Endorsements for *A New Social Contract Relating Mission Societies to Ecclesiastical Structures*:

Supporting the work of missiologist Ralph D. Winter (and lauding the precedent set by William Carey), in this book Robert A. Blincoe has done a thorough job amassing historical, sociological, biblical, and theological resources to make a solid case for the legitimacy of mission agencies that operate outside of ecclesiastical structures that might otherwise inhibit or compromise the work of getting out the Gospel. Those who take Blincoe's thesis to heart and put into practice what he has shown is a more biblical approach to mission work will do more to further the work of God's Kingdom than those who restrict their work within the bounds of the model that we inherited from the Protestant Reformers. In the end, Blincoe wisely calls for something like a partnership in mission between denominational missions and mission agencies with a specific focus.

Dennis Okholm, PhD. Azusa Pacific University

Robert A. Blincoe, in A New Social Contract, *has written one of the most engaging discussions of mission history of recent years. Blincoe begins with Ralph Winter's controversial theory developed in "Two Structures of God's Redemptive Mission," and "Protestant Mission Societies: The Other Protestant Schism", in which he had advanced an argument for the formation of mission agencies that operate independently from denominational structures and restrictions. Blincoe establishes clearly, through a thorough search of church and mission history, that Protestant mission agencies, following the example set by Catholic mission orders, have been successful in carrying the Gospel to every nation of the world.*

Blincoe writes with passion, but also with restraint, carefully documenting his study at every step. It is a pleasure to read his work. The product is a classic that will be used as a benchmark for years for research into the theory of mission agency development.

Dale W. Kietzman, PhD, Emeritus Professor Intercultural Communication, William Carey International University

A New Social Contract Relating
Mission Societies to Ecclesiastical Structures

By

Robert Alan Blincoe

A Dissertation presented
in partial fulfillment of the
requirements for the degree of
Doctor of Philosophy
William Carey International University
June 2012

Robert Alan Blincoe
A New Social Contract Relating Missions Structures to Ecclesiastical Structures
William Carey International University Press

1539 E. Howard Street, Pasadena, California 91104

E-mail: wciupress@wciu.edu

www.wciupress.org

Copyright © 2012 by Robert Alan Blincoe

Except as provided by the Copyright Act, no part of this publication may be reproduced, stored in a retrieval system or transmitted in any form or by any means without the prior written permission of the publisher.

All rights reserved

ISBN: 9780865850798

Library of Congress Control Number: 2013955410

Signature Page

We approve the dissertation presented by Robert Alan Blincoe on the subject:

"A New Social Contract Relating
Mission Societies to Ecclesiastical Structures"

_____   Jan. 3, 2011
Professor Dale W. Kietzman, Ph.D., Chairman   Date

_____   December 13, 2010
Professor Darrell L. Guder, Ph.D.   Date

_____   3 January 2011
Professor Dennis L. Okholm, Ph.D.   Date

Accepted by the University

_____   Aug 21, 2012
Provost Beth Snodderly, D. Litt. et Phil.   Date

WILLIAM CAREY INTERNATIONAL UNIVERSITY

ABSTRACT

The Protestant mission paradigm, as conceived by Luther and Calvin and taking classic shape in the generation of Reformers that followed them, assumed that church administrative bodies should retain for themselves the authority to initiate God's mission to all the world. However, another paradigm will be shown to be more biblical, more predictably effective as measured by an inductive study of mission history, and truer to what is "really there" in societies everywhere. Some early Protestant mission advocates, such as Justinian Welz and Adrian Saravia, opposed the Reformers' mission paradigm, but the church came down hard on them. Only with the publication of William Carey's *Enquiry* in 1792 did a more effective and biblical paradigm gain considerable acceptance, despite ecclesiastical adversity that continues today.

Ecclesiastical suspicion that mission agencies, however successful, are 1) a threat to church unity and 2) have no biblical basis has, unfortunately, aggravated the tension between them. Therefore, it is important to address these suspicions and, if possible, normalize the relationship between ecclesiastical hierarchies and mission agencies.

The research provides evidence-based support for the desired outcome of this thesis, that Protestant churches—modalities—should recognize the indispensable contribution of, and biblical basis for, sodalities—voluntary mission structures—thus bringing about the necessary favorable conditions to normalize a relationship between them.

The Table of Contents

The Table of Contents 4

Figures 7

Chapter 1: Introduction 10

    Statement of the Problem 11

    Background and Significance of the Problem 12

    Research Questions and Hypotheses 13

    Methodology and Procedures 15

    Assumptions 18

    Limitations of the Study 18

Chapter 2: A Review of Recent Literature 19

    Use of Historical Literature 19

    Use of Sociological Literature 20

Chapter 3: Design of Project Given by Ralph D. Winter 22

    3.1 Voluntary Associations Rising—Why Normalizing a Relationship between Ecclesiastical Structures and Voluntary Associations is More Necessary than Ever 23

    3.2 Organizing for Missio Dei, in Order to Close a Breach that has Opened in the Protestant Church 26

    3.3 Paradigm Shift and Resistance—Observations of Thomas Kuhn 35

Chapter 4: An Organizational Interpretation of Mission History 40

    4.1 The Biblical Literature 40

        4.1.1 The Jewish Structural Advantage 40

        4.1.2 Objections to Winter's "Two Structures" Thesis Considered 52

        4.1.3 Sending Paul and Barnabas—An Exegesis of Acts 13:1-3 Corrects a Misunderstanding 64

    4.2 The Celtic Church Advantage: Its Organizational Structure 71

    4.3 The Catholic Advantage: A Social Contract Recognizing Religious Orders 80

    4.4 The Protestant Disadvantage: Observations from the Reformation until 1792 .. 90

        4.4.1 Martin Luther: The Dissolution of the Religious Orders 92

4.4.2 John Calvin: His Understanding of Apostolos Reconsidered 96

4.4.3 Mission Thinking in the Era of Lutheran and Reformed Scholasticism 99

4.4.4 The Exceptional, Isolated Justinian Welz 104

4.5 William Carey's Paradigm: "The Use of Means" 109

4.5.1 The Appearance of Voluntary Societies after 1792 Enabled Protestants to Begin Achieving Their Mission Goals 116

4.5.2 Voluntary Societies Resemble Trading Companies, Carey Observed 132

4.5.3 Voluntary Societies as "The Fortunate Subversion of the Church"—Observations of Andrew Walls 139

4.6. Sodalities Everywhere: Special-Purpose Associations Among all Peoples 145

4.6.1 Ralph D. Winter's "Two Structures" Thesis as a Sociological Paradigm 148

4.6.2 The Voluntary Nature of the American People 152

4.6.3 A Brief Study of Foreign Voluntary Societies 160

4.6.4 Illustrating the Sodality-Modality Pairing as a Double Helix 167

4.6.5 The Term "Parachurch" in Light of the "Two Structures" Paradigm 172

4.6.6 Karl Barth's "Special Working Fellowships" 175

4.7. Presbyterian Mission History: Initiative, Reaction, and Desired Symbiosis 179

4.7.1 The Presbyterian Schism of 1837 181

4.7.2 Presbyterian Women's Societies from the Second Half of the 19th Century 188

4.7.3 Christian Endeavor and its Presbyterian Challenger, Westminster Fellowship ... 197

4.7.4 The Presbyterian Book of Order *Provision for "Special Organizations"* 201

4.7.5 Trends in Mission Giving: The Presbyterian Experience 205

4.7.6 The Conciliar Church Disadvantage 230

4.8. Mission Policies and Related Structural Issues—Findings in Seven Denominations 236

4.8.1 Anglican Mission Policy—The Church Mission Society 237

4.8.2 The Reformed Church of America Mission Policy 241

4.8.3 The Methodist Church Mission Policy 246

4.8.4 Quakers: The Friends Mission Policy 250

4.8.5 The Episcopal Church Mission Policy 251

4.8.6 American Baptist Mission Policy 253

4.8.7 The Lutheran Church Missouri Synod—A Model Mission Policy 254

CHAPTER 5: CONCLUSION TO THE DISSERTATION 263
    5.1 A New Social Contract for Presbyterians 264
    APPENDIX 1 Protestant missionary biographies before and after Carey in EDWM 271
    APPENDIX 2 Protestant missionary biographies before and after Carey in BDCM 275
BIBLIOGRAPHY 288

FIGURES

Figure 1. Jacob Baegert's region of Baja California--Guaycura 85

Figure 2. Timeline: Mission Biographies in EDWM 1752-1832 118

Figure 3. Mission Biographies in EDWM, 1752-1832 (2) 119

Figure 4. Timeline: Biographies in EDWM: 1522-1792, 1792-1998--A Comparison 120

Figure 5. Timeline: Mission Agencies in EDWM, 1752-1832 121

Figure 6. Timeline: Luther to Carey, plus 30 Remarkable Years 122

Figure 7. Timeline: Biographies in BDCM 1752-1832 124

Figure 8. Timeline: Mission Biographies in BDCM 1752-1832 (2) 125

Figure 9. Timeline: Biographies in BDCM 1522-1792, 1792-1998--A Comparison 126

Figure 10. Timeline: Biographies in BDCM 1522-1998 127

Figure 11. Modality and Sodality 148

Figure 12. Warp and Woof 151

Figure 13. Free-World Governments Respond to the Interests of their Citizens by Regulating Corporations 166

Figure 14. Double Helix: Sodality and Modality 168

Figure 15. Double Helix: Carey's Baptist Church and Carey's Baptist Mission Society 169

Figure 16. Double Helix Representation of Synagogue and Khevra 170

Figure 17. Double Helix: Two Structures in Islam 171

Figure 18. Double Helix Representation of Protestant "Sola Synodica" 172

Figure 19. Trends in Presbyterian Giving, Designated and Undesignated 210

Figure 20. Presbyterian Giving to 1) Presbyterian and 2) Non-Presbyterian Local Missions--A Comparison 212

Figure 21. Presbyterian Giving to 1) Presbyterian and 2) Non-Presbyterian Mission beyond Local--A Comparison 213

Figure 22. Ratio of Presbyterian Missionaries to Home Staff: Data 215

Figure 23. Ratio of Presbyterian Missionaries to Home Staff 216

Figure 24. Presbyterian Missionaries in the Middle East 217

Figure 25. US Frontiers Field Workers 218

Figure 26. US Missionary Totals by Affiliation 1918-2002 232

Figure 27. New Mission Initiatives, Lutheran Church World Mission 255

Figure 28. Four Kinds of Mission-Church Relationships 259

ABBREVIATIONS

ABCFM—American Board of Commissioners for Foreign Mission

AHMS—American Home Missionary Society

ALMA— Association of Lutheran Mission Agencies

BDCM—*Biographical Dictionary of Christian Missions*

BMS—Baptist Mission Society

CMS—Church Mission Society (previously Church Missionary Society)

ECO—Extra Commitment Opportunities (Presbyterian Church USA)

EDWM—*Evangelical Dictionary of World Missions*

IMC—International Missionary Council

LCMS—Lutheran Church Missouri Synod

NGO—Non-Governmental Organization

PHS—Presbyterian Historical Society

PCUSA—Presbyterian Church in the United States of America

RCA—Reformed Church of America

SAMS—South American Missionary Society

SPG—Society for the Propagation of the Gospel in Foreign Parts

SPCK—Society for the Promoting of Christian Knowledge

TDNT—*Theological Dictionary of the New Testament*

USAID—United States Agency for International Development

WCC—World Council of Churches

CHAPTER 1: INTRODUCTION

The Protestant mission paradigm, as conceived by Luther and Calvin and taking classic shape in the generation of Reformers that followed them, assumed that church administrative bodies should retain for themselves the sole authority to initiate God's mission to all the world. In Bishop Stephen Neill's words, this paradigm achieved "exceedingly little."[1] Though the doctrines developed by our Reformation fathers were thoroughly missional, in actuality the Protestant Churches endured a painful 275 year mission "ice age" beginning in 1517. Not even in the Dutch Golden Age of the late 16th and 17th centuries, when Protestant ships sailed to distant shores, did this paradigm produce results comparable to those achieved by Catholic orders sailing those same seas. Some early Protestant mission advocates, such as Justinian Welz and Adrian Saravia, opposed the administrative mission paradigm, but the church came down hard on them. Only in 1792, with the publication and widespread adoption of William Carey's "operating system"—the mission societies—did doctrinal *credenda* actualize in mission *agenda*.

Protestant administrations disapproved; Carey's paradigm, by which "a company of serious Christians" would "form themselves"[2] into a mission society, was incompatible

---

[1] Stephen Neill, *A History of Christian Missions*, 2nd ed. (New York: Penguin Books, 1986), 222.
[2] William Carey, *An Enquiry into the Obligations of Christians to Use Means for the Conversion of the Heathens*, Pre-1801 Imprint Collection (Library of Congress), ed. (Leicester: Baptist Missionary Society London; reprinted by Ann Ireland, 1792), 81.

with the Reformed mission paradigm (which I am calling *sola synodica*[3]). An undesirable pattern emerged: a few church members would form themselves into special-purpose associations that were independent of their churches administrations; then, church hierarchies would react negatively, basing their criticism on a dubious understanding of church unity and biblical teaching. Church leaders have even attempted to forbid their members from joining voluntary mission associations. However, in the late 18th century English Parliament and the United States Congress enacted laws guaranteeing the rights of their citizens to organize voluntary associations for causes important, perhaps, only to a few. Carey and others like him could now form themselves into mission societies, despite the wishes of centralized church administrations. Andrew Walls calls this "*the fortunate subversion of the church.*"[4] Church hierarchies, unable to prevent voluntary mission societies from forming, created their own centralized mission efforts and took on the identity of a mission agency. Proving one's church loyalty came to mean funding denominational missions programs.

Statement of the Problem

Ecclesiastical suspicion that mission agencies, however successful, are 1) a threat to church unity and 2) have no biblical basis has, unfortunately, aggravated the tension

---

[3] Medieval popes Leo IV and Urban II employed the term *Synodica* to denote the territory subject to the jurisdiction of a bishop. See *Charles George Herbermann and others, The Catholic Encyclopedia (New York: The Encyclopedia Press, 1913). s.v. "Diocese."*

[4] See Andrew F. Walls, "The Fortunate Subversion of the Church," in *The Missionary Movement in Christian History: Studies in the Transmission of Faith* (Maryknoll, NY: Orbis Books, 1996), 241-254.

between them. Therefore, it is important to address these suspicions and, if possible, normalize the relationship between ecclesiastical hierarchies and mission agencies.

Background and Significance of the Problem

In order for the people of God to create durable and effective solutions for many of humanity's greatest problems, it will be necessary for Protestant administrations to "shepherd the flock" by providing guidance to their members who are organizing or joining mission societies. Call this new relationship between administrative boards and mission societies *symbiosis*: "the intimate living together of two dissimilar organisms in a mutually beneficial relationship."[5] Research data presented in this dissertation indicates that voluntary associations are an "enabling technology,"[6] empowering ordinary citizens to initiate and sustain efforts that can identify and eradicate root problems, including injustice, slavery and war, racism, poverty, disease and repair of our families. By contrast, a five hundred year "experiment" during which Protestant administrative bodies have retained for themselves the authority to initiate mission efforts provides data indicating that this is fairly ineffective. Fortunately, comparative data is available from a second experiment that has been carried out by church governments that allow their citizens to form autonomous special-purpose associations. These "liberal" church governments—meaning that they permit and even encourage the decentralizing of

---

[5] Merriam-Webster Inc., *Merriam-Webster's Collegiate Dictionary*, 10th ed. (Springfield, MA: Merriam-Webster, 1997). s.v. "Symbiosis."

[6] This astute phrase is found in John Micklethwait and Adrian Wooldridge, *The Company: A Short History of a Revolutionary Idea* (New York: Modern Library, 2003), xx-xxi.

mission initiative—include Catholics, Celts, Jews and, after William Carey published his *Enquiry* in 1792, certain Protestants. A historical analysis, which comprises the major portion of this dissertation, allows us to determine that citizens whose hierarchies allow decentralization have an advantage over the churches whose hierarchies attempt to control mission initiative. In fact, this determination enables us to predict that church administrations which attempt to retain for themselves the exclusive rights to initiate mission efforts will do very little initiating, while church hierarchies that encourage their citizens to form special-purpose associations will initiate many mission efforts and greatly increase the probability of achieving their goals. For this reason church governing bodies should recognize and validate the mission agencies that their citizens are forming or joining.

Research Questions and Hypotheses

1. Does historical and biblical data support Ralph D. Winter's hypothesis that there are "Two Structures" of the church in the New Testament? Can a satisfactory response be made to Winter's critics?
2. Does the historical, theological and sociological data favor the "Two Structures" hypothesis sufficiently to persuade Protestant leaders to disagree with the organizational mission paradigm held by Luther and Calvin?

In this dissertation I provide data to support six propositions upon which my thesis rests:

1. For two and a half centuries Reformation churches could not initiate mission efforts because ecclesiastical hierarchies retained for themselves the authority to initiate them, thus deterring their members from organizing the needful voluntary mission structures.

2. The Roman Catholic Church, by contrast, could easily initiate new mission efforts on account of its validation of, and regulation of, voluntary structures.

3. Although Pietists had organized the first Protestant missions in the early 18th century, the *era* of Reformation missions began with the publication, and acceptance among Pietists, of William Carey's *Enquiry*.

4. Protestant Church hierarchies reacted against Carey's proposal by starting their own centralized mission structures and at times prohibiting their members from involvement in voluntary mission agencies.

5. Ralph D. Winter's thesis, described in "Two Structures of God's Redemptive Mission," and "Protestant Mission Societies: The Other Protestant Schism" has been proved valid and its critics have been satisfactorily answered.

6. The people of God, having gathered to hear God's word and to worship Him, and having heard God's "dismissal" to go into the entire world, will more effectively achieve the greatest good when ecclesiastical leaders recognize and regulate, but do not operate, the special-purpose associations that "the people of God" are organizing or joining.

Methodology and Procedures

There are five parts to the methodology I have used in this dissertation:

1. Use of Historical Missions Literature

2. Use of Sociological Literature

3. Use of Interviews

4. Use of Quantitative Data

5. A Study of For-profit Companies and their Relationship to Free-World Governments that Validate Them.

6. Report on the Relationship between Mission Structures and Ecclesiastical Hierarchies in Six Denominations

After reading all of the books and periodical that I could find on the subject of voluntary associations in the Protestant mission era, I decided to propose this thesis: Protestant churches—modalities—should recognize the indispensable contribution of, and biblical basis for, sodalities—voluntary mission structures—thus normalizing a relationship between them. I made use of interviews with key leaders in ecclesiastical hierarchies. Moreover, I was able to create timelines from data derived from standard reference books that provides evidence for a missions "ice age" that set in at the beginning of the Reformation and did not thaw until the time of William Carey's proposal to begin forming voluntary associations. Finally, I studied the relationship between ecclesiastical structures and voluntary associations in six Protestant denominations in order to test my thesis.

This dissertation employs a historical research methodology. I analyzed the relevant literature on the following subjects: 1) a history of Jewish mission in the first century AD, to determine a Biblical basis for Ralph Winter's "Two Structures" thesis; 2) a history of the Celtic and Catholic missions; 3) the resemblance of Carey's "company of serious Christians" to private trading companies, and, by corollary, 4) the resemblance of free-world governments to church governments in terms of guaranteeing the rights of their citizens to form special-purpose associations; 5) the history of Protestant missions, especially Presbyterian but also Lutheran, Methodist, Anglican, Friends, American Baptist and Dutch Reformed. Additional literature research from the field of social science yielded important information on the subject of the relationship between special-purpose associations and governments. Interviews with ecclesiastical leaders are also included. Finally, I analyzed key metrics to compare Protestant mission activity before and after 1792, the year William Carey published his *Enquiry into the Obligation to Use Means*. The research provides evidence-based support for the desired outcome of this thesis.

Definition of Terms. Technical terms the reader will encounter are:

- *Khevra*: the Hebrew word for special-purpose association. The plural is *khevrot*.

- *Paradigm shift*—In 1962 science historian Thomas Kuhn suggested this term to describe what he called the "revolutionary" moment when a scientist, bothered by the number or value of anomalies,[7] proposes a new, incompatible paradigm to explain what is "really there."[8]

- *Social Contract*: In political philosophy a social contract is an "actual or hypothetical compact, or agreement, between the ruled and their rulers, defining the rights and duties of each."[9] Thomas Hobbes, John Locke and Jean Rousseau wrote theories of government based on this concept, and, though they differed with each other on whether in the absence of government an individual life was "nasty, short and brutish" (Hobbes) or idyllic, (Rousseau), they agreed that populations form governments in order to safeguard some of their rights in exchange for surrendering some degree of individual freedom.

- *Sodality and Modality*: Roman Catholic academics were apparently the first to use the term *sodality*, referring to religious orders, convents, monasteries and other "pious associations."[10] Later, anthropologist Elman R. Service (d. 1996) applied a non-religious meaning to *sodality*; Service used it to describe "an association" that has "some corporate functions or purposes . . . Sodality is close in spirit to . . . 'special

---

[7] Thomas S. Kuhn, *The Structure of Scientific Revolutions* (University of Chicago Press, 1962), 53.
[8] Ibid., 206.
[9] Encyclopaedia Britannica Inc., *The New Encyclopædia Britannica*, 15th ed., vol. 10 (Chicago, Ill.: 1991). s.v. "Social Contract."
[10] See http://www.newadvent.org/cathen/14120a.htm. s.v. "Sodality." Accessed September 2010. From the Latin *sodalitatem* (nom. *sodalitas*) "companionship, a brotherhood," from *sodalis* "companion."

purpose group.'"[11] Ralph D. Winter used it in the way Elman R. Service did. Winter paired it with *modality*, a term he used to describe any general population, such as a high school student body or a church congregation.

- *Sola Synodica:* This new term describes the particular church paradigm by which ecclesiastical hierarchies retain for themselves the authority to initiate mission enterprises.
- *Symbiosis*: "the intimate living together of two dissimilar organisms in a mutually beneficial relationship."[12]

Assumptions

I have assumed that the reader is generally knowledgeable of the contribution of Catholic religious orders to missions.

Limitations of the Study

Describing either the remarkable record of the accomplishments of the missionaries, or the mistakes made by missionaries and mission agencies, for which criticism is due, is beyond the limits of this study.

---

[11] Elman Rogers Service, *Primitive Social Organization: An Evolutionary Perspective*, 2nd ed. (New York: Random House, 1971). 13. Robert Wuthnow also uses the term "special purpose groups." Robert Wuthnow, *The Restructuring of American Religion: Society and Faith since World War 2* (Princeton, NJ: Princeton University Press, 1988), 181-82.

[12] Merriam-Webster Inc., *Merriam-Webster's Dictionary of English Usage* (Springfield, MA: Merriam-Webster, Inc., 1994). s.v. "Symbiosis."

CHAPTER 2: A REVIEW OF RECENT LITERATURE

Because the research for this dissertation is an extensive discussion of the relevant books and periodicals, I have included here only an informal review of the literature.[13]

Use of Historical Literature

The relevant Jewish, Celtic, Catholic and Protestant mission literature was researched and referenced in this dissertation. In addition to Ralph D. Winter's large body of writing on the "Two Structures" paradigm, I will draw on pertinent historical observations, particularly those by Gerald H. Anderson, R. Pierce Beaver, David Bosch, Jonathan Brumberg-Kraus, Bruce Camp, David G. Dawson, Darrell L. Guder, George Marsden, John Pellowe, Dana L. Robert, J. Eckhard Schnabel, John V. Taylor, Eugene Teselle, and Andrew Walls.

I am indebted to several researchers. John Pellowe wrote a doctoral thesis on church-mission agency relations "and what they can do to improve their relations by thinking theologically about their ministry's practices."[14] William Douglas Mottinger gathered 61 key articles for his master's thesis, "Readings in Church/Mission Structures."[15] Bruce L. Bauer proposed a relationship between church and mission structures in his 1982

---

[13] By permission of my lead faculty advisor, there is no separate "review of the literature" in this dissertation.

[14] John Pellowe, "Leading Ministries into Christian Community: A Practical Theology for Church-Agency Relations" (D. Min. Dissertation, Gordon-Conwell Theological Seminary, 2008), 15. I quote from Pellowe's 2007 paper as well, also done at Gordon-Conwell: "A Practical Theology for Relations between Churches and Self-Governing Agencies." which is due to be published in 2011.

[15] William Douglas Mottinger, "Readings in Church/Mission Structures" (MA Thesis, Fuller Theological Seminary, 1986).

dissertation, "Congregational and Mission Structures."[16] Charles J. Mellis' fine book, *Committed Communities*,[17] covers the material on mission structures from Ralph D. Winter's history class at Fuller Seminary. And Cody U. Watson summarizes the importance of Winter's "Two Structures" thesis in his booklet, *Mission Orders and the Presbyterian Church (USA)*.[18] Most of all I am indebted to Ralph D. Winter, the greatest educator I have ever known. Albert Einstein said, "It is the theory that first determines what we can observe."[19] Because of Winter's "Two Structures" theory we are able to see things as they are.

Use of Sociological Literature

The relatively recent field of sociology has produced a considerable body of articles and books on special-purpose associations. Churches are a suitable subject of sociological study, as established by Ross P. Scherer in his article, "Sociology of Denominational Organization."[20] In my dissertation I refer to sociological research on voluntary societies in the United States, Asia, the Middle East, and Europe, and in the Jewish and Muslim

---

[16] Bruce L. Bauer, "Congregational and Mission Structures" (D. Miss. Dissertation, Fuller Theological Seminary, 1982).

[17] Charles J. Mellis, *Committed Communities: Fresh Streams for World Missions* (South Pasadena, CA: William Carey Library, 1976).

[18] Cody U. Watson, *Mission Orders and the Presbyterian Church* (Pasadena: Presbyterian Center for Mission Studies, 1989), 24-5.

[19] Werner Heisenberg recalled this quote from a private conversation with Einstein. Einstein's complete quote: "It is quite wrong to try founding a theory on observable magnitudes alone. In reality the very opposite happens. It is the theory which first determines what we can observe." Werner Heisenberg, *Physics and Beyond: Encounters and Conversations*, World Perspectives (London: G. Allen & Unwin, 1971), 63.

[20] Ross P. Scherer, *American Denominational Organization: A Sociological View* (Pasadena, CA: William Carey Library, 1980), 1-27.

religions. From this I have determined that sodalities—special-purpose associations—occur naturally in every population, and, therefore, occur naturally in the church as well.

Use of Interviews

I interviewed a mission leader from each of five denominational headquarters: the Presbyterian Church USA, the Lutheran Church Missouri Synod, the Reformed Church of America, the Quakers, the Methodist and the Episcopal churches in order to determine how new mission initiatives do or do not take place in hierarchical structures.

Use of Quantitative Data

Rodney Stark's essay, "Why Historians Ought to Count"[21] encouraged me to count the number of missionary biographies in two standard reference books; from this I created timelines and figures that present evidenced-based findings that support the effectiveness of Carey's enabling paradigm.

---

[21] Rodney Stark, *Cities of God: Christianizing the Urban Empire*, 1st ed. (San Francisco: Harper, 2006), 209-222.

CHAPTER 3: DESIGN OF PROJECT GIVEN BY RALPH D. WINTER

Ralph D. Winter was the chair of my dissertation committee until his death in May 2009. The project he designed is a review of the literature specializing in the relationship between mission societies and their relationship to church administrations. Winter wrote the following:

> The mentor has hoped for years to pull together a number documents shedding light on the above specialization. The associate's relationship to the mentor will consist in becoming the main editor, write brief summaries of each document, comparing them and ordering them, as well as writing an introduction to the entire volume. The mentor will write a foreword. This work will constitute a large portion of the mentor's dissertation activity and will be accompanied by a hundred page document which will be the basis for the introduction of the book. The purpose is to evaluate mission structures, their relevance and viability in contemporary use.[22]

This dissertation will be edited into the "hundred page document" which will be the basis for the introduction of the collection of articles. A book, whose working title is *Organizing for Mission*, is complete, and will, hopefully, be published. I have received written permission to republish the following articles (although the Guder, TeSelle, Taylor and Brumberg-Kraus articles have not previously been published):

1. Introduction by Robert A. Blincoe
2. "Some Questions Directed to Protestants" by Johann Baegert
3. "An Enquiry into the Obligation of Christians to Use Means" by William Carey
4. "Females Bring Their Mites" by R. Pierce Beaver
5. "A Plea for Mission Orders" by Ralph D. Winter
6. "The New Missions and the Mission of the Church" by Ralph D. Winter
7. "A Plea for a New Voluntarism" by R. Pierce Beaver
8. "The Planting of Younger Missions" by Ralph D. Winter

---

[22] Ralph D. Winter, "Doctoral Learning Contract," (Pasadena: William Carey International University, 2002).

9. "The Two Structures of God's Redemptive Mission" by Ralph D. Winter
10. "An Historical Comparison of American and British Voluntary Societies" by John V. Taylor
11. "Protestant Mission Societies: The American Experience" by Ralph D. Winter
12. "Why We Need a Second Mission Agengy" by Gerald H. Anderson
13. "Churches Need Missions because Modalities Need Sodalities" by Ralph D. Winter
14. "Special-Interest Groups and American Presbyterianism" by Gary Eller
15. "Parachurch Movements: The Religious Order Revisited" by Darrell L. Guder
16. "Church and Parachurch: Christian Freedom, Ecclesiastical Order, and the Problem of Voluntary Organizations" by Eugene TeSelle
17. "Missionary Societies and the Fortunate Subversion of the Church" by Andrew F. Walls
18. " The Monastic Rescue of the Church" by Mark Noll
19. "Were the Pharisees a Conversionist Sect?" by Jonathan Brumberg-Kraus

3.1 Voluntary Associations Rising—Why Normalizing a Relationship between Ecclesiastical Structures and Voluntary Associations is More Necessary than Ever

In recent years, citizens all over the world have been forming more voluntary associations than ever before. Peter Goldmark, president of the Rockefeller Foundation from 1988 to 1997, wrote:

> It's got to strike you that a quarter of a century ago outside the United States there were very few NGOs (nongovernmental organizations involved in development and social work) and now there are millions of them all over the globe. Nobody could make that happen at the same time. Why did they grow? They grew because the seed was there and the soil was right. *You have restless people seeking to deal with problems that were not being successfully coped with by existing institutions. They escaped the old formats and were driven to invent new forms of organizations.* They found more freedom, more effectiveness and more productive engagement [emphasis added].[23]

---

[23] David Bornstein, *How to Change the World: Social Entrepreneurs and the Power of New Ideas* (Oxford University Press, 2004), 4.

The whole world is feeling the effect of "restless people" forming themselves into new organizations. "Twenty years ago, for example," David Bornstein, in *How to Change the World*, writes,

> Indonesia had only one independent environmental organization. Today it has more than 2,000. In Bangladesh, most of the country's development work is handled by 20,000 NGOs. India has well over a million citizen organizations. Slovakia, a tiny country, has more than 12,000 . . . In Brazil, in the 1990s, the number of registered citizen organizations jumped from 250,000 to 400,000, a 60 percent increase. In the United States, between 1989 and 1998, the number of public service groups registered with the Internal Revenue Service jumped from 464,000 to 734,000, also a 60 percent increase.[24]

Without organizations, people who want to change the world are left wondering how to take action. For example, Bill Hybels, pastor of Willow Creek Church near Chicago, wrote a book called *Holy Discontent*. "Whether you're a high-powered market place person, a stay-at-home mom, a full-time student, or something altogether different," Hybels writes, "you can join God in making what is wrong in this world right!"[25] But how? Hybels does not guide his readers to that "enabling technology"—special-purpose associations—by which readers of Hybels' change-the-world pep talk would more likely make their dream of changing the world become a reality.

In his 1951 book *International Non-Government Organizations—their Purposes, Methods and Accomplishments*, Lyman White extolled the contribution to global development being made by voluntary societies. However, White observed, "Perhaps no

---

[24] Ibid.

[25] Bill Hybels, *Holy Discontent: Fueling the Fire That Ignites Personal Vision* (Grand Rapids: Zondervan, 2007), 25.

aspect of international relations has received less attention, even from students of international organization itself, than the part which non-governmental organizations have played in world affairs."[26] White attributes this inattention to

> the preoccupation of historians and political scientists with the rivalry between states and illustrates it by the political scientists' almost exclusive concern, several decades ago, with the formal organs of government to the exclusion of the role played by the trade unions, churches, etc.[27]

In their sociological study, *The Soul of Civil Society*, Don Eberly and Ryan Streeter show that voluntary associations "create the environment" in which *civility*—"that collection of the habits on which our democratic way of life depends"—can be fostered.[28] Civility—"respect and desire for dignity for other persons"—is "the sum of the many sacrifices we are called to make for the sake of living together."[29] The big idea of Eberly and Streeter's little book is that a general population achieves civil renaissance when

---

[26] Lyman Cromwell White, *International Non-Governmental Organizations; Their Purposes, Methods, and Accomplishments* (New Brunswick, NJ: Rutgers University Press, 1951), vii.

[27] Ibid. A remarkable number of Nobel Peace Prize recipients achieved their prominence by organizing special-purpose non-profit groups. They are: Wangari Maathai, Pan African Green Belt Network (2004); Shirin Ebadi, Association for Support of Children's Rights, Human Rights Defence Centre, Iran (2003); Médecins Sans Frontières (1999); Jody Williams, International Campaign to Ban Landmines (1997); Rigoberta Menchú, Committee of the Peasant Union (Guatemala) (1992); International Physicians for the Prevention of Nuclear War (1985); Mother Teresa, Sisters of Charity (1979); Amnesty International (1977); Betty Williams, Mairead Corrigan, Northern Ireland Peace Movement (1976); Martin Luther King, Jr. Southern Christian Leadership Conference (1964); Albert Schweitzer, Lambaréné hospital, Gabon (1952); Emily Greene Rich, Women's International League for Peace and Freedom (1946); John R. Mott, Young Men's Christian Associations, International Missionary Council (also 1946); Jane Addams, Women's International League for Peace and Freedom, Hull House (1931); Ferdinand Buisson, League for Human Rights (1927); Klas Pontus Arnoldson, Swedish Peace and Arbitration League (1908); Ernesto Teodoro Moneta, Lombard League of Peace (1907); Élie Ducommun, International Peace Bureau (1902); Jean Henry Dunant, Founder of the International Committee of the Red Cross (1901).

[28] Don E. Eberly and Ryan Streeter, *The Soul of Civil Society: Voluntary Associations and the Public Value of Moral Habits* (Lanham, Md.: Lexington Books, 2002), viii.

[29] Ibid.

citizens are free to organize themselves into voluntary societies. These societies identify a cause and apply all of the organizations' resources to achieving great ends.

Hoisting Many Sails. Starting voluntary associations resembles the hoisting of many sails on a fleet of ocean-going sailing ships. Consider how crews hoist the sails in order to catch the wind and sail out of the harbor. Today hundreds of "crews" are forming special-purpose associations. For the sake of achieving important tasks to which God calls His people, church governments must rethink their historic objection to mission societies. The interdiction that Luther and the Reformers ordered against religious orders still deters many church leaders from appreciating a biblical basis for, and proven effectiveness of, voluntary societies in changing the world. There is theological repair to be undertaken, and I believe the conditions for repair can be created by understanding the theology of *missio Dei.*

3.2 *Organizing for Missio Dei, in Order to Close a Breach that has Opened in the Protestant Church*

"Our task," writes Darrell L. Guder, "is to apply the theological understandings rooted in the *missio Dei* to the church's structures."[30] That is, our understanding of the missio Dei should make clear what structures the church needs in order to effectively engage in God's mission. The term *missio Dei* means "sending which is of God"; it was

---

[30] Darrell L. Guder, "Missional Structures: The Particular Community," in *Missional Church: A Vision for the Sending of the Church in North America.* (Grand Rapids: Eerdmans, 1998), 222.

probably coined by Karl Hartenstein,[31] who was clarifying Karl Barth's term *actio Dei,* a term which gave missiology a new grounding in the Trinity.[32] The term *missio Dei* was popularized by Georg Vicedom in his 1965 book, *Mission of God*.[33] Hartenstein wrote:

> When kept in the context of the Scriptures, *missio Dei* correctly emphasizes that God is the initiator of His mission to redeem through the Church a special people for Himself from all of the peoples (*ta ethne*) of the world. He sent His Son for this purpose and He sends the Church into the world with the message of the gospel for the same purpose.[34]

In his book, *Transforming Mission,* David Bosch explained how the meaning of *missio Dei* evolved over the last fifty years. "The classical doctrine on the *missio Dei,*" Bosch writes, "as God the Father sending the Son, and God the Father and the Son sending the Spirit was expanded to include yet another "movement": The Father, Son and the Holy Spirit sending the church into the world."[35] "Mission," wrote Bosch,

> is thereby seen as a movement from God to the world; the church is viewed as an instrument for that mission. There is church because there is mission, not vice

---

[31] See John G. Flett, *The Witness of God : The Trinity, Missio Dei, Karl Barth, and the Nature of Christian Community* (Grand Rapids, Mich.: W.B. Eerdmans Pub., 2010), 124ff.

[32] John G. Flett has demonstrated that Barth's role in coining the term *missio Dei* is a "popular account" that "demands significant revision." See "Barth and the Origins of Missio Dei" in ibid., 11ff.

[33] For more information on the development of *missio Dei* see Charles Edward Van Engen, *Mission on the Way: Issues in Mission Theology* (Grand Rapids: Baker Books, 1996), 27, 37ff. And Darrell L. Guder, *The Continuing Conversion of the Church*, The Gospel and Our Culture Series (Grand Rapids: Eerdmans, 2000), 19-21.

[34] Quoted in Van Sanders, "The Mission of God and the Local Church," in *Pursuing the Mission of God in Church Planting* (Alpharetta, GA: North American Mission Board (Southern Baptist Convention), 2006), 24. Near the end of his life, Ralph D. Winter published a collection of the writings titled, *Frontiers in Mission: Discovering and Surmounting Barriers to the Missio Dei*. This may have been Winter's only reference to the *missio Dei*; his biographer has not found any others (personal correspondence with Greg Parsons, August 13, 2010). So it is fascinating to realize that Winter summarized God's calling on him by testifying that his writings were all for the purpose of resolving certain obstacles to enable God's people to participate more effectively in the *missio Dei*. See Ralph D. Winter, *Frontiers in Mission: Discovering and Surmounting Barriers to the Missio Dei* (Pasadena: William Carey International University Press, 2005).

[35] David Jacobus Bosch, *Transforming Mission: Paradigm Shifts in Theology of Mission* (Maryknoll, NY: Orbis Books, 1991), 390.

versa. To participate in mission is to participate in the movement of God's love toward people, since God is a fountain of sending love.[36]

The early Protestants assumed that the entire *missio Dei* could be carried out by the instrument of the church governments. Bosch referred to this assumption:

> The fact is that, for more than a century after the Reformation, the mere idea of forming such "voluntary societies" next to the church was anathema in Protestantism. The institutional church, tightly controlled by the clergy, remained the only divine instrument on earth.[37]

In his 1971 article "Churches Need Missions Because Modalities Need Sodalities," Ralph D. Winter argued against the idea that the institutional church is the only divine instrument, as though "the church is the central and basic structure, whereas the mission is somehow secondary or perhaps merely a temporary aid in establishing churches [as though] the scaffolding must come down when the building is done."[38] Max Warren (d. 1977), director of the Church Mission Society, made an impassioned plea at the 1957 Ghana meeting of the World Council of Churches (WCC) when the proposal to subsume the International Mission Council (IMC) under the WCC was being debated. "Mission and Unity belong together, of course," said Warren, "but there is no obvious necessity for that belongingness to be stressed administratively."[39] Like Warren, Bishop Steven Neill opposed the merger:

---

[36] Ibid.

[37] Ibid., 329.

[38] Ralph D. Winter, "Churches Need Missions Because Modalities Need Sodalities," *Evangelical Missions Quarterly* Vol. 7, (1971, July): 194. (Winter originally titled this article, "The Legitimacy of So-called 'Para-Church' Structures in the Overall Christian Movement.")

[39] Quoted in Harvey Thomas Hoekstra, *The World Council of Churches and the Demise of Evangelism* (Wheaton, Ill.: Tyndale House Publishers, 1979), 42.

> The WCC is by its nature concerned with that third of the world's population which is nominally Christian, and in particular with that ten per cent of the world's population which belongs to the member churches of the WCC; whereas the IMC is concerned with the two-thirds of the world's population which is not and has never been Christian. This latter responsibility cannot possibly be brought under the heading of inter-church aid as is presently understood.[40]

Like Neill and Warren, Winter argued that the New Testament church did not retain control over the mission structures:

> When Paul and Barnabas departed from Antioch, their move and their new organizational relationship to each other were not regarded as a breakdown of unity in the body of Christ, but did clearly constitute a separation of functions . . . Both organization forms, the team and the church, were "church"; both the stationary Christian synagogue that remained in Antioch and the travelling missionary team (which, note well, no longer took its orders from the Antioch church) were essential elements in the body of Christ, the people of God of the New Covenant, and were equally the church.[41]

Church unity, then, is like a marriage (to borrow from the title of Winter's 1978 article "Ghana: Preparation for Marriage," from which the above quote is taken) because, as in a marriage, Winter explains,

> neither of the two structures could by itself effectively fulfill the functions of the other. Both were essential to the unfolding purposes of God . . . The writer is profoundly convinced that the very life of the church and its mission in history depends upon the existence and friendly, productive relationship between these two contrasting manifestations of the church.[42]

The findings in this dissertation indicate that the most promising future for the carrying out of the *missio Dei* is for the Protestant Church to carefully and finally decide

---

[40] Ralph D. Winter, "Ghana: Preparation for Marriage," *International Review of Mission* 17, (1978): 347. 347, quoting Stephen Neill in an article by Karsten Nissen, "Mission and Unity: A Look at the Integration of the International Missionary Council and the World Council of Churches," *International Review of Mission*, 63, no. 252 (October 1974), 546.
[41] Ibid., 339.
[42] Ibid., 339-40.

to replace its *sola synodica* paradigm with the "Two Structures" paradigm proposed by Ralph D. Winter.[43] This would mean that church governing structures would recognize and sanction the special-purpose associations that their members are joining or forming. Such a social contract would be similar to the relationship between a city government and its activist associations. Here is an example from the city of Detroit.

"Private Groups Push Detroit Ahead"

In a 2008 Detroit *Free-Press* newspaper story, "Private Groups Push Detroit Ahead," reporter John Gallagher writes,

> To get something done in Detroit, you traditionally went to City Hall. In recent years, more and more you went to a foundation, a nonprofit agency, or a quasi-public authority. It's a part of a trend that has seen Detroit's civic-minded leaders evolving a new model for operating a town chronically short of cash and beset with a fractious political culture.[44]

The trend in Detroit to privatize certain government functions has apparently been positively received, according to the news article. "Although fraught with political sensitivities," the article continues,

> the privatization of traditional city oversight of some functions is a trend that is by now too strong to ignore. "What you've seen over the last few years has been a continuing acceleration of public-private partnerships, and you're going to see that trend going forward," Doug Rothwell, president of the corporate leadership group Detroit Renaissance said recently.

---

[43] Ralph D. Winter, "The Two Structures of God's Redemptive Mission," *Missiology* 2, no. 1 (1974).
[44] John Gallagher, "Private Groups Push Detroit Ahead," *The Detroit Free Press*, April 6, 2008, 1. All quotes concerning this story are from Gallagher's news article.

The article then explains the "efficiency" advantage that private associations enjoy over government:

> Charlie Williams, a former top aide to Mayor Coleman A. Young and now president of an environmental firm in Detroit, said the inability of the city's bureaucracy to move as quickly as private entities has also pushed the trend forward. "Implied in that is that the government doesn't do an effective job in terms of efficiency," he said. "You're overwhelmed by the bureaucracy." Many leaders, including those in city government itself, acknowledge that there really is little alternative given the bleak outlook for city finances.

In sum, private citizen groups and Detroit's city government are negotiating a new social contract. This trend was observed by Stanley H. Skreslet in his article, "Impending Transformation: Mission Structures for a New Century." Skreslet writes,

> Numerous social commentators have pointed to the phenomenon of decentralization as a distinctive mark of economic and political activity today. This trend may be seen, for instance, in the push to privatize many of the functions that used to be performed by governments.[45]

In the Detroit story the reader observes that 1) private citizens have organized special-purpose associations to solve some of the problems that until recently were the domain of Detroit's city government. We also read of 2) the reluctance of Detroit's City Hall to surrender the initiative to private interest groups. However, 3) the shift to private initiative will continue because 4) private initiative, such as the RiverFront Conservancy and the Kresge Foundation, are more effective at solving some problems. Moreover, we read that 5) governments should recognize and regulate, but not administrate, the private sector. Finally, City Hall is not going away. "No one should think the public sector can

---

[45] Stanley H. Skreslet, "Impending Transformation: Mission Structures for a New Century," *International Bulletin of Missionary Research* 23, no. 1 (1999): 2.

be dispensed with entirely," said Rip Rapson, president of the Kresge Foundation. From fixing roads and sewers to assembling tax-foreclosed land he said, municipal governments remain essential. However, there is a new social order afoot relating the citizen sector and the municipal government in Detroit and nearly everywhere in the free world. This is because, as Bornstein writes,

> While governments must be held responsible for translating the will of the citizenry into public policy, they are not necessarily the most effective vehicles, and certainly not the sole legitimate vehicles, for the actually delivery of many social goods, and they are often less inventive than entrepreneurial citizen organizations.[46]

A year after the April 2008 *Detroit Free Press* story, *Time* magazine compared Detroit's public high schools to that city's only Jesuit high school, the University of Detroit High School:

> Lunch period at an inner-city all-boys school is an event usually associated with the sounds of chaos, not classical music. And yet there are definitely strains of Beethoven coming from the piano in the cafeteria at the University of Detroit Jesuit High School and Academy. Behind the pianist, another student waits patiently for his turn. Upstairs in the art room, a senior is using the lunch hour to apply more brushstrokes to a portrait. A few kids are playing pickup ball in the gym, but more are crowded in the library. In a city where 47% of adults are functionally illiterate and only 25% of high school freshmen make it to graduation, U of D is the chute through which bright young men can get to college. *The school boasts a near perfect graduation rate and sends 99% of its graduates on to higher education.* (In 2009 the one student who didn't go to college turned down a scholarship from the University of Michigan to sign a seven-figure contract with the Detroit Tigers) [emphasis added].[47]

---

[46] Bornstein, 8.

[47] Amy Sullivan, "Jesuit Message Drives Detroit's Last Catholic School," *Time Magazine*, November 10 2009.

It is desirable that Detroit's city council continue recognizing and regulating, but not administrating, special-interest citizen groups that are initiating all manner of good works. In this way, some of problems that the city faces are more effectively addressed. There is a bright future because the government is offloading responsibilities to the private sector. I would like to offer a personal example.

How the US Government and an NGO Changed the Future in Kurdistan. I lived in Kurdistan of northern Iraq from 1991 to 1996. There I directed a relief effort initiated by Medical Teams International,[48] a non-profit organization based in Portland, Oregon. Times were tough; in a deliberate attempt to punish the Kurdish people Saddam Hussein's government in Baghdad ordered the electricity turned off the electricity in all of Kurdistan (it remained off for five years) and halted the livestock vaccination program. In 1992 I hired two unemployed Kurdish veterinarians and began purchasing livestock vaccine in Mosul, where there was still electricity. For a year we improved the health of the herds and flocks in our region. Our vaccination program caught the attention of the US Agency for International Development (USAID); in 1993 the USAID director in Iraq offered Medical Teams International a contract to vaccinate animals all over Northern Iraq for a population of four million people. We accepted. Working through the Kurdish Veterinary Association, a local civic agency, we put a hundred veterinarians and assistants to work. Every week for the next three years they vaccinated thousands of

---

[48] To learn more about this non-profit organization, visit www.medicalteams.org

sheep, cattle and goats. As the health of the flocks and herds improved, the number of animals increased. Moreover, animal owners sold the wool from their sheep and turned goat milk into cheese and yogurt. The price of meat dropped to where consumers could buy it. In short we made a better future for millions of Kurds.

In this example, the American government negotiated a contract with a non-profit organization to initiate and implement an effective solution to a problem. A government agency—the USAID—monitored our vaccination program but did not manage it. In a similar way church governments should recognize and regulate, but not manage, the initiatives that its members want to begin or join.

There are lots of "restless persons" in the church who want to change the world. We have heard Peter Goldmark say that they "invent new forms of organizations" to achieve more effective outcomes. In the 1990s I started two special-purpose associations: the Kurdish Literature Association and Friends of the Kurds. I joined three additional special-interest groups that others founded: Medical Teams International and the Presbyterian Order for World Evangelization (POWE)[49] and Frontiers.[50] A board of directors for each agency holds the chief executive officer accountable for a certain mission that is defined in the agencies' founding documents.

---

[49] To learn more about the Presbyterian Order for World Evangelization, visit www.reconsecration.org. Accessed November 2006.
[50] www.frontiers.org

3.3 Paradigm Shift and Resistance—Observations of Thomas Kuhn

William Carey's paradigm will be shown to be more biblical, more predictably effective as measured by an inductive study of mission history, and truer to what is "really there" in societies everywhere. Here, I will put forward a theory to explain the church's resistance to Carey's paradigm. In 1962 Thomas Kuhn wrote his landmark book, *The Structure of Scientific Revolutions.*[51] In it, Kuhn, professor of History of Science at the University of California at Berkeley, popularized the term *paradigm* and coined the term *paradigm shift*. It seems to me that Kuhn's explanation of *paradigm shift* helps demonstrate what was revolutionary about Carey's structural theory. Furthermore, Kuhn's theory of "resistance" helps the reader explain the inclination of some ecclesiastical leaders to oppose William Carey's paradigm.

Paradigms, explains Kuhn, are "scientific achievements that for a time provide model problems and solutions to a community of practitioners."[52] A paradigm does not provide solutions to all problems—"it need not, and in fact never does, explain all the facts with which it can be confronted."[53] The unresolved problems are called "anomalies." An anomaly is "the recognition that nature has somehow violated the paradigm-induced expectations that govern normal science."[54] A crisis occurs when a scientist is bothered by the number or importance of these anomalies. "Discovery commences with the

---

[51] Kuhn, 85.
[52] Ibid., preface.
[53] Ibid., 18.
[54] Ibid., 52-3.

awareness of anomaly."[55] When this crisis occurs a scientist may propose a revolutionary paradigm. Such a scientist—Kuhn mentions Copernicus, Newton, Darwin, Lavoisier, and Einstein—proposes a new theory that is incompatible with a time-honored paradigm which the science community of its day regards as normal:

> Probably the single most prevalent claim advanced by the proponents of a new paradigm is that they can solve the problems that have led the old one to a crisis. People are persuaded to change paradigms if they believe that the new model is closer to nature, closer to what is "really there."[56]

Upon hearing of a new paradigm, the community of scientists is pushed to choose between the new and old paradigms, and to be persuaded that one explains nature better than the other. A scientist's claim to have reconciled the crisis-provoking anomalies is, however, rarely persuasive by itself, even if it resolves the anomalies unexplained by the older paradigm. According to Kuhn some scientists *resist* a better paradigm (that is, resist a "paradigm shift") for psychological reasons. Some scientists are "intolerant of those theories invented by others."[57] Kuhn theorizes that scientists make "quasi-metaphysical commitments"[58] to their own familiar but anomaly-ridden paradigm. Sometimes, writes Kuhn, scientists "do not treat anomalies as counter-instances, though in the vocabulary of philosophy of science that is what they are."[59] Normal science "often suppresses fundamental novelties because they are necessarily subversive of its basic

---

[55] Ibid., 52.
[56] Ibid., 206.
[57] Ibid., 24.
[58] Ibid., 41.
[59] Ibid., 77.

commitments."[60] In other words, some scientists hold on to what they are familiar with and disregard contrary evidence. This "unscientific" resistance to paradigm shift is of great interest to Kuhn. "Professionalization leads to . . . a considerable resistance to paradigm change."[61] Kuhn says that older adherents tend to resist more than younger people. "Almost always," he writes,

> The men who achieve these fundamental inventions of a new paradigm have been either very young or very new to the field whose paradigm they change. These are the men who, being little committed by prior practice to the traditional rules of normal science, are particularly likely to see that those rules no longer define a playable game and to conceive another set that can replace them.[62] . . . There are always some men who cling to one or another of the older views, and they are simply read out of the profession, which thereafter ignores their work.[63]

Kuhn quotes Charles Darwin who wrote, "I look with confidence to the future—to young and rising naturalists, who will be able to view both sides of the question with impartiality."[64] And Max Planck remarked that "a new scientific truth does not triumph by convincing its opponents and making them see the light, but rather because its opponents eventually die, and a new generation grows up that is familiar with it."[65] Kuhn concludes, "The transfer of allegiance from paradigm to paradigm is a conversion experience that cannot be forced."[66] "Kuhn even uses religious language," writes David Bosch, "to describe what happens to the scientist who relinquishes one paradigm for

---

[60] Ibid., 5.
[61] Ibid., 64.
[62] Ibid., 90.
[63] Ibid., 19.
[64] Ibid., 151.
[65] Ibid.
[66] Ibid.

another. It is a case of 'scales falling from the eyes,' of responding to 'flashes of intuition,' indeed of 'conversion.'"[67] When a new paradigm is "intuitively obvious," Kuhn writes, some scientists may embrace it, yet other scientists will retain faith in a familiar paradigm because their minds are not acting on logic but on psychological factors; "such scientists are not yet and may never be 'converted.'"[68]

Paradigm Shift and Resistance, Applied to Social Sciences. Do Kuhn's scientific observations apply to the social sciences? Kuhn, writing in 1962, states that his observations "have parallels in the pre-paradigm periods of fields that are today unhesitatingly labeled science."[69] *Social science* is "a scholarly or scientific discipline that deals with such study, generally regarded as including sociology, psychology, anthropology, economics, political science, and history."[70] I will consider Carey to be a social scientist who proposed a paradigm that subsequent social scientists tested and debated and accepted.

Kuhn's Theory Explains the Resistance to Carey's Paradigm Shift. Luther and the Reformers embraced a mission paradigm by which the advancement and fulfillment of the *missio Dei* depended entirely on the initiative of church administrations. By 1792 this paradigm was quite mature, having been the accepted model for two and a half centuries.

---

[67] Ibid., 122, 123, 151. Quoted also in Bosch, 184.
[68] Kuhn, 150.
[69] Ibid., 160.
[70] *The American Heritage Dictionary of the English Language*, 3rd ed. (Boston: Houghton Mifflin, 1996), s.v. "Social Science".

But Carey's proposal to democratize mission initiative quickly gained a following. Unlike previous generations, new laws enabled Christians in late 18th century England to organize societies without approval of the established Church. This was crucial because even when Carey's paradigm proved effective, the hierarchies resisted it. In their book *Voluntary Religion*, editors W. J. Sheils and Diana Wood make this relevant comment: "Ecclesiastical authority is particularly liable to feel itself under threat from religious activity outside its control, and the reactions of authority have often turned into counter-church movements."[71] For example, in 1960 Presbyterian Church U.S. reminded its members that non-Presbyterian mission agencies, including CARE, World Vision and Christian Children's Fund, "are not related to our Church and are not recommended as the approved channel for the relief activities of our own people. All members of our Church are urgently requested to send their relief funds through their churches."[72]

Historical and exegetical research validates, I believe, William Carey's "company of serious Christians" paradigm and, by corollary, Ralph D. Winter's "Two Structures" paradigm. It follows, on account of accepting Winter's thesis, that the *sola synodica* model by which church administrations retain for themselves the authority to initiate mission can be predicted to fail.

---

[71] W. J. Sheils and Diana Wood, eds., *Voluntary Religion*, vol. 23 (Oxford: UK: Published for the Ecclesiastical History Society by B. Blackwell, 1986), xiii.

[72] Robert Weingartner, "Missions within the Mission," in *A History of Presbyterian Missions, 1944-2007* (Louisville: Geneva Press, 2008), 112.

CHAPTER 4: AN ORGANIZATIONAL INTERPRETATION OF MISSION HISTORY

In this section I will set out evidence that Ralph D. Winter's "Two Structures" paradigm is soundly based on what was really there in the first century Christian church. In addition, objections to Winter are considered and refuted. I hope to help the reader understand a New Testament basis for a second New Testament church structure, the mission agency. "The missionary movement must become more theological," John A. Mackay said, "not primarily for those to whom missionaries go, but for the Church herself and the missionaries who represent her."[73]

4.1 The Biblical Literature

Many church leaders are inclined to assume that the local church is the sole legitimate structure found in the New Testament—"the only divine instrument on earth,"[74] as David Bosch characterized the perspective of the Reformers. That the local church borrowed its practices from what was already there in the Jewish synagogue is well-known. What is less well-known is that Paul's missionary band had its roots in the contemporary Jewish mission experience.

4.1.1 The Jewish Structural Advantage

"Very few Christians, casually reading the New Testament," Winter wrote:

---

[73] John A. Mackay, "The Evangelistic Duty of Christianity," *The Christian Life and Message in Relation to Non-Christian Systems of Thought and Life,* vol. 1 of *The Jerusalem Meeting of the International Missionary Council*, March 24-April 8, 1928 (New York: IMC, 1928), p. 390. Quoted in Gerald H. Anderson, "American Protestants in Pursuit of Missions: 1886-1986," *International Bulletin of Missionary Research* 2, no. 3 (1988): 106.

[74] Bosch, 329.

and with only the New Testament available to them, would surmise the degree to which there had been Jewish evangelists who went before Paul all over the Empire, people whom Jesus himself described as "traversing land and sea to make a single proselyte." Paul followed their path; he built on their efforts and went beyond them with the new gospel he preached.[75]

When occasion demanded, Winter writes, "Paul established brand new synagogue-type fellowships of believers as the basic unit of his missionary activity. The first structure in the New Testament scene is thus what is often called the *New Testament church*. It was essentially built along Jewish synagogue lines [emphasis is in original]."[76] The defining characteristic of this structure "is that it included old and young, male and female."[77] Then Winter describes a second, "quite different" Jewish structure active in the first century:

> While we know very little about the structure of the evangelistic outreach within which pre-Pauline Jewish proselytizers worked, we do know, as already mentioned, that they operated all over the Roman Empire. It would be surprising if Paul didn't follow somewhat the same procedures.[78]

Paul's team "may certainly be considered a structure," Winter asserts.[79] "While its design and form is not made concrete for us on the basis of remaining documents, neither, of course, is the New Testament church so defined concretely for us in the pages of the New

---

[75] Winter, "The Two Structures of God's Redemptive Mission," 121.

[76] Latourette wrote that "the synagogue . . . was to have a profound effect upon the nascent Christian Church . . . Both in Palestine and among the Jews of the 'dispersion' scattered through much of the Mediterranean world and Western Asia, the synagogues were the places where most of the Jews worshipped and taught." Kenneth Scott Latourette, *A History of Christianity*, Revised ed., 2 vols. (New York: Harper & Row, 1975), 13-14. Winter wrote that the Christian church model was "obviously borrowed" from the synagogue. Ralph D. Winter, "The Anatomy of the Christian Mission," *Evangelical Missions Quarterly* 5:74-89, (1969): 75.

[77] Winter, "The Two Structures of God's Redemptive Mission," 122.

[78] Ibid.

[79] Ibid.

Testament."[80] Thus, two kinds of Jewish social structures existed, both of which were adopted by Christians. "The structure we call the New Testament church," Winter summarizes, "is a prototype of all subsequent Christian fellowships where old and young, male and female are gathered together as normal biological families in aggregate."[81] On the other hand, Paul's missionary band "can be considered a prototype of all subsequent missionary endeavors organized out of committed, experienced workers who affiliated themselves by making a second decision beyond membership in the first structure."[82] These two structures "have continuously appeared across the centuries":

> The New Testament is trying to show us *how to borrow effective patterns*; it is trying to free all future missionaries from the need to follow the precise forms of the Jewish synagogue and Jewish missionary band, and yet to allow them to choose comparable indigenous structures in the countless new situations across history and around the world—structures which will correspond faithfully to the *function* of the patterns Paul employed. As Kraft has said earlier, we seek *dynamic equivalence* not formal replication [emphasis is in original].[83]

Pharisees were a Khevra: A Jewish Mission Agency. The Hebrew term for a voluntary mission structure is *khevra* (khev-RAH). Winter references a type of *khevra* (though he does not use this term) when he mentions "the structure of the evangelistic outreach within which pre-Pauline Jewish proselytizers worked."[84] There were several *khevrot* (plural of *khevra*) in New Testament times: Pharisees, of which more will be said, as well

---

[80] Ibid.

[81] Jewish women and children were members of synagogues, a convention first practiced in ancient Greece, where "all members of the family take part in the συναγωγή." Wolfgang Schrage, "Synagogue," in *Theological Dictionary of the New Testament* (Grand Rapids: Eerdmans, 1965), 800.

[82] Winter, "The Two Structures of God's Redemptive Mission," 122.

[83] Ibid. Winter is referencing Charles H. Kraft, *A Hausa Reader; Cultural Materials with Helps for Use in Teaching Intermediate and Advanced Hausa* (Berkeley, CA: University of California Press, 1973).

[84] Winter, "The Two Structures of God's Redemptive Mission," 121.

as Essenes, Sadducees, and others, some quite informal, comprised of a rabbi and his chosen disciples.[85] *Khevrot* still exist today.[86] *Khevra* is the Hebrew word for "membership society," "association," "fraternity," "guild." It is related is *khaver* ("kha-VER*)* meaning "friend." The Pharisees were a *khevra*, organized to perform tasks and achieve certain goals. F. F. Bruce says the Pharisees "banded themselves together in local fellowships or brotherhoods."[87] In a chapter called "The Fraternity of Pharisees" Alfred Edersheim writes that "the Pharisees were a regular 'order,' and that there were many such 'fraternities.'"[88] If we do not see them explained as such in the New Testament, it is because "the New Testament simply transports us among contemporary scenes and actors, taking the then existent state of things, so to speak, for granted."[89]

Sadducees and Essenes were also *khevrot*. We don't know much about the wandering band of exorcists in Acts 19 but they were on a mission to cast out demons. It is reasonable to say that John the Baptist invited "disciples" to join his *khevra*. Jesus called

---

[85] The literature of the Qumranic community describes the Pharisees, Sadducees and "Essenes." "The monastery at Qumran was probably the extreme expression of Sadduceeism" and its members probably "partisans of Judas Maccabee," differing from the "normative Sadduceeism of the Herodian period." Robert Eisenman, *The Dead Sea Scrolls and the First Christians* (Rockport, MA: Element Books, 1996), 51.

[86] For examples of modern day *khevrot*, google *khevra* or *chabura, chevra* or *havurah*.

[87] F. F. Bruce, *New Testament History* (London: Nelson, 1969), 78. Also Ralph P. Martin, *New Testament Foundations: A Guide for Christian Students* (Grand Rapids: Eerdmans, 1975), 86. Also Alfred Edersheim, *Sketches of Jewish Social Life in the Days of Christ* (London: The Religious Tract Society, 1876), 169ff. Students of the New Testament would be more open to the "two structures" paradigm if a study Bible explained the term *khevra* in the same way that a study Bible explains "Essene," "Maccabean" and other Jewish terms that do not appear in the New Testament.

[88] Edersheim, 169.

[89] Ibid.

twelve to go with him on a preaching mission that he organized; his disciples would have recognized themselves as members of a *khevra*, as would the Jews who met them.

While all Jews could belong to a synagogue, only some Jews met the requirements (or had the inclination) of joining a *khevra*. These two kinds of organizations—synagogue and *khevra*—are two distinct structures with which Jews like Peter and Paul would have been familiar.

In sum, Winter theorized that in the New Testament we observe "the pre-existence of a commonly understood pattern of relationship, whether in the case of the church [patterned after the Jewish synagogue] or the missionary band [patterned after the Jewish Pharisees] which Paul [had] employed earlier as Saul the Pharisee."[90] "We will consider the missionary band," Winter writes, "the second of the two redemptive structures in New Testament times."[91] For Winter, Pellowe says, "Neither structure is more central than the other, although the church structure regulates the specialized structure, on the principle that the specialized reports to the more general."[92]

Jewish Voluntary Societies Today

In his article, "Jewish Organization Patterns in the United States," Daniel J. Elazar observes that Jews in the United States belong to all manner of membership societies that are voluntary and task-oriented. Jews do not demean these voluntary structures as "para-

---

[90] Winter, "The Two Structures of God's Redemptive Mission," 122.
[91] Ibid., 124.
[92] John Pellowe, *A Practical Theology for Relations between Churches and Self-Governing Agencies* (Gordon-Conwell Theological Seminary, 2007), 80-81.

synagogue" organizations, as though the synagogue were the center of the Jewish activities. Membership in Jewish special-purpose associations is often more important than membership in the synagogue, with the result that "the essential community of interest and purpose is reflected in a well-nigh complete panoply of organizations."[93] Elazar explains this social characteristic:

> It is *not simply* association with a *synagogue* that enables a Jew to become part of the organized Jewish community. Affiliation with *any of a whole range of organizations*, ranging from clearly philanthropic groups to "secularist" cultural societies, offers the same option [emphasis is in original].[94]

In fact, writes Elazar, the synagogue since 1960 has become *less* important in the Jewish life, while the standing of Jewish organizations has increased in importance,[95] especially in America:

> The American Jewish community is built upon an associational base to a far greater extent than any other in Jewish history. That is to say, not only is there no inescapable compulsion, external or internal, to affiliate with organized Jewry, but there is no automatic way to become a member of the Jewish community. All connections with organized Jewish life are based on voluntary associations with some particular organization or institution, whether in the form of synagogue membership, contribution to the local Jewish Welfare Fund (generally considered to be an act of joining as well as contributing) or affiliation with *B'nai Brith* Lodge of Hadassah (the Women's Zionist Organization) chapter.[96]

Without its associational base, "there would be no organized Jewish community at all," Elazar writes. "With it, the Jewish community attains the kind of social status (and even a

---

[93] Daniel J. Elazar, "Patterns of Jewish Organization in the United States," in *American Denominational Organizations* (Pasadena: William Carey Library, 1980), 132.
[94] Ibid., 133.
[95] Ibid.
[96] Ibid.

certain legal status) that enables it to fit well into the larger society of which it is a part."[97] The Jewish congregation "is a very flexible device that can accommodate all those services and more, usually through a system of *hevrot* (fellowships) or committees."[98] Jews can organize these services, or missions, *whether or not there is a synagogue*. Indeed, members of the *hevrot* may be members of more than one synagogue or of no synagogue at all.

Pluralism in a Jewish congregation assures that no central governing power would ever deny its members their liberty to organize special-interest associations. "The new voluntarism," Elazar writes, "extended itself into the internal life of the Jewish community as well, generating pluralism *even within previously free* but relatively homogeneous and monolithic community structures [emphasis is in original]."[99] Elazar describes this arrangement as "pluralistic federalism," a kind of creative chaos that "substantially eliminates the neat patterns, the kinds which are easily presented on organizational charts."[100] A hierarchical organizational structure "does not offer an accurate picture of the distribution of powers and responsibilities in the Jewish community today":

> There is *no* functioning, organizational *pyramid* in Jewish life; no national organization able to issue directives to local affiliates; and no local "judicatory" organization able to order others within its "jurisdiction" into line. In sum, there is no *central* governing agent in most Jewish communities which serves as the point

---

[97] Ibid., 134.
[98] Ibid., 135. *Hevrot* is an alternative spelling to *khevrot*. See 2.1.
[99] Ibid.
[100] Ibid.

at which authority, responsibility, and power converge, even at the local level [emphasis and parentheses are in original].[101]

Attempts at centralization were unlikely to succeed, considering the pluralism in the American Jewish experience:

> From the late 1850s to the early 1880s, the growing American Jewish community experimented with a representative Board of Deputies of American Israelites, modeled after the Board of Deputies of British Jews in the United Kingdom. The experiment was launched with great difficulty and failed almost immediately. Neither it nor its more narrowly based successor, the Union of American Hebrew Congregations (the very name reveals how contemporaries still conceived of Jewish life as concentrated in the synagogue and potentially unifiable on the congregational basis), ever came close to achieving universality.[102]

Thus, the different interests of Jewish traditionalists and liberals, Elazar states, were too great for control by any Jewish hierarchy.[103]

Kinds of Organizations in the Jewish Community. Elazar lists and describes four kinds of Jewish organizations[104]:

1. Government-like organizations
2. Localistic institutions and organizations
3. General purpose, mass-based organizations
4. Special interest organizations

Then Elazar combines the first two and the last two: "The first two are essentially embodied in the institutions which form the structural foundations of the community, and the last two essentially in organizations which function to activate the institutional

---

[101] Ibid., 135-36. "Judicatory," Elazar explains, "is a Presbyterian term widely adopted to refer to generic, regional, ecclesiastical authority structures."
[102] Ibid., 139.
[103] Ibid.
[104] Ibid., 137ff.

structure and give it life."¹⁰⁵ Elazar refers to the first pair as "organic" and the second pair as "associational."¹⁰⁶ Thus, two types of structure in the Jewish congregation have been described. These two kinds of structure are the same that Ralph Winter and Jonathan Brumberg-Kraus observed in the New Testament Jewish culture—1) the synagogue and 2) the special-purpose associations.

I take the opportunity here to introduce Jonathan Brumberg-Kraus, professor at Wheaton College ("the other Wheaton," he told me, a four year liberal arts college in Norton, Massachusetts). In 2002, Brumberg-Kraus wrote a remarkable paper, "Were the Pharisees a Conversionist Sect?"¹⁰⁷ Brumberg-Kraus' observations will help reply to objections raised against Winter's thesis, objections to be considered in section 4.1.2.

Jewish Missionary Societies—Observations of Jonathan Brumberg-Kraus

In his paper Brumberg-Kraus explains the purpose of one first century Jewish voluntary society, the Pharisees. He writes,

> Though early Christian literature represents the Pharisees as perhaps their greatest religious rival—in the conflict stories and other anti-Pharisee polemic in the Gospels, in Paul's dramatic disavowal of his former life as a Pharisee—most have dismissed Matthew's claim, that Pharisees 'traverse sea and land to make a single proselyte' (Mt 23:15) as polemical hyperbole.¹⁰⁸

---

¹⁰⁵ Ibid., 137.
¹⁰⁶ Ibid., 132.
¹⁰⁷ Jonathan Brumberg-Kraus, "Were the Pharisees a Conversionist Sect? Table Fellowship as a Strategy of Conversion" http://acunix.wheatonma.edu/jkraus/articles/Pharisees.htm. In this remarkable article (available only online) Brumberg-Kraus establishes the Pharisees as a "holiness movement" actively competing against the "mercy movement" of Jesus. Accessed October 2003.
¹⁰⁸ Ibid., 1. Brumberg-Kraus cites Gal 1:11-24, Phil 3:4-9, Acts 9:1-19, 22:1-21, 26:12-23 (Paul's conversion); I Thessalonians 1:4-10, Acts 2 (success of the conversion mission). See also Alan F. Segal,

But in fact, Brumberg-Kraus states, the Pharisees actively sought "converts" to Pharisaism. He continues,

> Their primary target group was not Gentiles, as Matthew's use of the term "proselyte" implies. The terms "proselyte" and "proselytism" usually refer to a conversion from one ethnic community to another. That is, proselytes to Judaism have "converted" from being Gentiles to being members of the Jewish ethnic group. Likewise in Pauline Christianity, one "converts" from being a Gentile or a Jew into a new kind of community in which "there is neither Jew nor Gentile." The Pharisees however seemed to have *confined their active efforts to win new followers to ethnic Jews* [emphasis added].[109]

Thus, Brumberg-Kraus begins his explanation of a holiness renewal mission to convert fellow Jews. (This is against Josephus, who left a lasting, wrong impression by describing Pharisees, Sadducees and Essenes as "schools of philosophy"[110] after Greek fashion). Brumberg-Kraus concurs with Winter's thesis. "While the popularity of the Pharisees does not prove conclusively that they conducted any sort of missionary campaign (Mt 23:15 is the only explicit contemporary reference to such a mission)," Brumberg-Kraus writes, "one could reasonably hypothesize that their popularity was the

---

Paul the Convert: The Apostolate and Apostasy of Saul the Pharisee (New Haven: Yale University Press, 1990), 6.

[109] Brumberg-Kraus. 1. The Pharisees resembled the Lubavitch Jews, who make every effort "to proselytize the Jews, attempting to convert the non-orthodox to a more Torah-observant way of life" (See Martin Gilbert and Josephine Bacon, *The Illustrated Atlas of Jewish Civilization* (London: A. Deutsch, 1990), 88.

[110] Josephus emphasized features of the Jewish religious orders which "he judged would make the greatest impression on his Gentile readers." See F.F. Bruce, 78. Thus, when historians read Josephus at face value they are led away from thinking of the Pharisees, Sadducees and Essenes as New Testament-era Jewish *khevrot*. J. Gresham Machen in his book *The Origin of Paul's Religion*, has not a word on the origin of Paul's missionary strategy or field-governed autonomy. Instead, relying on Josephus for his single reference to the Pharisees, Machen simply says that Josephus distinguishes three Jewish sects, the Pharisees, the Sadducees, and the Essenes. See J. Gresham Machen, *The Origin of Paul's Religion* (New York: Macmillan, 1921), 177.

result of active missionizing . . . How the Pharisees got so popular is precisely the question an analysis of their 'strategy of conversion' tries to answer."[111]

Brumberg-Kraus then describes this fascinating "strategy of conversion." A Pharisee delegation would go to a synagogue and ask for permission to address the congregation on the Sabbath. The Pharisees would describe their understanding of how to keep the Torah; interested Jews would be invited to a meal at which the food would be prepared according to the requirements of the Torah. The food would be "tithed" and ritual purity would be observed. Even the spices would be tithed before they were prepared, a practice to which Jesus referred.[112] Pharisees dined together in order to ensure that every member of the community was following the dietary regulations. After the meal the guests would be invited to join the *khevra*. Presumably some of the newly-initiated members would participate in the mission to invite more Jews to consider the way of holiness upheld by the Pharisees. Conformity to these distinctive practices, Brumberg-Kraus states, "was the prerequisite for different levels of membership in Pharisaic 'associations' (*khevrot*)."[113]

Next, Brumberg-Kraus references Paul's letter to the Galatians and Josephus' *Autobiography* to lend support, unintentionally, to Winter's thesis that Paul's experience as a Pharisee suggested to him the form of his mission in the New Testament. Brumberg-Kraus writes,

---

[111] Brumberg-Kraus. 2.
[112] "Woe to you, scribes and Pharisees, hypocrites! For you tithe mint, dill, and cumin, and have neglected the weightier matters of the law: justice and mercy and faith. It is these you ought to have practiced without neglecting the others."—Matthew 23:23
[113] Brumberg-Kraus. 2.

> If Paul himself had not been a proselytizing Pharisee before his conversion, at least his post-conversion opponents in Galatians (e.g., in Gal 2:12) could be plausibly identified as Jewish missionaries who are of the Pharisaic persuasion. Moreover, both Paul's and Josephus' description of themselves as Pharisees stress that the designation applies to their outward behavior: Paul says he was "*as to the law* a Pharisee" (Phil. 3:5); and Josephus says he chose to "govern himself *(politeusthai,* lit., to conduct himself in public*)* according to the school of thought of the Pharisees" (*Life* 12) . . . Josephus characterizes the Pharisees as one among several *haireseon* to which *one could convert*, even if he [Josephus] himself did not take that step. Therefore, if one takes seriously the cumulative testimony of Josephus, Paul, the Synoptic Gospels and their prior Christian traditions, one would have to agree that the Pharisees' near contemporaries perceived them as a popular religious-philosophical movement in 1st century Judaism, whose "mission" seemed to consist of getting other Jews to participate in their distinctive practices of table fellowship, tithing, and ritual purity; and which was a community to (or from) which people could convert [emphasis is in original].[114]

Brumberg-Kraus offers further proof to his thesis that the Pharisees had a "conversionist agenda" when he points to the Gospel texts in which Jesus and his followers dispute with the Pharisees. Brumberg-Kraus writes,

> In my view, the relationship between these practices [purity rituals, tithing, including tithing of food, and table fellowship] and a conversionist agenda becomes clear when they are contextualized in terms of the early church's concerns. What did the composers of the Gospels have to fear from the Pharisees? That a programmatic policy of tithing, purity rituals, and table fellowship would steal away potential converts? How could these early Christians possibly have viewed the observance of tithing and purity rules, and restrictive table fellowship as competition to their mission? The answer is that the particular *behaviors* of tithing, observance of purity laws, and table fellowship themselves functioned as *means of proselytizing* [emphasis is in original].[115]

---

[114] Ibid., 3. Brumberg-Kraus here cites Scot McKnight, *A Light among the Gentiles: Jewish Missionary Activity in the Second Temple Period* (Minneapolis: Fortress Press, 1991), 104, 152.

[115] Brumberg-Kraus. 6.

Brumberg-Kraus' paper lends support to Winter's "Two Structures" thesis. In the next section we will consider the arguments of missiologists who object to Winter's thesis.

4.1.2 Objections to Winter's "Two Structures" Thesis Considered

In the twentieth century many missiologists supported of the historic "one structure" paradigm of the churches in the Reformed tradition. These missiologists include Roland Allen,[116] Harvie Conn,[117] Orlando Costas,[118] George W. Peters,[119] Paul A. Beals,[120] J. H. Bavinck,[121] J. Eckhard Schnabel[122] and Bruce Camp.[123] They hold that the New Testament admits only the congregation, and, presumably, its eventual superstructure, the denomination. Thus Peters: "It must be stated, however, that they [mission societies] are not of Biblical origin, for they are not divine institutions of the same order as churches[124]

---

[116] Roland Allen, *The Spontaneous Expansion of the Church and the Causes Which Hinder It* (London: World Dominion Press, 1927).

[117] Harvie M. Conn, *Theological Perspectives on Church Growth* (Nutley, NJ: Presbyterian and Reformed, 1976), 122.

[118] Orlando E. Costas, *The Church and Its Mission: A Shattering Critique from the Third World* (Wheaton, IL: Tyndale House Publishers, 1974), 159-67.

[119] George W. Peters, *A Biblical Theology of Missions* (Chicago,: Moody Press, 1972), 226.

[120] Paul A. Beals, *A People for His Name: A Church Based Missions Strategy*, Rev. ed. (Pasadena, CA: William Carey Library, 1985), 111-36.

[121] Johan Herman Bavinck, *An Introduction to the Science of Missions* (Philadelphia: Presbyterian and Reformed, 1960), 60.

[122] Eckhard J. Schnabel, *Early Christian Mission*, 2 vols. (Downers Grove, Ill.: InterVarsity Press, 2004); Eckhard J. Schnabel, *Paul, the Missionary: Realities, Strategies and Methods* (Downers Grove, IL: IVP Academic, 2008).

[123] Bruce Camp, "A Theological Examination of the Two-Structure Theory," *Missiology* 21, no. 2 (1995). And Bruce Camp, "Scripturally Considered, the Local Church Has Primary Responsibility for World Evangelization," in *School of Intercultural Studies* (La Mirada: Biola University, 1992).

[124] Peters, 229.

... mission societies are a historical abnormality."[125] Roland Allen said as much in a chapter called "Missionary Organizations" when he maintained that the Early Church was itself a mission agency.[126] "The organization of missionary societies," Allen wrote, "was permitted for the hardness of our hearts, because we had lost the power to appreciate and to use the divine organization of the Church in its simplicity for the purpose for which it was first created."[127] Orlando Costas asserts that the success of "nonchurch" structures—his term for independent mission agencies—is God's judgment on the church and a sign of the church's failure to be the church.[128] Ironically, J. I. Packer observes the very same success of the voluntary structures, "but interprets it as God's blessing rather than his judgment."[129] "The Church," says Packer, "manifests its reality in local churches (gatherings committed to do all the things the Church does) and also in parachurch bodies (associations committed to do some of the things the Church does)."[130] Furthermore, "Packer believes that any time believers gather to do what scripture says the church does, there is the church made visible."[131] This includes small groups of special

---

[125] Ibid., 214.

[126] Allen, 97.

[127] Ibid., 161.

[128] Costas, 168. On page 162 Costas is critical of Ralph D. Winter, "The Planting of Younger Missions," in *Christian/Mission Tensions Today* (Grand Rapids: Moody Press, 1972).

[129] J. I. Packer, "Crosscurrents among evangelicals." In Charles W. Colson and Richard John Neuhaus, *Evangelicals and Catholics Together: Toward a Common Mission* (Dallas: Word, 1995). Quoted in Pellowe, "Leading Ministries into Christian Community: A Practical Theology for Church-Agency Relations", 49. (unpublished dissertation)

[130] J. I. Packer, "Crosscurrents among evangelicals." In Colson and Neuhaus. 150-51, quoted in Pellowe, "Leading Ministries into Christian Community: A Practical Theology for Church-Agency Relations", 412.

[131] J. I. Packer, "Crosscurrents among evangelicals." In Colson and Neuhaus. 161-62. Quoted in Pellowe, "Leading Ministries into Christian Community: A Practical Theology for Church-Agency Relations", 412ff.

purpose. Karl Barth has a similar opinion, supportive of "special working fellowships," as we will read in section 4.6.6.

J. Eckhard Schnabel's Objection Considered

J. Eckhard Schnabel criticized Winter's "Two Structures" paradigm by averring that Winter based it on a false premise. Schnabel holds that there was apparently no apparent Jewish mission in the first century. If Schnabel is correct, then Winter's thesis—that Paul patterned his mobile missionary teams after what he was familiar with as a Pharisee—would be invalidated. In his book *Paul the Missionary* Schnabel writes that "Paul's missionary work provides neither a paradigm" to justify the existence of mission agencies "nor principles or rules"[132] which mission agencies today could employ. Schnabel cites "Ralph Winter's argument that the modern mission society resembles the missionary team of Paul and his coworkers" as "a well-known example of using the New Testament for contemporary missiological purposes."[133] Schnabel is particularly distressed because Winter uses the Pharisees of the New Testament to validate his "Two Structures" theory:[134]

> Ralph Winter argues that the church always has two structures that are legitimate and that contribute to the fulfillment of the Great Commission: the church or local congregation, which uses the model of the Jewish synagogue; and the mission society, which uses the model of Jewish and early Christian teams of missionaries. He suggests that the church can be understood, from a sociological perspective, as a "modality," a structured community in which there are no

---

[132] Schnabel, *Paul, the Missionary: Realities, Strategies and Methods*, 393.
[133] Ibid.
[134] Ibid.

differences of gender or age, while the missionary team is a "sodality," a structured community in which membership is determined by a second "decision" and limited as a result of age, gender or marital status. He argues that theologically the function of the church is important, not its form or structures. This analysis has been criticized[135]... It also needs to be noted that the early Christian missionary teams did not adopt the form of similar Jewish "teams" of missionaries, as there is no evidence for a missionary movement in Second Temple Judaism.[136]

Schnabel must somehow set aside Jesus' reference to the Pharisees' mission and does so by calling it "polemical" and "hyperbolic"[137]:

> Nothing in this comment [by Jesus] forces us to interpret it in terms of a "burning zeal of the Pharisaic mission," since no Jewish, Greek or Roman texts unambiguously prove the existence of Jewish missionary work among Gentiles. Assertions such as that of Walter Grundmann, who states that Jewish missionary activity "reached its climax at the time of Jesus and the apostles,"[138] are sheer inventions.[139]

In contrast to Schnabel, Brumberg-Kraus believes, as we have seen, that the Pharisees were a first-century voluntary mission society. And Richard De Ridder writes, "The word of Jesus in Matthew 23:15 would make no sense at all if the Jews never sought to win converts."[140] The Roman poet Horace (d. 8 BC) said that Jews forced people to become Jews.[141] This indicates, at least in Horace's mind, that Jews were inviting Gentiles to join them in the faith. De Ridder believes that "the Jews were motivated to some form of

---

[135] Schnabel, *Early Christian Mission*, 1578. Schnabel adds, "For some of the arguments that follow above see B. Camp 1995." This reference is to an April 1995 *Missiology* article by Bruce Camp, "A Theological Examination of the Two-Structure Theory." I respond to Bruce Camp later in this section of the paper.
[136] Ibid.
[137] Ibid., 163-4.
[138] Quoted in ibid., 490.
[139] Ibid., 164.
[140] Richard De Ridder, *Discipling the Nations* (Grand Rapids: Baker Book House, 1975), 94.
[141] "*veluti te Iudaei cogemus in hanc concedere turbam.*" Horace and John Carew Rolfe, *Q. Horati Flacci Sermones Et Epistulae*, Allyn and Bacon's College Latin Series (Boston: Allyn and Bacon, 1901), Book 1.4.142.43.

witness to their Gentile neighbors[142] . . . [and] to others besides the members of the dispersed communities of the Jews."[143]

In a 1995 *Missiology* article, "A Theological Examination of the Two Structure Theory,"[144] and also in his doctor of ministry dissertation,[145] Bruce Camp argued against Winter's "Two Structures" paradigm. We turn to Bruce Camp's argument next.

Bruce Camp's Objection Considered

Bruce Camp believes that mission agencies are a "scriptural abnormality."[146] Camp states that the local church has primary responsibility for world missions, though primary responsibility does not mean sole responsibility.[147] It is important that "local churches, mission agencies, missionaries, and planted (national) churches should relate to each other," he writes.[148] "The idea that an expression (a sodality) of the universal church may limit its constituency based on sex, age, talent, gifts, or other criteria is completely foreign to Christianity. It violates both scriptural teaching (1 Corinthians 12:21) and early

---

[142] De Ridder, 121.

[143] Ibid., 122. The validity of Winter's "Two Structures" paradigm does not depend on resolving the problem of the whether the outcome intended by the mission of the Pharisees was laudable.

[144] Camp, "A Theological Examination of the Two-Structure Theory." Camp is founder of DualReach.[144] Ralph D. Winter's endorsement is on the DualReach website.

[145] Camp, "Scripturally Considered, the Local Church Has Primary Responsibility for World Evangelization."

[146] Camp, "A Theological Examination of the Two-Structure Theory," 197. Camp is quoting Harry Boer and agreeing with him. See Harry R. Boer, *Pentecost and Missions* (Grand Rapids: Eerdmans, 1961), 214. 214. But Camp also believes agencies are "a gift from God to help local churches fulfill their Great Commission mandate." Bruce Camp, "Paradigm Shifts in World Evangelization," *Mobilizer* 5, no. 1 (1994): 3.

[147] Camp, "Scripturally Considered, the Local Church Has Primary Responsibility for World Evangelization," 4.

[148] Ibid., Abstract.

church practice (Acts 1-2)."[149] For these reasons Camp objects to Ralph Winter's "Two Structures" thesis. Mission agencies can be valid, Camp says, on condition that they derive their legitimacy from local churches, "not usurping the local church's biblical mandate."[150] Camp cites missiologists who believe that mission agencies are "not biblical."[151] He takes issue with a 1979 article "Paul and the Regions Beyond," in which Winter wrote that "Paul's missionary band was as much the church (that is, as much the *ecclesia*) as were the synagogue structures which supported him and which were in turn created by his ministry."[152] Camp suggests:

> that a theological error is involved when mission agencies (sodalities) are presented as another expression of the universal church . . . It is biblically unwarranted to suggest that missionary bands are another expression of the universal church.[153]

Camp employs the term "universal church" several times; Winter does not use this term at all, and it is somewhat difficult to find its equal in Winter's body of writings. I

---

[149] Camp, "A Theological Examination of the Two-Structure Theory," 203.

[150] Ibid., 207.

[151] Ibid., 197.

[152] Ralph D. Winter, "Paul and the Regions Beyond," *Asia Missions Advance*, (1979 July 11-15): 7. "The English word 'church,'" writes Winter, "is most likely traceable back to a Greek word (*kuriakon*) which is not even to be found in the New Testament. Nevertheless, most evangelicals go along with the exegetical sleight of hand that takes place when our references to denominational organizations as churches is substituted for the Greek word *ecclesia* in the New Testament, which more accurately refers primarily to a people, a community, a multitude, a movement and not to a specific type of organizational structure." Ibid., 6. For more on *kuriakon* as the probable root word for *kirche*, *kirk* and *church* see K. L. Schmidt, "Ekklesia," in *Theological Dictionary of the New Testament* (Grand Rapids: Eerdmans, 1965), 531-2. (Foerster, in his article on *kuriakos* in the same volume of *TDNT* does not comment on the etymology of *kirche/church*. 1095-1096.)

[152] Similarly, "Martin Luther "detested the old German word *Kirche*," writes Charles van Engen "because of its institutional and hierarchical associations, preferring such words as crowd (*Haufe*), convocation (*Versammlung*), assembly (*Sammlung*), and congregation (*Gemeinde*)." Van Engen, 105. These German terms more closely resemble the ecclesia of the New Testament.

[153] Camp, "A Theological Examination of the Two-Structure Theory," 201.

think that Winter would use the term "largest Christian modality" to mean what Camp means by "universal church." If this is so, then the question can be framed thus: "Did Ralph Winter's "Two Structures" paradigm refer to missionary bands as an expression of the universal church?" The answer, "No" seems clear; missionary bands are comprised of subsets of the universal church.

John Pellowe is helpful in framing a reply to Camp's objection. In his dissertation on agency-church relations, Pellowe writes:

> The temptation is to resort to scriptural precedent because evangelicals agree that scripture is authoritative; but even this seemingly safe route crosses a minefield. People resort to scripture with different assumptions about how to apply it. The pre-study survey includes a perfect illustration. One pastor answered a question about [the] legitimacy of unaffiliated agencies by asking, "Where in scripture was that again?" while another used the reverse argument, "I cannot think of a passage of scripture that disallows an independent ministry." Both appealed to scriptural authority with different outcomes![154]

David Bosch agreed. "We usually assume far too easily," he wrote, "that we employ the Bible as a kind of objective arbitrator in the case of theological differences," without fully realizing that we "approach the Bible with [our] own set of preconceived ideas about what it says." This means that "it is of little avail to embark upon a discussion of the biblical foundations of mission unless we have first clarified some of the hermeneutical principles involved."[155]

---

[154] Pellowe, *A Practical Theology for Relations between Churches and Self-Governing Agencies*, 3.

[155] Bosch, David J. "The Why and How of a True Biblical Foundation for Mission." Quoted in Van Engen, 35. To clarify my hermeneutics, then, I believe that a unity of the Bible presents itself when the authors are read in the spirit of trying to discover what they intended, a discovery that is most likely made through a historico-grammatical hermeneutic.

For Camp, the controlling principle is the importance of the "body of Christ" metaphor. The body of Christ, the most prominent of nearly 100 images used in the New Testament to describe the Church, "stresses the unity of the Church, whether local or universal, and particularly the fact that this unity is organic, and that the organism of the Church stands in vital relationship to Jesus Christ as her glorious head."[156] The church is "the unity of a living organism."[157] It follows, Camp believes, that there can be only one structure, the one revealed in the New Testament, what we normally think of as church.

On the other hand, Charles van Engen believes that "Paul's definition of church" was "based on the Old Testament concept of the people of God."[158] If the "people of God" in the Old Testament and the New Testament are a continuum, the question of church structures appears in a new light. Hans Küng writes that the "people of God" image is the oldest and most fundamental concept of the early church's self-understanding. Compared to "people of God," Pellowe says of Küng's thinking, "the image of the body of Christ, a temple and so on are secondary."[159] Pellowe's extensive literature review and attitude survey (chapters two and five of his dissertation) determined that

---

[156] Camp, "Scripturally Considered, the Local Church Has Primary Responsibility for World Evangelization," 31. Bruce is quoting Louis Berkhof, *Systematic Theology*, 2d rev. and enl. ed. (Grand Rapids, Mich.,: Wm. B. Eerdmans publishing co., 1982), 557.

[157] Camp, "Scripturally Considered, the Local Church Has Primary Responsibility for World Evangelization," 33. Quoted in Archibald Robertson and Alfred Plummer, *A Critical and Exegetical Commentary on the First Epistle of St. Paul to the Corinthians*, 2nd ed., The International Critical Commentary on the Holy Scriptures of the Old and New Testaments (Edinburgh: T. & T. Clark, 1914), 269-70.

[158] Van Engen, 105.

[159] Pellowe, "Leading Ministries into Christian Community: A Practical Theology for Church-Agency Relations", 89. Quote is from Hans Küng, *The Church* (London: Burns & Oates, 1967), 162. Unfortunately Camp did not quote any Catholic sources because, he wrote, "local autonomous churches did not exist in

people who question the validity of [mission] agencies tend to identify the *organized* church (local churches and denominational offices) as the church, placing the focus on structure and subordinating people to structure. People who support the validity of agencies tend to focus on *the people of God* as the church, emphasizing people and subordinating structure to people[160] [emphasis is in original].

Pre-existing beliefs about the nature of the church may have influenced people to hold opposing viewpoints. It is Camp's position that the church began on the Day of Pentecost.[161] But the apostles were familiar with the term *ecclesia* from the Septuagint, where it means "assembly," and is used in that way more than a hundred times. My position is that at Pentecost (a pre-New Testament feast of the people of God) the God of Joel came again with power and fire and wind.[162] "Pentecost is an equipping, not a birthing . . . The church was actually born with Abraham's call."[163] "Since Pentecost," Pellowe added, "the people of God and the church are one and the same. The two terms

---

Catholicism for many centuries." Camp, "Scripturally Considered, the Local Church Has Primary Responsibility for World Evangelization," 6.

[160] Pellowe, "Leading Ministries into Christian Community: A Practical Theology for Church-Agency Relations", 78.

[161] Camp, "Scripturally Considered, the Local Church Has Primary Responsibility for World Evangelization," 5.

[162] "As the feast of the celebration of first-fruits, Pentecost symbolized the beginning of the great redemptive harvest long anticipated in the OT (Is. 49:22; 66:18-21; Ze. 14:16). We also see the fulfillment of Isaiah's prophetic vision of the remnant from among the nations (Is. 2:2-4; Acts 2:10-11). And the agricultural celebration of Pentecost itself echoes Isaiah's feast on the Mountain of God (Is. 25:6-8). The presence of the Lord through the advent of the spirit at Pentecost, visiting the newly constituted church in Jerusalem, suggests the new Jerusalem of Zechariah (Ze. 12:7-9). Perhaps more significant is the resulting fire and wind phenomenon, imagery suggestive of Sinai and the coming of Yahweh to his people. On the day of Pentecost the church became the object of the fulfillment of these prophecies as well as others such as Psalm 96:7-9, Ez. 36:25-28 and Jeremiah 31:33,34." Don R. Golden, "A Study of the Local Church in Evangelical Cross-Cultural Mission" (University of Wales, 1998), 7.

[163] John Pellowe, *A Theological Understanding of the Place of Independent, Organized Ministry in Relation to the Institutional Church* (Canadian Councl of Christian Charities, 2007), 2.

are interchangeable."[164] Pentecost, for Peter, was another chapter in the history of the people of God:

> All the prophets, as many as have spoken, from Samuel and those after him, also predicted these days. You are the descendants of the prophets and of the covenant that God gave to your ancestors, saying to Abraham, 'And in your descendants all the families of the earth shall be blessed.'"—Acts 3:25.[165]

"The origin of the Christian identity," Pellowe wrote, "lies not in Jerusalem but in Haran, where God called Abraham."[166] Paul understood his mission as a continuation of the mission to preach the gospel that God gave "beforehand" to Abraham.[167] While Jesus Christ immeasurably added to God's glory by proving the one virtue which God's incarnation alone could demonstrate—the depth of God's sacrifice, love, judgment and mercy—Jesus did not bring "another gospel." At Pentecost the apostles received new power, but the Holy Spirit moved them to preach the continuation of the mission that began when God "dismissed" Abraham from Haran.[168] New believers, as sons and daughters of Abraham and Sarah, gain immediate access to the blessing of God Himself,

---

[164] Pellowe, "Leading Ministries into Christian Community: A Practical Theology for Church-Agency Relations", 421.

[165] The chiefs of all the people, of all the tribes of Israel, presented themselves in the assembly of the people of God.—Judges 20:2. See also 2 Samuel 14:13. For a Mennonite perspective on the central understanding of the Church as the "people of God" see Wilbert R. Shenk, *Write the Vision: The Church Renewed*, 1st U.S. ed., Christian Mission and Modern Culture (Valley Forge, Pa.: Trinity Press International;, 1995), 81ff.

[166] Pellowe, "Leading Ministries into Christian Community: A Practical Theology for Church-Agency Relations", 86.

[167] Galatians 3:8.

[168] Jesus Christ glorified the Father by magnifying infinitely what God had meant when He said to Abraham, "I will bless you, and in you shall all the families of the earth be blessed. (Genesis 12:3). Walter C. Kaiser of Gordon-Conwell Seminary calls this "the gospel encapsulated." Walter C. Kaiser, Jr., "Israel's Missionary Call," in *Perspectives on the World Christian Movement*, ed. Ralph D. Winter and Steve Hawthorne(Pasadena: William Carey Library, 1999), 16.

not through the mediation of the church. God is the herald who calls all of the "saved on earth" into the great *ecclesia*. When God's people respond to this call, they gather as the *ecclesia* in localities, in congregations. But they do not remain gathered; the Lord dismisses the people of God to take the *missio Dei* to the world. "The decisive point is not that someone or something assembles; it is who or what assembles. The explicit or implicit addition *tou theou* or *tou kuriou* tells us who assembles, or who causes men to assemble."[169] It is plain, Georg Schmidt adds, that the familiar image in Greek literature of a herald assembling the citizens of a community is now being given sacred meaning: God in Christ is the herald, "calling men out of the world,"[170] assembling His own. The size of the gathering is not important: "Where two or three are gathered together in my name, there am I in the midst of them."[171] Writing to Timothy, Paul describes the *ecclesia* as the *oiko theou*, household of God.[172] The creation of a "people of God" is the fundamental reality which 96 New Testament metaphors illuminate but never supplant.[173]

---

[169] Schmidt, 505.

[170] Ibid., 513.

[171] Matthew 18:20. "More recently," writes van Engen, "Hendrik Kraemer came close to Luther's simplicity of definition when he said, 'Where there is a group of baptized Christians, there is the church." Quoted in Van Engen, 115.

[172] "If I am delayed, you will know how people ought to conduct themselves in God's household, which is the church of the living God." 1 Timothy 3:15.

[173] Van Engen write that "Paul Minear (1960) found ninety-six different images of the church in the New Testament." Van Engen, 106. During Vatican II the Catholic Church changed its understanding of nature of the church, Pellowe writes, from "an institutional-hierarchic ecclesiology" (pyramid structure) to the "dynamic people of God" notion in which the church is seen first of all as a pilgrim people." Pellowe, "Leading Ministries into Christian Community: A Practical Theology for Church-Agency Relations". 101, quoting Veli-Matti Kärkkäinen, *Introduction to Ecclesiology: Ecumenical, Historical & Global Perspectives* (Downers Grove, Ill.: InterVarsity Press, 2002), 28. This correction brought the Catholic understanding of the church closer to the biblical framework.

In summary, over tens of centuries God's covenant love has created a great "assembly,"[174] the sons and daughters of Abraham; God calls them together to hear His word, "You will be my people, and I will be your God" (Jeremiah 30:22, etc.). God dismisses His people from the assembly "with grace and apostleship to bring about the obedience of faith among the nations/*ethnesin*" (Romans 1:5). This dismissal concludes the ministry of one church structure and the beginning of the other. With Guder, I hold that "the Scriptures function authoritatively in the formation of the churches' structures."[175] With Camp I believe a relationship between ecclesiastical hierarchies and special-purpose associations must be normalized, a cause for which Camp has provided important leadership.[176] The *khevra* pattern of voluntary mission societies should be accepted as a biblical basis for the "second structure" of God's redemptive mission. Winter's "Two Structures" paradigm is an appropriate and true explanation of "what is really there" in the nature of the church. In his *The Dynamics of Christian Mission*, Paul Pierson offers an apt summary of my position. "Some say that if the Church were completely healthy," Pierson writes,

> it would not need such mission structures. That is clearly wrong. A healthy church will constantly form teams that are called to specific projects, whether at the local level, focusing on special groups in its own area; or at the international level,

---

[174] *Ecclesia* has several meanings, even within the book of Acts. Schmidt notes that in Acts 19:32-40, the *ecclesia* in Ephesus is angry crowd. "Here *ecclesia* is a secular term in the full sense." Schmidt continues: "If we follow the fundamentally necessary and reasonable principle that the same word should be rendered consistently in the same author, this excludes the use of 'Church.' On the other hand, it also excludes the English 'congregation.' This leaves us with very little option but the simple rendering 'assembly' or 'gathering.'" Schmidt, 505.
[175] Guder, "Missional Structures: The Particular Community," 222.
[176] Camp, Bruce is founder of DualReach.[176] Ralph D. Winter's endorsement is on the DualReach website.

> focusing on distant culture. In the latter case, it will probably cooperate with other congregations of the same heritage in a denominational mission board, or with a multi-denominational mission structure. Both are legitimate.[177]

We must recognize, Pierson adds, "that when a theology says only the organized Church should be involved in mission, that theology has a very serious quarrel with history."[178]

For the reasons offered here I think I have answered Eckhardt's and Camp's criticism of Ralph Winter's "Two Structures" thesis. All the critics—Camp, Schnabel, Conn, Costas, Peters—are answered satisfactorily as well if the Jewish "two structures" pattern has been observed in the New Testament. As Darrell L. Guder has said, "We have both modality and sodality in the Antiochene church."[179] Everyone can observe "two structures" of God's redemptive mission in the New Testament, and discover them in succeeding generations of church history, but it was Ralph Winter's theory that allowed us to see it.

4.1.3 Sending Paul and Barnabas—An Exegesis of Acts 13:1-3 Corrects a Misunderstanding

The reason for exegeting Acts 13:1-3 is to demonstrate that this passage does not support the widely held understanding that the Antioch church sent out Paul and

---

[177] Paul E. Pierson, *The Dynamics of Christian Mission: History through a Missiological Perspective* (Pasadena, CA: William Carey International University Press, 2009). 33. Pierson also says, "I do not want to denigrate the institutional churches. We need them. They often provide stability, continuity and a system of checks and balances needed in every enterprise. However, even while we recognize their importance we must also be open to the Holy Spirit, who constantly surprises us and works outside these structures." 33.
[178] Ibid., 33.
[179] Guder, *The Continuing Conversion of the Church*, 185.

Barnabas. Protestant church leaders such as Camp and others[180] have based their claim for a "one structure" church paradigm on this understanding. I believe a careful reading will make clear that this assumption is doubtful; while churches today may properly see themselves as "sending churches," this passage does not lend support to them. In exegeting Acts 13:1-3 Harold Cook gives a helpful answer to the question, "Who Really Sent the First Missionaries?"[181] Cook first describes an understanding of the view he wishes to correct. In this view, "the Antioch church," it is said,

> exercised its proper place as the local body of Christ by recognizing and assessing the gifts of Paul (and others). It then was informed about the needs of other areas. Because of this it enlisted men who could meet the need; it authorized, then commissioned them to go, identifying itself with them, and then sent them out to the work.[182]

In this view one is to imagine that in the 11th chapter of Acts "Barnabas heard of Paul, sought him out, brought him to Antioch and helped him serve an internship in that church of not less than one year."[183] But reading of the actual account in Acts reveals, Cook says of the author whom he is quoting, "that he didn't get all of this from that account."[184] These assumptions, writes Cook, "merit serious consideration because they

---

[180] George Miley, *Loving the Church--Blessing the Nations: Pursuing the Role of Local Churches in Global Mission* (Waynesboro, GA: Gabriel, 2003).
[181] Harold R. Cook, "Who Really Sent the First Missionaries?," *Evangelical Missions Quarterly* 11, no. 4 (1975): 233.
[182] Cook is quoting from David H. Clark, in the *United Indian* missions magazine, "Editorial," Spring, 1971.
[183] Ibid.
[184] Cook: 233.

represent a trend in current evangelical thinking about missions."[185] An exegesis of Acts 13:1-3 follows.

Luke tells us "there were prophets and teachers," five of them.[186] He tells us their names. The Holy Spirit set apart[187] two of them, Barnabas and Saul, "for the work" (a phrase that Luke uses three times to describe the missionary task of church planting[188]). "Note first," Cook writes, "that the church as such was not involved in this action." Five prophets and teachers prayed and fasted and heard from the Holy Spirit. "Some would contend," Cook writes, "that the church was involved by implication, since these were the leaders in the church. But this is pure presumption . . . [as the five] are not named as elders or bishops of the church."[189]

The text indicates that three men laid hands on two colleagues. The "laying on of hands" in this narrative could have one of two meanings; Cook argues that the three meant to bless Paul and Barnabas (in the manner of Christ laying hands on children in Matthew 19:13-15), rather than to appointment them to an office (as when church leaders

---

[185] Ibid., 234.

[186] "Now there were in the church at Antioch prophets and teachers, Barnabas, Simeon who was called Niger, Lucius of Cyrene, Manaen, a member of the court of Herod the tetrarch, and Saul. While they were worshiping the Lord and fasting, the Holy Spirit said, 'Set apart for me Barnabas and Saul for the work to which I have called them.' Then after fasting and praying they laid their hands on them and sent them off." (Acts 13:1-3).

[187] The text says they were "set apart by" the Holy Spirit (Acts 13:2), and "sent out by" (εκπεμφέντες) the Holy Spirit" (Acts 13:4). That the reader of Acts 13 is meant to concede the field-governed nature of Paul and Barnabas' teams is carefully and convincingly argued in Joseph and Michele C., "Field-Governed Structures: New Testament," *International Journal of Frontier Missions* 18, no. 2 (2001).

[188] "From Attalia they sailed back to Antioch, where they had been committed to the grace of God *for the work* they had now completed" (Acts 14:26). "But Paul did not think it wise to take him, because he had deserted them in Pamphylia and had not continued with them *in the work* (Acts 15:38)." [emphasis added]

[189] Cook: 234. 234.

appointed deacons in Acts 6:6, and elders—implied in Paul's caution to Timothy not to lay hands on anyone in undue haste—in 1 Timothy 5:22. "Appointment presupposes superior authority to make the appointment," Cook comments. "But the three certainly did not have any authority other than that which Barnabas and Saul also enjoyed."[190] This group of three "sent" Paul and Barnabas "off," (*apelusan*). "This verb is never once used," Cook writes, "in the sense of an authoritative sending of individuals on a mission, or with a task to perform. *Apoluo* is translated "divorce" in Matthew 5:32 and as "set free" from prison in Acts 2:32. "So it really should be translated," Cook believes, "'they let them go,' or more freely, 'they wished them Godspeed.'"[191]

Later Paul felt obligated *to report* to the church in Antioch all that he was doing,[192] but he evidently was not governed by a sending church. Paul and Barnabas understood themselves to be authorized to dismiss John Mark from their team without referring this decision to the Antioch church. Furthermore, "it should be observed," writes Frank Severn, "that neither Antioch nor Jerusalem determined who should join the Pauline team."[193] "If the missionary work of Paul and Barnabas was a ministry of the Antiochian church," Pellowe writes,

---

[190] Ibid., 235.
[191] Ibid., 236.
[192] Acts 14:26-27—"From there they sailed back to Antioch, where they had been commended to the grace of God for the work that they had completed. When they arrived, they called the church together and related all that God had done with them, and how he had opened a door of faith for the Gentiles."
[193] Frank M. Severn, "Mission Societies: Are They Biblical?," *Evangelical Missions Quarterly* 36, no. 3 (2000): 323.

then one might wonder what the relationship of the team was to the other churches from which Paul drew his team?[194] . . . Was the team's ministry their ministry too? Did they have as much control as the Antioch church? If so, how would competing priorities of the various churches be resolved?[195]

Moreover, Cook writes, "If the Antioch church had constituted itself a missionary sending agency, surely there would be some further evidence of its missionary activity after this one trip. But this is completely lacking."[196] Appealing to Acts 13:1-3 to secure a biblical basis for today's church assessment and funding and oversight of missionaries seems to be treading on thin ice. Yet books promoting the so-called Antioch missions model abound.[197]

When Paul started his second trip, intending to retrace the route of his first trip (Acts 14:26), the Antioch church commended him to God. But in Acts 16:6 Luke records that the Holy Spirit changed Paul's plans, "the same plans," Pellowe writes, "the Antiochian church expected him to fulfill when they commended him."[198] Paul

> immediately and without consultation with his church changed his mission and followed God's direction (Acts 16:9-10). He did not go back to his church or the

---

[194] Pellowe writes, "A search on the names mentioned in Acts 20:4 shows they came from churches in Berea (Sopater), Thessalonica (Aristarchus), Galatia (Gaius and Timothy), Ephesus (Trophimus) and an unspecified location in Asia (Tychicus). It appears that, like Timothy in Acts 16:1, these were men whom Paul met and enlisted on his mission trips (since it appears he left Antioch with only Barnabas)." Pellowe, *A Practical Theology for Relations between Churches and Self-Governing Agencies*, 107.

[195] Ibid., 115.

[196] Cook: 234. 234

[197] The author of *Antioch Revisited,* Tom Julien, speaks for many when he writes: "As the believers of the [Antioch] church worshiped and fasted, the Holy Spirit said, 'Set apart for me Barnabas and Saul' . . . They laid hands on the two men, as a sign both of their recognition of God's call and of their responsibility as a church . . . It was a divinely inspired model of how the church ought to function." Tom Julien, *Antioch Revisited: Reuniting the Church with Her Mission* (Winona Lake, IN: BMH Books, 2006), 15-16. Tom Julien has inserted his interpretation of who was fasting and worshipping, changing the reference from five men to "all the believers of the Antioch church." See also Miley, 81ff.

[198] Pellowe, *A Practical Theology for Relations between Churches and Self-Governing Agencies*, 108.

churches of any of his team members for a discernment process or for approval to change the mission. There is no record of any dissension from the team about the process Paul followed.[199]

The apostle understood his authority to make strategic decisions "for the work."[200] It is not possible for missionaries and their sending churches today to follow an "Antioch pattern" if that presumes the existence of a pattern in 13:1-3 for today.[201] What shall we conclude? "Is it then wrong for the church to send out missionaries?" Cook asks:

> Far from it! Our only contention in this article is that it is wrong to claim that the organized church is the one agency prescribed in the New Testament for the sending of missionaries. On the contrary, the one indispensable is the sending by the Holy Spirit. If the church acts in accord with the Holy Spirit, well and good. But if not, the Spirit will still send forth his missionaries, whether individually, as in the early centuries, or through independent societies, as in more recent years.[202]

---

[199] Ibid.

[200] Apparently Paul could conclude his work in a region and move on (Romans 15:18-23). Not that the work of the gospel was completed, only that he had brought the work to "the end of the beginning." By baptizing new believers (Acts 8:12) and appointing elders in every place (Acts 14:23) and authorizing other church planters to appoint elders (Titus 1:5; 1 Timothy 5:21-22) Paul could finish the task of church planting in one area and lead his team to the regions beyond (2 Cor. 10:16).

[201] Today, a church missions pastors or a committee takes responsibility for assessing a member's calling to mission; that is a good idea, but not an idea modeled on the Antioch church. The church today is likely to fund the missionary from its budget; this requires a complex administrative function unimagined in the first century. With the Bible as our source and authority for doctrine and practice we can state that the Holy Spirit sent Paul and Barnabas, as He had sent Philip to the Ethiopian eunuch (Acts 8:29) and Peter to Cornelius Acts 11:12), as He kept Paul from going into Bithynia (Acts 16:7), but led him to Macedonia (v. 10). Alex Rattray Hay adds, "We can hardly conceive of Paul, Luke and Timothy having to write back to a 'Mission Board' in Jerusalem to ask permission to follow the leading of the Spirit to go over to Macedonia." Alexander Rattray Hay, *The New Testament Order for Church and Missionary* (Temperley, Argentina ; St. Louis: New Testament Missionary Union, 1947), 500. Churches today still hear the Holy Spirit say that He is sending forth members "for the work" of planting churches "where Christ is not known" (Romans 15:20) or for other mission tasks.

[202] Cook: 239.

These societies "are not an aberration, as some would have us believe," Cook concludes. "Rather, they are modern attempts (often faulty, to be sure) to follow the scriptural principle of letting the Spirit do the sending as in the early days."[203]

Cook supports Winter's observation that "the travelling missionary team . . . no longer took its orders from the Antioch church."[204] Craig van Gelder also supports Winter, noting that "once Barnabas and Paul were sent out by the Antioch church, they were basically on their own. They were neither under the control of Antioch in decision making, nor were they dependent upon Antioch for financial support."[205] Moreover, "at least 30 mobile men sent out from 14 different local assemblies, other than the twelve apostles, worked apart from, alongside of and with Paul."[206] By these findings I believe there is adequate data to disagree with Bruce Camp and other critics who derive the idea of a sending church's authority to govern mission agencies from Acts 13:1-3.

This concludes my attempt to reply to the critics of Winter's "Two Structures" paradigm.

---

[203] Ibid.

[204] Winter, "Ghana: Preparation for Marriage," 339.

[205] Craig Van Gelder, "Local and Mobile--a Study of Two Functions (Unpublished Dissertation)," (Jackson, MS: Reformed Theological Seminary, 1975), 24.

[206] Ibid., 25. Paul's teams were field-governed; so was Patrick's mission. On this subject Joseph and Michele C. have written five helpful articles on "Field-Governed Mission Structures." Ralph D. Winter has written "William Carey's Major Novelty," the account of the joint venture agreement signed by the Baptist Missionary Society (BMS) in England and the Serampore Brotherhood in India.

4.2 The Celtic Church Advantage: Its Organizational Structure

For a long time—the sixth through the ninth century held administrative authority over dioceses and abbots governed bishops in a large and diverse region of Europe. I refer to the era of the expansion of the Celtic Church. There is apparently nothing inherently better or natural about the Roman pattern of rule by *alicubi regionum*—territorial church government.[207] In fact, William Marnell suggest a Celtic advantage: *"In a missionary country the monastery and not the parish is the obvious pattern of organization* [emphasis added]."[208] Arguably, every country is still a missionary country, as the recent missional church movement seems to demonstrate.

While Roman-Empire Christianity was perfectly suited to rule where the Roman Empire had administrated rule by regional *dioceses*, Ireland/Hibernia was something different. In fact, *diocese* was a term used

> to designate the administration of a territory dependent on a city. . . as the Christian bishop generally resided in a *civitas*, the territory administered by him, being usually conterminous with the juridical territory of the city, came to be known ecclesiastically by its usual civil term, *diocese*.[209]

This governance model "presupposed," George Hunter wrote,

> an organized town or village, with a parish church at the town's center. It also presupposed a network of towns, connected by roads within a geographic political

---

[207] Schmidt, 502.

[208] William H. Marnell, *Light from the West: The Irish Mission and the Emergence of Modern Europe* (New York: Seabury Press, 1978), 27.

[209] Herbermann and others, s.v. "Diocese". All of the "citizens" of a Roman "city" came to be regarded as "Christians."

unit, like a county, that could double as a bishop's diocese. Celtic Ireland had no established towns however, only temporary settlements of tribal groups.[210]

But in Ireland there were no towns, no provinces, and no fixed boundaries, "and therefore a diocesan episcopacy was unsuitable."[211] The characteristic indicators of Roman dominion and civilization—Fletcher mentions "towns, roads, coinage, written law, bureaucracy, taxation"[212]—were absent in Ireland. Fletcher then dryly adds, "One might reasonably guess that Patrick's congregations were a good deal less touched by *Romanitas* than the Tervingi of Dacia among whom Ulfilas had ministered."[213] "In consequence of the predominance of the clan," Workman writes, "diocesan episcopacy, such as we find early developed in Italy and Gaul, did not exist, or, rather, existed only in a subordinate tribal form."[214] The Celts monastic leaders established a tribal, hereditary pattern of rule over a great expanse of Europe:

> Monasticism obtained a speedy mastery over Celtic minds not only by reason of its emotional appeal and its severe ideal of renunciation, but even more because of its perfect adaptation to the Celtic genius, *and by its power of falling in with the clan or sept system under which the Celts were organized* [emphasis added].[215]

---

[210] George G. Hunter, *The Celtic Way of Evangelism: How Christianity Can Reach the West Again* (Nashville, TN: Abingdon Press, 2000), 27.

[211] Nora K. Chadwick, *The Celts* (Harmondsworth, England: Penguin Books, 1970), 198.

[212] R. A. Fletcher, *The Barbarian Conversion: From Paganism to Christianity*, 1st American ed. (New York: H. Holt and Co., 1998), 89. Also John Thomas McNeill, *The Celtic Churches; a History A.D. 200 to 1200* (University of Chicago Press, 1974), 69-70.

[213] Fletcher, 89.

[214] Herbert B. Workman, *The Evolution of the Monastic Ideal from the Earliest Times Down to the Coming of the Friars* (London: C. H. Kelly., 1913), 193.

[215] Ibid., 184. "*Sept*: a division of a family, especially a division of a clan." It is a philosophical question of no small consequence to decide whether any country is ever no longer "a missionary country."

The effect of "falling in with the clan or sept system" was this: clan leaders would choose the ruling abbots from among their sons. These abbots were not subject to Rome's bishop, even if that bishop were Patrick himself. For, despite Patrick's best effort to spread the Roman form of administration—he had been appointed bishop by Pope Celestine I before returning to Ireland in 433—the Celtic Christians preferred, even insisted on, a hereditary pattern of governance. Of the diocesan model, historian Nora Chadwick writes, "Within a comparatively short time in Celtic Britain and Ireland this system proved incapable of adaptation to a tribal system of society."[216] The diocese "gave way to the federation of monastic communities, each with its *paruchia* under the supreme jurisdiction of the 'heir' of the founder-saint."[217] In his superb book, *The Barbarian Conversion*, Richard Fletcher describes this Celtic version of church governance:

> In Ireland the fundamental political unit—the very word 'political' is perhaps something of a misnomer in this context—was the *tuath* (plural *tuatha*), a human grouping held together partly by kinship, partly by clientage, in occupation of a shifting zone of territory under the presidency of a dynasty of kings maintained by tribute in land.[218]

Upon an abbot's death the governance over his monastery transferred to a younger male relation. For example, at least ten of the first thirteen abbots of Iona were kin of Saint Columba.[219] The monastic pattern made its appeal in Ireland largely because it proved capable of accommodating itself to this version of governance, which is to say, de-

---

[216] Chadwick, 197.
[217] Ibid.
[218] Fletcher, 89. Nora Chadwick writes, "Beyond the boundaries of the *tuath* an individual could not rely on legal protection." Chadwick, 104.
[219] Fletcher, 181.

centralized governance. Monasticism was "the one distinctive Christian institution which proved itself brilliantly capable of meshing and marrying with Irish social habits."[220] Patrick's accommodation to the Irish social mores may perhaps be seen in his reference to "the sons of kings who travel with me."[221] Marnell provides a seventh century account of the hereditary nature of Celtic abbatial succession:

> The lord of Trim gave the land for the monastery and its church, with the proviso that the monastery was to educate the children of the district. To perpetuate the monastery, one child in seven so educated was to enter the monastic life. A member of the founder's family was to be abbot if a member was available; the hereditary nature of the position was one of its marked Irish peculiarities.[222]

What then the role of the Catholic bishop of a Celtic diocese? Workman writes:

> The clan or monastery was supreme. Bishops there were in abundance, but they were incidental rather than essential. The ecclesiastical jurisdiction was in the hands of the abbots of the great monasteries who administered the districts subject to them, the bishops being merely members of the monastic bodies, and as such subject, even as regards the exercise of their Episcopal functions, to the authority of the abbot, in virtue of the vow of monastic obedience.[223]

Ordinations and other episcopal functions were performed by the bishop, but "under the direction of the abbot and convent."[224]. Bishops alone "could ordain to clerical office, confirm the faithful and consecrate church properties."[225] But a bishop as such had no voice in the affairs of the convent, or in the administration of the district. Workman adds,

---

[220] Ibid., 90.
[221] Ibid.
[222] Marnell, 29.
[223] Workman, 193-34.
[224] Ibid., 194.
[225] McNeill, 69-70.

> *The abbot, in fact, represented the tribe of the saint; the bishop did not.* In the cases where the abbot might chance to be a bishop, he exercised his jurisdiction not as bishop but as abbot. For the head of a Celtic monastery admitted no superior; he considered himself, like Henry VIII, supreme head next after Christ [emphasis added].[226]

Thus did a second version of church government endure for a long time and over a great part of northern Europe.

Despite Patrick's effort to "establish a ruling episcopate such as existed in Roman Britain"[227] it was, in the end, an unrealizable goal. After Patrick's death (461), the governance of the monasteries reverted to the clan. "The Irish Church lost much of such Episcopal authority that Patrick had imposed on it," Herbert Workman remarked. "Under the pressure of its tribal feuds, for some centuries [governance] continued to be predominantly 'monastic,' if indeed that is the right word to apply to these cases of the clan turned 'religious.'"[228] "The abbot and not the bishop," wrote David Bosch of the Celtic Church, "was the real source of authority; in fact, the bishop was often a subordinate member of the monastic community."[229] In summary, Irish clans rebuffed the attempt by Roman representatives to impose a hierarchical, centralized version of church order. While it is true that eventually (after several centuries!) the Celtic church adopted

---

[226] Workman, 194.
[227] McNeill, 69.
[228] Workman, 190.
[229] Bosch, 235.

the Catholic version of church order, the Celtic advantage was "not without a logic of its own in a land where the process of conversion was continuing:"[230]

> *There is no particular paradox in a bishop being under the administrative authority of an abbot in a missionary country* in which the Church is organized on a monastic basis. Bishop and priest do the work of Mary; the abbot can do the task of Martha [emphasis added].[231]

When Celtic missionaries sailed from Ireland to Iona and Lindisfarne in Scotland they extended the order of rule they preferred—abbot over bishop, autonomous over hierarchical, local over distant. From Scotland, the *peregrini* expanded the Celtic movement southward. Inevitably, this brought the freewheeling Celtic monks into contact, and conflict, with the Catholic monks whom Pope Gregory had sent to Canterbury in 596. Though Augustine had arrived in England a century before the Celts, his missionaries did not advance far from their base. Marnell contrasts the "stability" of Catholic monasticism and the "mobility" of Celtic in the strongest terms when he writes:

> We have now passed two decades the date of the Synod of Whitby. There was still nothing one could truly call an English Church. Northumbria was converted as was Scotland, and Christianity was strongly entrenched in much of East Anglia and in parts of Mercia. *This was almost entirely the work of the Irish monks and stemmed from Iona and Lindisfarne* [emphasis added].[232]

Thus, McNeill could state that "the Christianization of the English kingdoms in the seventh century was mainly the work of Irish monks and their English pupils. By comparison the Roman mission in England was carried on less extensively and with less

---

[230] Marnell, 28.
[231] Ibid.
[232] Ibid., 67.

local continuity."²³³ Thomas Cahill wrote that on account of the Celtic zeal the first abbot of Lindisfarne, Aidan, "has far better claim than Augustine of Canterbury to the title Apostle of England, for, as the Scottish historian James Bulloch has remarked, 'All England north of the Thames was indebted to the Celtic mission for its conversion.'"²³⁴

The full measure of monastic autonomy is indicated by the fact that Celtic missionaries broke off communication with their sending monasteries; missionaries were not directed by or expected to make periodic reports to a home base.²³⁵ One imagines that the practice of trusting young apprentices to fear God and lead, without reporting upwards, would provoke and perturb leadership in hierarchical structures; however, if we are going to admire their enduring and extensive achievements, we are going to have to respect the Celtic church governance code.

How Theodore of Tarsus Resolved a Governance Conflict Between Celtic and Roman Patterns of Administration

Advancing Celtic missionaries provoked a confrontation when their string of monasteries reached the Catholic region in southern England. The dispute between Roman and Celtic Christianity was not simply about hair style of the monks or the date of Easter, though Bede said as much.²³⁶ "This was, of course, only a superficial cause of

---

[233] McNeill, 118.
[234] Thomas Cahill, *How the Irish Saved Civilization: The Untold Story of Ireland's Heroic Role from the Fall of Rome to the Rise of Medieval Europe*, 1st ed. (New York: Nan A. Talese, Doubleday, 1995), 200.
[235] McNeill, 155-56.
[236] Bede, *A History of the English Church and People* (Harmondsworth, Middlesex: Penguin Books, 1968), 186-87.

trouble."[237] The real struggle arose *"from radical differences in Church organization, especially in the relations of bishop and abbot, of clan and of diocese* [emphasis added]."[238] Nor must we forget, Workman reminds us, "that rigid uniformity, the mark of Rome, has never been a distinguishing feature of the Celtic temperaments."[239]

The objective of the Roman Church hierarchy became to unite—by winning over—the Celtic Christians into one English church. A synod, convened at Whitby in 664, decided in favor of the Roman version of church order, requiring Celtic abbots to submit to Roman bishops, to ask for permission before beginning new monasteries and to conform to Roman rituals and church calendar. But the Celtic abbots did not abide by the Synod's pronouncements; thus the very peace of the church depended on whether the affections of the Celts could be won. Enter Theodore of Tarsus, appointed to be Archbishop of Canterbury by Pope Vitalian in 668. (Vitalian had chosen as archbishop an English priest, Wighard, but Wighard died in Rome earlier in 668.) An African monk, Hadrian, recommended Theodore as the man for this task.[240] Ralph D. Winter calls this "a master stroke" because Theodore of Tarsus was an acceptable intermediary to the apprehensive Celtic abbots.

> Theodore hailed from the eastern end of the Roman Empire, the source of much of what was Celtic Christianity. Thus, just as the Jerusalem Council asked

---

[237] Chadwick, 193.
[238] Workman, 193.
[239] Ibid., 194.
[240] Jerald C. Brauer and B. A. Gerrish, *The Westminster Dictionary of Church History* (Philadelphia: Westminster Press, 1971), s.v. "Theodore of Tarsus".

Barnabas (who was both Greek and Jewish in culture) to go to Antioch to see to things there, Theodore was asked to go to Britain.[241]

Theodore, who was sixty-six years old, accepted the bishopric. Gregory ordered Hadrian, the African monk, to go with him "to ensure," Bede tells us, "that he [Theodore] did not introduce into the Church which he was to rule any Greek customs which conflicted with the teachings of the true Faith."[242] Together these two outsiders offered the Roman English and the non-Roman Celts a disinterested benevolence that brought about a climate that could resolve their differences.

Upon arriving in Canterbury, Theodore "found the church in a bad way, for a recent pestilence had carried off many clergy and populace and only three bishops were left."[243] In 673 he presided over the Synod of Hertford which ruled against certain persisting Celtic customs. In 680 he drew up and sent to Rome a statement of the incorporation of Celtic Christianity into English Church's orthodoxy; this represented his greatest success. Until his death at the age of eighty-eight Theodore continued laboring to unify the English Church and bind it firmly to Rome. His was "the firm hand effecting a melding of the virile Celtic Christianity and the prestigious Latin Roman version, a

---

[241] Ralph D. Winter, "Theodore of Tarsus," in *Evangelical Dictionary of World Missions* (Grand Rapids: Baker House, 2000), 493.

[242] Bede, 204. The customs in the Celtic Church were nearer to Greek and Egyptian customs; this explains Bede's comment on the Pope's reason for sending Hadrian to accompany Theodore. "The Celts owed more to the Copts than to Constantine," quipped David Marshall. David Marshall, *The Celtic Connection* (Grantham, Lincolnshire, England: The Stanborough Press, 1994), 15.

[243] Latourette, 347.

contextualization which was to last for many centuries."[244] Through his efforts the Celtic monastery outposts became Roman dioceses. For this the Venerable Bede admired him, "the first archbishop whom the entire Church of the English obeyed."[245] In 731, when Bede wrote the closing words of his *Ecclesiastical History*, "he rested happy," Nora Chadwick wrote, "in the reflection that all the countries of Britain and Ireland, with the exception of the Welsh, had forsaken their former separatism and accepted the Roman obedience."[246]

We can say in concluding this section that the Celtic version of the "Two Structures" paradigm endured for hundreds of years and advanced the Celtic mission to France, Switzerland, Belgium, and Italy.[247] Does the Celtic pattern of governance in a "missionary country" resemble the subversive, disturbing sodalities which Andrew Walls has suggested we need today?

4.3 The Catholic Advantage: A Social Contract Recognizing Religious Orders

The Catholic Church also developed a version of the "Two Structures' paradigm to its own advantage. The autonomous nature of Catholic religious orders has enabled hundreds and thousands of likeminded women and men to form themselves into religious

---

[244] Winter, "Theodore of Tarsus," 493. For more on Theodore's achievements in reforming the Catholic Church in England, see my paper, "Benedictines, Cistercians, Friars—A Long Obedience in the Same Direction." www.pcms-usa.org.
[245] Bede, 206.
[246] Quoted in Marshall, 5.
[247] Marnell, 2.

orders and initiate new missions efforts as needed. In his book *Sisters,* a history of nuns in America, John Fialka writes:

> The fact that hundreds of different orders of sisters could carry out independent missions, working with, working around or working despite the orders of their bishops gave the church a *flexible, innovative structure* that coped well with the extreme challenges and opportunities in the new nation [emphasis added].[248]

This elastic structure gave the Catholic Church "a resilience to flow over obstacles and an innovative drive that had it constantly reaching out to new members and colleting arriving immigrants."[249] These are "characteristics that many Catholic historians fail to appreciate. They simply baffle most non-Catholics, who continue to view the Church as a monolith."[250] In her book, *The Missionary Movement in American Catholic History*[251], Angelyn Dries praises the achievements of Catholic missionaries in the New World: Catholic monastics drew the first maps; they discovered the rivers, explored the forests, and walked the deserts and the plains and, yes, educated and baptized the Native Americans. Jesuits brought to the New World peoples the music, literature, and visual arts and the science, astronomy and arithmetic of Europe. The missionaries learned the

---

[248] John J. Fialka, *Sisters: Catholic Nuns and the Making of America*, 1st ed. (New York: St. Martin's Press, 2003), 121-22.
[249] Ibid., 122.
[250] Ibid.
[251] Angelyn Dries, *The Missionary Movement in American Catholic History*, American Society of Missiology Series; No. 26 (Maryknoll, NY: Orbis Books, 1998).

languages of the New World peoples: seminarians who sought ordination could not pass their exams without knowledge of at least one Indian dialect.[252]

Later generations of Catholic orders accomplished still more: They built America's largest private school and nonprofit hospital systems.[253] At its peak, in the 1950s, the Catholic parochial school system contained 11 percent of America's students. And the financial and managerial innovations of sisters made possible one out of every five hospital beds in the United States.[254] One nun co-founded with Dr. Bob Smith the meeting later known as Alcoholic Anonymous;[255] another, Mother DePazzi, worked with the United Railways Company in St. Louis to develop the first prepaid health insurance plan in the United States.[256] The common asset in all these achievements is the Catholic Church's social contract by which it licenses its members to organize semi-autonomous special purpose structures.

The normal sequence in the Catholic Church, going back to Francis of Assisi, is to organize first, then ask permission. In 1209 Francis set off for Rome, where Innocent III approved the Rule that Francis and eleven other men had already begun obeying. Upon leaving Rome Francis felt authorized to accept new members, hear confessions, appoint

---

[252] Ibid., 13. But I would be remiss to admire the Catholic orders only for their good works without adding praise for their work of prayer, for the monastic life is primarily this. See Ambrose Tinsley, *Pax: The Benedictine Way* (Collegeville, MN: The Liturgical Press, 1994).
[253] Fialka, 1.
[254] Ibid., 3.
[255] Ibid., 12-13.
[256] Ibid., 131.

leaders for new houses of Franciscans, and start an order for women.[257] In 1948, Mother Teresa organized the Sisters of Charity in Calcutta. On October 7, 1950 Mother Teresa received approval from the Vatican to do what she was already doing. When she was awarded the 1979 Nobel Peace Prize it was not because she herself gave aid to the dying in Calcutta for thirty years, but because she persuaded hundreds of women to join her in doing good in Calcutta and in dark corners all over the planet. The first Catholic order founded in the United States to focus specifically on overseas missions was the Maryknoll Society. Three lay people created Maryknoll: Thomas Frederick Price (1860-1919), James A. Walsh (1867-1936), and Mary Josephine Rogers (1882-1955). Price, Walsh and Rogers moved with a few followers to a hill overlooking the Hudson River near Ossining, New York, in September 1912. The group was recognized by Rome as a Pious Society without vows. Five years later, in 1917 and, after much difficulty in obtaining ecclesiastical approval as a religious congregation, the Foreign Mission Sisters of St. Dominic—The Maryknoll Sisters—received Rome's authorization in 1920.[258] Then there is Opus Dei, the Catholic lay mission order. According to John L. Allen, Jr. "Opus Dei does not want to stifle creativity and initiative by suggesting that one needs to wait for orders from headquarters before proceeding" because "that would contradict

---

[257] For more on the beginning of the Franciscans see John R. H. Moorman, *A History of the Franciscan Order: From Its Origins to the Year 1517* (Chicago, Ill.: Franciscan Herald Press, 1988), 10-19.
[258] Dries, 77.

[founder] Escriva's emphasis on the freedom of members to act as they see fit in temporal affairs."[259]

The sequence by which restless people organize themselves for mission and then ask permission is what Ralph D. Winter called "the enviable Roman Catholic Synthesis."[260] The harmony between the modality and the sodality achieved by the Roman Church, Winter wrote, "continues to be Rome's great organizational advantage to this day."[261]

One Jesuit with keen insights into the Catholic advantage was Johann Jacob Baegert (d. 1777). Twenty-one years before William Carey wrote his *Enquiry* Baegert wrote a history of his experiences as a Jesuit missionary to the Guaycura people in what is today Baja California.

---

[259] John L. Allen, *Opus Dei: An Objective Look Behind the Myths and Reality of the Most Controversial Force in the Catholic Church*, 1st ed. (New York: Doubleday, 2005), 36-37.

[260] Ralph D. Winter, "Protestant Mission Societies and the 'Other Protestant Schism'," in *American Denominational Organization* (Pasadena: William Carey Library, 1980), 196.

[261] Winter, "The Two Structures of God's Redemptive Mission," 128.

(Figure 1)

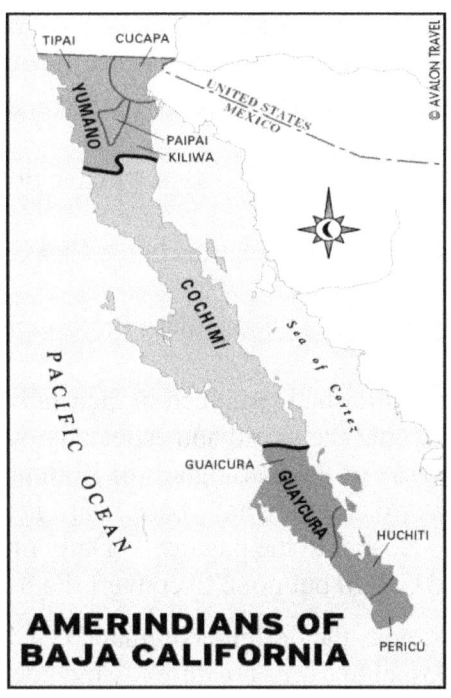

Figure 1. Jacob Baegert's region of Baja California--Guaycura[262]

Jacob Baegert's "Questions Directed to Protestants." From 1751 to 1768 Jacob Baegert lived at a mission called San Luis Gonzaga. When King Charles III of Spain ordered the Jesuits expelled from the New World in 1767, Baegert returned to Germany, settling in his native Bavaria. In 1771 Baegert published his memoirs, *Observations in Lower California.*[263] In one chapter, after describing the martyrdom of two Jesuit missionaries, he directs six questions "to any Protestants who may happen to read this." Baegert's questions are candid and illuminating. They help us understand the contrast between the

---

[262] Joe Cummings, "Jacob Baegert's Region of Baja California--Guaycura," (Avalon Travel, 2008).
[263] Jacob Baegert, Brandenburg, M. M., Baumann, Carl L., *Observations in Lower California* (Berkeley: University of California Press, 1952), 156-65.

Catholic and the Protestant mission experiences during the 18th century. "The Protestants have the best opportunity of carrying out the work of converting nonbelievers in both the West and the East Indies," Baegert writes, "for there, as everyone knows, their trade and power is very great. Nevertheless," he says, "I have not heard or read anything up to now about Protestant missions or missionaries in the East or West Indies." "With their permission," Baegert continues, "I ask these Protestant gentlemen":[264]

> First: If the Apostles had remained in their fatherland, sitting at home behind the stove, where would the world and especially our Germany be today? When will one be able to say of the theologians of Wittenberg and Geneva: Their call went out into the world and they have been heard in all the corners of the earth preaching the Gospel to the pagans.[265] Daily preachers are born to take the place of Luther and Calvin but none to convert the heathen.

> Second: I ask, does the definite command of Christ, "Go ye into all the world and preach the Gospel to every creature"[266] include Protestant preachers, or does it not? If Christ's command has no meaning for them, then they cannot be counted among successors of the Apostles, but only as followers and partisans of Luther and Calvin.

> Third: I shall not speak of the hundred other prophecies concerning the conversions of heathens. (They would all have to be false if it depended upon Protestants.) But what of the particular prophecy of Christ in Matthew 24 that, before the end of the world arrives, the Gospel shall be preached everywhere and to all nations? It is certain that if, on the one hand, the Protestants have the only true Gospel and religion in their possession, and on the other hand, their preachers will not do better in the future than they have done in the past two and a half centuries in preaching the Gospel among the heathen, then the Judgment Day will never dawn.

> Fourth: I am asking what you think of Christ's saying in Luke 11: "He who is not with Christ is against Him, and he who does not help Him to gather, scatters and destroys?" The Protestant pilots and seamen have been trying to find a northern route to the Orient for almost two hundred years, so that their merchant ships may

---

[264] Ibid., 157-58.
[265] Psalm 19:4 (Baegert references Psalm 18, the Catholic numbering of the Psalms)
[266] Mark 16:15

reach Japan and China in less time; but their preachers do not search for any ways to penetrate into Abyssinia, Tibet, the Great and Lesser Tartary, there to enlighten age-old heretics or to baptize idolaters or other unbelievers. What conclusion may be drawn from that?

Fifth: Why do the Dutch conceal their Calvinistic religion before the Japanese? They deny their own religion; they do not wish to be known as Christians, but solely as Dutchmen. The English and the Dutch (in particular the latter) trade in all things in all the corners of the globe, and they will do anything for profit. But the one thing they do not wish to export and bring to the market, however, is their religion.

Sixth: If Protestant preachers fear misfortune and death, and perhaps for this reason lack courage and do not dare to venture among foreign nations and barbarians, why then do they not show any concern for the eternal salvation of their colonial slaves in America and the Negro slaves from Guinea and elsewhere. Surely from them they have nothing to fear.

These, then, are Baegert's six objections to two and a half centuries of Protestant mission inactivity, which he contrasts to the achievements of the Catholics, who "travel throughout the world, penetrating into regions where no profit-hungry merchant or daring pioneer has ever been before." Like Paul the apostle "they fear no dangers, but suffer shipwreck, hunger, and thirst, and dwell in deserts. They risk their lives a hundred times and spill their blood in a hundred different ways."[267] Meanwhile, Baegert continues, "the Protestant lip servant puts his hands in his pockets and watches indifferently the horrors of idolatry in so many lands. He lets millions of black and white pagans perish . . . in spite of God's explicit command to help them and save them from eternal damnation."[268]

---

[267] Baegert, 165.
[268] Ibid.

The Catholic Advantage was Structural. Baegert's questions were delivered at a time when Catholic missionaries were sailing from Europe to all the continents. But from the beginning of the Reformation Lutherans and Calvinists were, according to Baegert, "sitting at home behind the stove." Luther's well-known rejection of the church's monastic structures brought about an unforeseen, injurious effect. John Calvin as well pressed for the end of monastic structures.[269] Subsequent Reformers deterred their citizens from forming Protestant equivalents. Catholics, meanwhile, pushed beyond their frontiers until they reached new populations in India (Robert de Nobili, 1605); China (Matteo Ricci, 1582); Japan (Francis Xavier, 1549; Franciscans, 1593); Vietnam (Alexander de Rhodes, 1620); the Philippines (Domingo de Salazar, 1588); West Africa (Dominicans, 1486); Brazil (Manuel de Nóbrega, Jesuits 1549[270]); California (Franciscans, 1514; Nova Scotia (Jesuits, 1611); Mexico (Juan de Padilla 1528) and Venezuela (Franciscans, 1508); southwestern United States (Eusebio Kino, 1687); Baja California (Baegert, 1751); and California (Junipero Serra, 1769). The Jesuit Robert Bellarmine (1542-1621) argued in a series of papers published between 1586 and 1593 that the Roman Catholic Church is the true church because it sent missionaries while the Protestants did not.[271] No wonder Rufus Anderson wrote, "The monasteries were Papal

---

[269] Calvin has his defenders, including Scott Simmons, who has pulled together a history of Calvin's missionary efforts. Scott J. Simmons, "John Calvin and Missions: A Historical Study," *www.aplacefortruth.org/calvin.missions1.htm*. See also R. Pierce Beaver, "The Genevan Mission to Brazil," *The Reformed Journal* 17, no. 6 (1967).
[270] Dale Kietzman, private correspondence December 21, 2009

forms of missionary societies," and "it was by means of associations such as these that the Gospel was originally propagated among our ancestors, and over Europe."[272]

The Catholic Church, characterized as centrally administrated, has proven sufficiently flexible to permit its members to begin voluntary societies in order to start good works. Peter Wyatt, Catholic professor of mission at Emmanuel College in Toronto, explains the relationship between bishop and religious orders in Toronto:

> One of the auxiliary bishops has as one of his responsibilities the task of keeping track of these various ministry groups. One of the reasons he does so is simply to know what kinds of ministry and activity these groups are doing. The hierarchy is not interested *prima facie* in controlling them. It simply wants to know what ministry is going on in the name of the Catholic Church in the local diocese. An advantage of knowing what the groups are doing is that they can be aware of each other and perhaps can pool their resources.[273]

The Toronto bishop *regulates, but does not administrate,* the voluntary ministries in his area; Wyatt cites an occasion when the bishop issued a statement disassociating his office from the Army of Mary because it "no longer represents itself as truly Catholic" since "its leaders teach a doctrine that is contrary to that of the Catholic Church" on fundamental points.[274] In this "enviable Catholic synthesis" we discover a pattern for Protestants.

---

[271] Kenneth B. Mulholland, "From Luther to Carey: Pietism and the Modern Missionary Movement," *Bibliotecha Sacra* 156, no. 1 (1999): 86.

[272] R. Pierce Beaver, *To Advance the Gospel; Selections from the Writings of Rufus Anderson* (Grand Rapids: Eerdmans, 1967), 64-5.

[273] Pellowe, "Leading Ministries into Christian Community: A Practical Theology for Church-Agency Relations", 313. The number of religious groups that the bishop of Toronto has tallied, Pellowe reports, on page 313, is "between 265 and 280."

[274] Ibid., 457.

4.4 The Protestant Disadvantage: Observations from the Reformation until 1792

Historians offer several explanations for the 275 year Protestant era of near paralysis. "Virtually no Protestant missionary activity took place between 1517 and 1792," Ken Mulholland writes, "Yet those years constituted the golden age of Roman Catholic missions . . . Why is that?"[275] Some historians mitigate the lack of Protestant mission by suggesting that Protestants lacked the finances or the ships to send missionaries. This is contraindicated by the rise of the Dutch Golden Age in 17th century Holland, when Dutch trading ships plied the oceans of the world and Dutch settlers colonized the East Indies and West Indies.[276] Stamoolis notes that "when Holland became a world power, chaplains were sent to its colonies. However, any missionary effort was to come after their primary task of meeting the needs of the colonists."[277] Ralph Winter contrasts the reception of the Catholic traders to the Dutch traders in Japan:

> A chief example of the difference between Protestant and Catholic relationships to the non-Western world might be that situation in Kyushu where the extensive influence of the Catholic missions had converted several hundred thousand of the Japanese. Their influence was so extensive that the emperor eventually prohibited any Portuguese or Spanish ships from landing in Kyushu, since they all carried missionaries and were permanently involved in mission work. The emperor didn't see any reason, however, to restrict the Dutch from landing, *since Dutch ships had no missionary mechanism of this variety and were thus no problem to the*

---

[275] Mulholland: 85. 85

[276] Chaplains were on board the Dutch East India ships, and some of these men, such as Georgius Cadidius, and Robert Junius who labored for fourteen years among the Taiwanese, brought great numbers of Asian people to faith. For a brief account of certain Dutch and English chaplains who were also missionaries see Samuel H. Moffett, *A History of Christianity in Asia Vol. 2*, vol. 2 (Maryknoll, NY: Orbis Books, 2005), 213-46.

[277] James J. Stamoolis, "History of Missions," in *Evangelical Dictionary of World Missions* (Grand Rapids: Baker Books, 2000), 444.

Japanese. They were simply commercial people, and they were not restricted during this period when all Christian influence was banned [emphasis added].[278]

Rewarded with trade privileges, Protestant merchants in Japan enjoyed a commercial advantage over their Catholic counterparts who sailed with missionaries.

The impediment to sending Protestant missionaries was structural. Even today, many Protestant leaders are not eager to close the breach that has opened, a breach separating the Reformers' mission ideals from what actually happened. Luther believed in the church's mission to the world.[279] That is, Luther *expected* the entire world to hear the gospel.[280] He said, "Before the last day comes, church rule and the Christian faith must spread over all the world."[281] Calvin too preached that "our duty everywhere is to make known among the nations the greatness of God."[282] But historian Stephen Neill says that Luther and the Reformers did "exceedingly little" to put realize this expectation.[283] Here is Neill's quote in context:

> It is clear that the idea of the steady progress of the preaching of the Gospel through the world is not foreign to his [Luther's] thought. Yet, when everything favourable has been said that can be said, and when all possible evidences from the writings of the Reformers have been collected, it all amounts to exceedingly little.[284]

---

[278] Ralph D. Winter, "Opening Remarks," in *Consultation on Voluntary Societies* (First Presbyterian Church, Evanston, IL: Unpublished, May 22, 1975).

[279] John Calvin made a bold attempt to begin send a mission to Brazil in 1555.

[280] For a fine selection of Luther's mission expectations see Lyle L. Vander Werff, *Christian Mission to Muslims: The Record: Anglican and Reformed Approaches in India and the near East, 1800-1938* (South Pasadena, CA: William Carey Library, 1977), 11-12.

[281] Ibid., 11.

[282] Sermon by Calvin from Isaiah 12:4-5. Quoted in Moffett, 213.

[283] Neill, 222.

[284] Ibid.

To understand Neill's critique we begin with the Reformers' decision to dissolve dissolution the Catholic religious orders in the early days of the Reformation.

4.4.1 Martin Luther: The Dissolution of the Religious Orders

Luther and the Reformers adopted what Paul Pierson calls "the medieval model of the territorial church."[285] Luther believed that the entire mission of the church should be borne by local churches and their regional administrative structures.[286] Luther dissolved the monasteries "even though," writes Paul Pierson, "monastic communities had been the primary vehicle of mission since the fourth century."[287] Here is Luther in 1520:

> The pope must be forbidden to institute, or set his seal on, any more of these Orders. Indeed, he must be ordered to dissolve some, or force them to reduce their numbers. For faith in Christ, which is alone the supreme good, and which exists apart from any of the Orders, suffers no small danger. The many different works and customs may easily lead men rather to rely on these works and customs than to care for faith.[288]

Dennis L. Okholm says that the Reformers thought monasticism to be "salvageable, to a degree." He writes:

> Calvin and Luther both praised the early founders of religious orders—especially folks like Antony, Augustine and Francis . . . Calvin suggests, as Luther did, that

---

[285] Paul E. Pierson, "The Reformation and Mission," in *Evangelical Dictionary of World Missions* (Grand Rapids: Baker Books, 2000), 813.

[286] Luther seems to have unacquainted with the durable Celtic tradition, by which the bishop was subordinated to the abbot. In this respect the Celtic tradition was "much less ecclesiastical" than the Anglo-Saxon, as David Bosch has pointed out. Bosch, 235. Also Neill, 50.

[287] Pierson, "The Reformation and Mission," 813. The *Oxford Encyclopedia of the Reformation* estimates the number of monasteries in England and Wales, Ireland and Scotland at the beginning of the 16th century to be thirteen hundred, accommodating approximately fifteen thousand men and women, though by this time the monasteries in Scotland were "in a state of serious decline." *The Oxford Encyclopedia of the Reformation*, ed. Hans J. Hillerbrand (New York: 1996), Volume 3: 72, 76.

[288] Martin Luther and John Dillenberger, *Martin Luther, Selections from His Writings*, 1st ed. (Garden City, NY: Doubleday, 1961), 446.

Augustine's description of early monastic practice should function as the norm by which to judge defects in the monasticism of his day.[289]

But to Melanchthon the monastic vows which were a form of slavery "at variance with faith and freedom of the spirit."[290] Zwingli was blunter still, attacking monasticism for enriching the monks and because they pursued a false god of salvation through outward works.[291] In any case, Luther adopted the Catholic rule by synod, but denied his ministers the Catholic advantage of semi-autonomous abbots authorized to initiate new efforts. Had Catholic bishops retained for themselves the sole authority to initiate mission, they would have disabled the mission capacity of the Catholic Church. Herbert Workman put it aptly:

> *The Church has never yet directly founded one religious order.* These have not sprung from the authoritative acts or provisions of councils or popes; *in every case they have been the outcome of individual consecration and enthusiasm, seeking for itself some outlet that it could not find in the channels provided by the Church* [emphasis added].[292]

There is no need to agree with Gustav Warneck's assertion that Luther was indifferent to missions.[293] In 1523, Martin Luther wrote a missionary hymn based on Psalm 67. It stirs the blood:

---

[289] Dennis L. Okholm, *Monk Habits for Everyday People: Benedictine Spirituality for Protestants* (Grand Rapids: Brazos Press, 2007), 129.

[290] *The Oxford Encyclopedia of the Reformation*, s.v. "Monasticism" 80.

[291] Ibid., s.v. "Monasticism" 81.

[292] Workman, 12.

[293] Gustav Warneck, *Outline of a History of Protestant Missions from the Reformation to the Present Time* (New York: Revell, 1901), 9-11. Hans Kasdorf classifies the set of missiologists that present the Reformers as indifferent to mission as in "the Warneck Tradition." Hans Kasdorf, "The Reformation and Mission: A Bibliographical Survey of Secondary Literature," *Occasional Bulletin of Missionary Research* 4, no. 4 (1980): 170. For a refutation of Warneck see Bosch, 243ff.

May God bestow on us His grace, With blessings rich provide us,
And may the brightness of His face To life eternal guide us
That we His saving health may know, His gracious will and pleasure,
And also to the heathen show Christ's riches without measure
And unto God convert them.[294]

Luther *expected* that the world would hear the gospel.[295] Though Warneck criticized the Reformers "because fundamental theological views hindered them from giving their activity, and even their thoughts, a missionary direction,"[296] later scholars demonstrated that Luther's theology and understanding of church and kingdom was "an essentially missionary theology."[297] In fact, Bosch adds, "he [Luther] provided the church's missionary enterprise with clear and important guidelines and principles . . . The starting point of the Reformers' theology was not what people could or should do for the salvation of the world, but what God has already done in Christ."[298] James Scherer writes,

> For Luther, mission meant reestablishing the church on its true evangelical foundation in Jesus Christ and the gospel . . . The church, missionary in its very nature, is God's instrument sending out his Word into the world. Every baptized believer has both a right and a duty to witness to Christ.[299]

---

[294] "Es woll' uns Gott Genädig Sein" William Gustave Polack, *The Handbook to the Lutheran Hymnal* (Saint Louis, Mo.,: Concordia Publishing House, 1942), 349.

[295] However, Hans Kasdorf has written that When Luther spoke of mission he meant mission to the "repaganized" (*verheindischte*) Catholic Church of Europe. Hans Kasdorf, *Christian Conversion in Context* (Scottdale, Pa.: Herald Press, 1980), 170.

[296] Warneck, 9.

[297] Bosch, 245.

[298] Ibid.

[299] James A. Scherer, "Lutheran Missions," in *Evangelical Dictionary of World Missions* (Grand Rapids: Baker Books, 2000), 585.

Sails on the Deck. Historians now concur with David Bosch, that the theology of the Luther and Calvin, at least, was "fundamentally missionary."[300] But even the Lutheran Philip Nicolai (1556-1608), whom Bosch calls "exceptionally important" on account of writing about the need for *propagatio*[301]—extending the gospel because God would have us love others—offered no means to actualize his ideas. In other words, the Lutheran version of missions was like a fleet of sailing ships in the harbor with their sails lying on the deck. How can such a fleet catch the wind? Ralph D. Winter has suggested that the suppression of orders was "the greatest error of the Reformation and the greatest weakness of the resulting Protestant tradition."[302] The first Protestants, Winter said,

> unwittingly created another and even more significant *internal* schism deriving from and resulting in a truncated view of the church: this other organizational hiatus resulted as the Reformers conceived of an overall church structure getting along nicely without any voluntary sub-communities worthy of being part of the church [emphasis is in original].[303]

"Soon after Luther tacked his Ninety-Five Theses to the church door at Wittenberg," Kenneth Mulholland wrote whimsically,

> there came a tremendous explosion of missionary expansion in the wake of the Reformation, as missionaries almost immediately began to go to the ends of the earth. Correct? Wrong. Virtually no Protestant missionary activity took place between 1517 and 1792. Yet those years constituted the golden age of Roman Catholic missions.[304]

---

[300] Bosch, 247.
[301] Ibid., 249.
[302] Winter, "The Two Structures of God's Redemptive Mission," 130.
[303] Winter, "Protestant Mission Societies and the 'Other Protestant Schism'," 202.
[304] Mulholland: 85.

"It would take centuries, David Bosch wrote, "before anything remotely as competent and effective as the monastic missionary movement would develop in Protestantism."[305] A missionary ice age had set in.

4.4.2 John Calvin: His Understanding of Apostolos Reconsidered

John Calvin (d. 1564) considered the apostolic age and office to have ceased in the first century. Since then, "in a duly constituted church it has no place,"[306] Calvin wrote (some irony should be allowed, since it was apostles who appointed persons to the office that Calvin esteemed above all others: presbyters, or elders[307]). In his commentary on *Ephesians* Calvin wrote:

> I take the word "apostles" not in that general sense which the derivation of the term might warrant, but in its own peculiar signification, for those highly favored persons whom Christ exalted to the highest honor. *Such were the twelve, to whose number Paul was afterwards added.* Their office was to spread the doctrine of the gospel throughout the whole world, to plant churches, and to erect the kingdom of Christ [emphasis added].[308]

One wishes that Calvin had understood the link between apostleship and mission which recent research has made available. In his article on *apostolos* in the *Theological Dictionary of the New Testament,* Karl Rengsdorf wrote that long before first century Christian apostles began their mission, *apostoloi* referred to ships sent by owners to

---

[305] Bosch, 245.

[306] Jean Calvin, *Institutes of the Christian Religion*, vol. 2 (Philadelphia: Westminster Press, 1960), 1057.

[307] "And they [the apostles] appointed elders"—Acts 14:24

[308] In his commentary on Romans 16:7, Calvin again confines the age of apostleship to the earliest days of the church. Of Andronicus and Junia he writes, "But as they had embraced the gospel by faith before Paul, he hesitates not to set them on this account before himself." 546

distant harbors.[309] The word was often combined with *ployon* to mean a freighter or transport ship.

> It then came to be applied to the fleet itself and it thus acquires the meaning of a naval expedition. In this way it came to be applied on the one side to a group of *men sent out for a particular purpose*, and on the other to the commander of an expedition, e.g. the admiral [emphasis added].[310]

Thus, Greeks understood *apostoloi* to be persons on a mission. When we look for a Hebrew or Aramaic antecedent to "apostle" we discover the Hebrew word *shaliakh*. Church father Jerome tells us that "apostle" is simply a Latinized form of the Hebrew *shaliakh* (pronounced *sha-LEE-akh*). In the Syriac Church today an apostle is still called a *shaliakh*. *Shaliakh* is also used in Judaism.[311] Perhaps Jesus used the Aramaic *shalikha* in sending out the twelve and the seventy; they went out as though the one sending was coming in person ("He who hears you hears me"[312]). "The rabbis summed up this basis of the *shaliakh* in the frequently quoted statement: '*the one sent by a man is as the man*

---

[309] Karl Heinrich Rengstorf, "Apostolos," in *Theological Dictionary of the New Testament* (Grand Rapids: Eerdmans, 1965), 407.

[310] Ibid.

[311] By searching *shaliakh* on Google, one may find such references as: "Eren Rosenberg has served as a *shaliakh* for the Jewish Agency for Israel and frequently leads workshops and activities throughout the Greater Columbus Jewish Community"; "The leader in a synagogue service is usually called the *shaliakh tzibbur*/messenger of the community"; "'He was a great *shaliakh*,' said Dov Paritzky, the B'nai Akiva-Israel official who was in charge of Karni while he served as emissary." Here is an illustration of the special role played by a *shaliakh*: "In the ancient Jewish community, were a man's house to burn down and he lose everything, an appeal for charity was made through the dispatch of an emissary, known as *shaliakh*, or several of them, who would travel from town to town and plead for donations for the homeless victims. The emissaries carried letters from the town rabbi, usually in Hebrew, detailing the extent of the disaster, expounding the virtues of *Tsedaka* (charity) with citations from the Talmud, and appealing for help. Upon arrival in each town the letter was presented to the local rabbi, who would read it from the pulpit to his congregation in the synagogue, adding his own appeal for generosity as a great *mitzva*. The *Shaliakh* too would make a statement and answer questions from the audience, and often go from house to house to make the collection." Jacob Auerbach *The Undying Spark*. Long Beach, N.Y. Copyright @ 1992. Online at http://www.pruzhanydistrict.com.ar/people_sub/CHAPTER%20TWO.htm. Access date: November 2006.

[312] Luke 10:16

himself.'"[313] A sending king expects the hearers ("those who have ears") to listen as though the king himself had arrived. The Palm Sunday crowd understood Jesus as God's man, shouting "Blessed is the one who comes *in the name of the Lord.*"[314] This is precisely Paul's understanding of his apostolic commissioning, "as though God were making His appeal through us."[315] "What characterizes the *shaliakhim* of every period is that *they leave their own homes* to bring a message from one who sends them [emphasis added]."[316] Thus, Stephen, a Greek-speaking Jew, uses the word "apostle" in the identical way that *shaliakh* is used in the Old Testament: Moses was a messenger of the king of glory to the king of Egypt. The messenger may be plain (a stutterer, as was Moses), but he delivers the message with the authority of the one who sends. The messenger may have "no form or majesty that we should look at him, nothing in his appearance;"[317] No matter; the decisive thing "is their authorization. The task as such is of no significance for the quality of [the designation of] *shaliakh*."[318] In the Intertestamental Period a rabbi would send two or more together—*shalokhim*—as his messengers.[319] Rabbis would lay hands on the emissaries; but this did not confer a perpetual office on those setting out. Upon completing his duty the emissary would not be a *shaliakh* any longer. "The NT

---

[313] Rengstorf, 415.
[314] Matthew 21:9
[315] 2 Corinthians 5:20
[316] Rengstorf, 415.
[317] Isaiah 53:3
[318] Rengstorf, 415.
[319] Ibid., 417.

apostle always denotes *a person who is sent,* and "sent with full authority."[320] In this sense Paul appealed to Philemon, through his runaway slave, Onesimus, writing, "So if you consider me a partner, welcome him as you would welcome me."[321]

Johannes Nissen describes two apostolates, the first being Peter's "pillar apostolate" (Galatians 2:9). "Obviously, the purpose and nature of the bishop's office is modeled on this apostolate, he writes."[322] The second is Paul's "mobile apostolate, demonstrated through his missionary travels." Nissen aptly cautions,

> In the church today Paul's apostolate has gone virtually unrecognized, [while] the pillar apostolate has won the day everywhere . . . In the course of history the Petrine apostolate has been overemphasized at the expense of the Pauline apostolate, and mission as local church growth [has been overemphasized] at the expense of mission through the 'traveling apostolate.'"[323]

One wonders whether Calvin, had he the information on *apostolos* available today, might have understood God's calling upon "some to be apostolic" today and always, to the end of the age.[324]

4.4.3 Mission Thinking in the Era of Lutheran and Reformed Scholasticism

Though the Reformers agreed to dissolve the monasteries, they disagreed on what was the nature of the congregation and its administrative superstructure, the synod.

---

[320] Ibid., 421.
[321] Philemon 17
[322] Johannes Nissen, *New Testament and Mission: Historical and Hermeneutical Perspectives* (Frankfurt am Main; New York: P. Lang, 1999), 116-17.
[323] Ibid.
[324] Don R. Golden remarked on the fact that Rengstorf's research on *apostolos* "does not appear in the bibliographies of the missiological textbooks written by noted scholars such as Kane, Bosch, Winter, Peters and Verkuyl." Golden, 13.

"When the Reformation shattered the ancient unity of the Western church," writes Bosch, "each of the fragments into which it was divided was obliged to define itself over against all the other fragments."[325] Opposing factions adopted competing, incompatible creeds. But "in all these instances," deplores Bosch, "the church was defined in terms of what happens inside its four walls, not in terms of its calling in the world."[326] Robert Glover writes,

> There is all too abundant evidence that most of the leaders of the Reformation, including Luther, Melanchthon, Calvin, Zwingli and Knox, seem to have had no serious sense of responsibility for direct missionary efforts on behalf of heathen or Moslem. Despite their clear conceptions and statements of the fundamental doctrines of evangelical faith, they showed a remarkable ignorance of the scope of the divine plan and of Christian duty in relation to the gospel.[327]

Little scholarship was devoted to missiology; but one Reformed scholar—Gisbert Voetius (1588-1676) of the Dutch Reformed Church—did articulate a theology of missions. Voetius wrote that "the first goal of missions is the conversion of the heathen; the second the planting of churches; and the highest the glory of God."[328] But Voetius held that "*only the institutional church—local church council, presbytery, or synod—*

---

[325] Bosch, 248.

[326] Ibid. Bosch points the reader to the passive voice of the verbs used to describe the church in the Augsburg Confession (1530): "the church is where the gospel *is taught* purely, and the sacraments *are administered* rightly. It is a place where something is done, not a living organism doing something [emphasis is in original]." 249

[327] Robert H. Glover, *The Progress of World-Wide Missions* (New York: Harper, Brown 1953), 68.

[328] Moffett, Volume 2, 216.

could act as sending agency [emphasis added]."³²⁹ Thus, the lengthy Protestant era of *sola synodica* that began in 1517 wore on.

Some Explanations for the Scarcity of Early Protestant Missions. Bosch gathers the several explanations for the failure of early Protestant missions and cites them in *Transforming Mission*.³³⁰ Hans-Werner Gensichen suggests four reasons why the Protestants remained at home "behind the stove":³³¹

1. A desperate shortage of preachers at home.
2. No Protestant monastic orders
3. Preoccupation with the Protestant struggle for existence in Europe
4. Lack of contacts with non-Christian lands and peoples.

James Stamoolis adds that "internal squabbles as well as pressure from the Catholic Church made missions impossible. The response of the Reformers was to teach that the obligation for missionary work had ceased with the apostles."³³² However, the Anabaptists sent missionaries outside of Christian Europe, overcoming the same

---

³²⁹ J. van Oort and Rijksuniversiteit te Utrecht. Faculteit der Godgeleerdheid., *De Onbekende Voetius: Voordrachten Wetenschappelijk Symposium, Utrecht, 3 Maart 1989* (Kampen: J.H. Kok, 1989), 126. Quoted in Bosch, 328.

³³⁰ Bosch, 45. Other explanations, somewhat contrived, supported the Lutheran conviction that the Great Commission had already been fulfilled; in 1598 Philip Nicholai presented a survey of the Christian presence in the Near East, China, India, and Ethiopia, concluding that the kingdom of Christ had indeed extended to the ends of the earth. Justinian Ernst von Welz, Scherer, James A., *Justinian Welz: Essays by an Early Prophet of Mission* (Grand Rapids: Eerdmans, 1969), 27. In addition, the greatest Lutheran theologian of the 17th century, Johann Gerhard (1582-1637) staunchly held that the apostolic calling was unique to the original disciples and to Paul; there were no successors. Ibid., 27-28. Moreover, the Wittenberg Opinion held that Christians of Europe were not responsible for the loss of the heathen, though heathen may be ignorant of the gospel, since God will judge all humanity on the basis of what light they have. Ibid., 32-3.

³³¹ Hans Werner Gensichen, *Missionsgeschichte Der Neueren Zeit* (Göttingen,: Vandenhoeck & Ruprecht, 1961), 5-7. Quoted in Neill, 222. Neill comments that Gensichen "carefully sets out everything that can be said" to apologize for Luther's ineffectual affirmation that the ideals of Jesus should expand to the ends of the world. Ibid.

³³² Stamoolis, 444.

obstacles said to render the Reformation mission effort impossible.[333] Bosch then offers a candid summary statement:

> In spite of what Holl, Holsten, Gensichen, Scherer, and others have identified as the fundamental missionary thrust of the Reformer's theology, very little happened in the way of missionary outreach during the first two centuries of the Reformation.[334]

Dubious doctrines seemed to inhibit Protestants from reading the Bible for what is said, doctrines such as 1) The Great Commission had been fulfilled by the first century apostles; 2) Predestination suggested that God in his sovereignty would see to the conversion of souls; and 3) The depravity of the world is a sign of God's mercy to the elect. "It was almost as if pastors and theologians feared that the world would improve," wrote Bosch.[335] "This 'practical heresy,'[336] as Beyreuther calls it, led to profound pessimism and neutralized any thought of an attempt at changing structures and conditions."[337] Only with the Great Awakenings of the 17th century was this pessimism challenged and displaced by a joyous and expectant belief that the people of God can overcome evil with good. Thus, John Eliot, member of "The Company for the

---

[333] Bosch, 245-6. David Bosch writes: "Whereas the Reformers no longer considered the 'Great Commission' as binding (cf. Warneck 1906:14, 17; Littell 1972:114-16), no biblical texts appear more frequently in the Anabaptist confessions of faith and court testimonies than the Matthean and Markan versions of the 'Great Commission,' along with Psalm 24:1. They were among the first to make the commission mandatory for all believers" ibid., 246.

[334] Ibid., 245.

[335] Ibid., 250.

[336] Ibid. Bosch's reference to "practical heresy" is from Erich Beyreuther, *Zinzendorf Und Die Christenheit 1732-1760* (Marburg an der Lahn: Francke, 1961), 3.

[337] Bosch, 250.

Propagation of the Gospel in New England—commonly called the New England Company[338]— began to receive support from his fellow New England Calvinists:

> The sense of being elected by God was thus channeled into new avenues. Such a shift can be detected time and again in Calvinist groups. The emphasis on predestination leads to active involvement in mission; the elect of God cannot remain inactive.[339]

It is noteworthy that John Eliot was a missionary of the Society for the Propagation of the Gospel in New England. It "was founded in England," Bosch wrote, "to underwrite the missionary enterprise in the transatlantic colonies. It was the first Protestant missionary society exclusively devoted to missionary purposes."

Adrian Saravia's Great Commission Society and His Opponents. Adrian Saravia, (1531-1613) was a younger contemporary of Calvin, and a professor of theology in Leyden.[340] Like Welz, below, Saravia promoted the idea of the "Great Commission as binding on the Protestant Church."[341] He maintained, Bosch wrote, "that we could only appropriate the promise of Jesus in Matthew 28:20 if we also obeyed the commission of Matthew

---

[338] Ibid., 257. The name of the New England Company on its charter was "The Company for the Propagation of the Gospel in New England." E. L. Frizen, *75 Years of I.F.M.A., 1917-1992: The Nondenominational Missions Movement* (Pasadena, CA: William Carey Library, 1992), 51-2.

[339] Bosch, 258.

[340] Assisting Guido de Bres, Saravia and two other theologians wrote the Belgic Confession of 1561. D. G. Hart and Mark A. Noll, eds., *Dictionary of the Presbyterian & Reformed Tradition in America* (Downers Grove, IL: Intervarsity Press, 1999), 30.

[341] Bosch, 247. Bosch adds, "Communication between Saravia and his opponents was compounded by the fact that he had based his views regarding the continued validity of the 'Great Commission' on the conviction that only those bishops who indubitably stood in the apostolic succession were heirs to the commission to the apostles. In a sense this issue was even more important to him than that of enkindling a renewed interest in mission. His views on apostolic succession later made him move to England and join the Anglican Church."

28:19."³⁴² Saravia's views were, however, were "fiercely opposed by Theodore Beza, Calvin's successor in Geneva, as well as by the Lutheran Johann Gerhard."³⁴³ A century later, Justinian Welz encountered the same resistance, as the following section indicates.

4.4.4 The Exceptional, Isolated Justinian Welz

In 1663-1664 Welz (d. 1666) described what Hans-Werner Gensichen called "nothing less than a detailed blueprint for a mission society, somewhat similar to the cultural and scientific societies of the baroque age but unique in its focus on foreign missions."³⁴⁴ The members would go overseas as hermit-missionaries. Bosch remarked on Welz's proposal:

> Such hermit-missionaries should be people marked by holiness and personal piety and should be sent out under the auspices of a "Jesus-Loving Society."³⁴⁵ Welz was, however, ahead of his time; much of what he stood for was to be brought to fruition only a generation later, when Pietism irrupted on the German Lutheran scene.³⁴⁶

But a Lutheran contemporary of Welz, the well-regarded superintendent of Regensburg and theologian Johann Heinrich Ursinus (d. 1667), opposed Welz's mission. Here is what happened.

As a university student at the age of 20, in 1641, Justinian Welz had written a critique on social injustice and political reform.³⁴⁷ But following his student years Welz took up

---

³⁴² Ibid.
³⁴³ Ibid.
³⁴⁴ Hans-Werner Gensichen, "Justinian Von Welz," in *Biographical Dictionary of Christian Missions*, ed. Gerald H. Anderson(New York: Simon and Schuster, 1998). 722
³⁴⁵ Welz, 38-45, 62-68, 70-76.
³⁴⁶ Bosch, 251-52. Welz was probably inspired by the "Society of Jesus"—Pope Paul III had recognized the Jesuit order in 1540—when Welz started the "Jesus-Loving Society."
³⁴⁷ Welz, 13.

with bad company and spent perhaps 20 years among carefree and sensuous friends. When he writes again it is to tell of his repentance. Then, late in 1663, Welz published *A Brief Report on How a New Society is to be Established Among Orthodox Christians of the Augsburg Confession*. In it the author states his intention to found a new society that promotes ecumenical brotherhood and mission to the heathen.[348] James Scherer writes that in the spring of 1664 Welz published a second tract, *A Christian and Sincere Admonition to All Orthodox Christians of the Augsburg Confession Concerning a Special Society Through Which with the Help of God our Evangelical Religion May Be Spread*.[349] Three kinds of members would comprise the society:[350]

1. *Promotores*, or wealthy patrons and sponsors, including kings and princes who would subsidize the major cost of the society's work.
2. *Conservatores,* the full-time supervisors of the society, some living abroad, some at home. These supervisors would report to the patrons
3. *Missionarii,* the volunteers who were to be trained and sent out.

At the conclusion of his tract Welz related his society to previous ones:

> You should not, gracious reader, put the wrong construction on the term "new society," and imagine that I am trying to bring to pass something entirely new. No, that is not my intention. Rather, I seek to renew the ancient and honorable enterprise of propagating the gospel through a society, and that I call new.[351]

Another mission enthusiast, Johann Gichtel (1638-1710), soon joined Welz. But first Welz had to persuade the higher echelons of the Lutheran Church. To that end Welz canvassed the members of the Imperial Diet, laying the groundwork for a presentation.

---

[348] Ibid., 15.
[349] Ibid., 16.
[350] Ibid., 41. See 63-4.
[351] Ibid., 76.

But his proposal was neither rejected nor accepted, Welz wrote a scathing attack on his opponents; those who had supported him now turned against him. The church leaders received an anonymous rebuke of Welz; It was probably written by Johann Ursinus.[352] Thus, Welz suddenly found himself isolated, except for the unwavering support of Gichtel. Welz then uttered a series of "Woes" upon the clergy, scholars, and rulers of his day, losing any chance of further influencing his opponents.[353]

Ursinus, writes Scherer, "was considered one of the most enlightened leaders of Lutheran orthodoxy in his day."[354] In his day, Lutheran orthodoxy "was more flexible and open to ideas of reform than in earlier years" and "Ursinus represented this reformist attitude. Yet even he failed to recognize the moment of truth in Welz's proposal."[355] Ursinus, if he is the author of the anonymous rebuke to Welz written in 1664, did not hold back: "Dear Justinian," he wrote, "stop dreaming, lest Satan deceive you":

> Stay in the land, in the calling to which God has called you; do not think beyond your ability. Be merciful; always love your neighbor as yourself. But act according to the example of the faithful Samaritan, who represents the image of love to us, who did not wander around the world to bind up all the wounded, but only those whom God set before his eyes as he went on his way.[356]

> The Jesus Society sought by you has a nice appearance but is un-Christian, without command, promise, precedent, yes, clearly against God and our Savior Jesus. O Justinian! May the dear Lord God preserve us from your Jesus-Society! Those who truly love Jesus already see where Satan is leading, and because they

---

[352] Ibid., 19.
[353] Ibid.
[354] Ibid., 20.
[355] Ibid.
[356] Ibid., 102.

love Jesus they guard against allowing their reason to be maddened by the roguishness and deception of men and of the devil himself![357]

Ursinus' objection, Bosch observed, "contains virtually all the features of orthodoxy's interpretation of mission":

> Obstacles to the conversion of pagans are insurmountable and the task is impossible; God has already made himself known to all nations, in various ways; the "Great Commission" was for the apostles only and it is presumption on our part to arrogate it to ourselves; the pagan nations are, in addition, impervious to the gospel since many of them are savages who have absolutely nothing human about them.[358]

As for Welz's Jesus-Loving Society, Ursinus wrote, "Such an agency is clearly un-Christian and against God and our Savior, since Jesus can tolerate no partners. All that is called for is for everyone to "mind his own door, and everything will be fine."[359] Ursinus' objection derived from his understanding of Luther's idea that the instrument of mission was from first to last the active Word, which, as Scherer wrote, "traversed the world and awakened faith wherever it went."[360] The church "was *sui generis* a kind of missionary structure."[361] Each Christian layman, as a priest before God, "was obligated to make the name of Christ known among non-Christians. God needed no professional missionary agents."[362] But "Luther's great missionary insights did not, unfortunately, come to fruition in the church of his own time."[363] In terms of mission beyond the state church,

---

[357] Ibid. 107
[358] Bosch. 252
[359] Ibid. 252
[360] Welz, 26.
[361] Ibid.
[362] Ibid.
[363] Ibid.

"the priesthood of believers, despite the fine theory, became largely a dead letter. Thus, we cannot speak of missions in this period as arising out of the life of local congregations, or the concern of ordinary Christians."[364]

The Lutheran Church condemned Welz as a heretic.[365] But "driven by the passion of his convictions," Welz sold his possessions and left for Surinam in South America in 1666 "where he died, probably in that same year, a sacrifice to orthodox intransigence. No trace was left of his missionary ministry."[366]

The Reformed leaders invested considerable energy deterring imitators of Justinian Welz from organizing mission initiatives. In 1651, just three years after the Peace of Westphalia, "the highly influential and respected Lutheran faculty of the University of Wittenberg issued a classic statement about the continuing validity of the Great Commission."[367] This became the dominant view—the mission paradigm— in the Lutheran Church and many of the Reformed churches for the next 150 years. The Wittenberg statement emphasized three points:

> First, only the apostles were privileged to fulfill the Great Commission. *Therefore missions are not the responsibility of the church.* Second, no person is excused before God because of ignorance of the gospel. Those who do not believe are presumed to have rejected the gospel when it was preached to them by the apostles during New Testament times. *Therefore European Christians have no need to assume responsibility for the lostness of the heathen.* Third, rulers are responsible to propagate the gospel in their own territories alone. The Wittenberg

---

[364] Ibid.
[365] Scherer, "Lutheran Missions," 586.
[366] Bosch, 251-52. Welz's name is not mentioned in the four volume *Oxford Encyclopedia of the Reformation*.
[367] Mulholland: 90. Welz, 28.

fathers were satisfied that the rulers had faithfully carried out this duty [emphasis added].[368]

Summary. The Protestant mission record from 1517 to 1792 indicates that the *sola synodica credenda* did not produce a mission *agenda*. There was an operating system failure; the Protestants denied themselves the structural advantage that had enabled the Jews, and the early church, and the Celtic Church and the Catholic Church to begin achieving their goals. "Because Martin Luther believed in the priesthood of all believers," Mulholland explained, "he saw no need for the monasteries. *Thus by closing down monasteries he dismantled a potential sending structure for Protestant missions* [emphasis added]."[369] For 275 years, until William Carey penned the paragraph beginning with the word "Suppose," Protestantism "failed to develop a missionary structure that was reproducible and sustainable. Protestants had no structure through which to send missionaries."[370] But in 1792 William Carey took a Pietist's passion and proposed a new operating system that would enable citizens everywhere to organize themselves to send the light.

4.5 William Carey's Paradigm: "The Use of Means"

On May 30, 1792, William Carey preached, along with several others, at the Kettering meetings in Nottingham, Midlands, England. He took as his text "Enlarge the

---

[368] Mulholland: 90. Welz, 28.
[369] Mulholland: 87. There were Protestant mission structures before William Carey; Carey praised as early adopters the Danish-Halle Mission and the Moravian and Wesleyan missions. Carey, 10, 35, 36.
[370] Mulholland: 87.

place of thy tent, and let them stretch forth the curtains of thine habitations; and thy seed shall inherit the Gentiles, and make the desolate cities to be inhabited."[371] According to Carey's nephew, Eustace, who did not get around to writing a biography of his uncle until 1837, William Carey preached that in this text

> the church was here compared to a poor desolate widow, who lived alone in a small tent; that she who had thus lived in a manner childless, was told to expect an increase in her family, such as would require a much larger dwelling; and this because her Maker was her husband, the Holy One of Israel, and the God of the whole earth. The discourse was very animated and impressive. After it was concluded, the ministers resolved that at the next Kettering minister's meeting, on the first of October of the same year, the plan of a society should be brought forward and, if found practicable, a society formed.[372]

Carey Cites the "Former Undertakings": Moravians and Wesleyans. In his Enquiry, Carey lavished praise on the voluntary societies that he had heard of, and cited them as precedents. Of the Moravians Carey writes, "Have not the missionaries of the *Unitas Fratrum*, or Moravian Brethren, encountered the scorching heat of Abyssinia, and the frozen climes of Greenland, and Labrador, their difficult languages, and savage manners?"[373] And there was John Wesley's mission "amongst the Caribs and Negroes"; and there were the "former undertakings" of John Elliot, David Brainerd, the Danish-Halle mission and the missionary training school in Leyden, 1722-1733. Carey refers to

---

[371] Isaiah 54:2-3

[372] Eustace Carey and Jeremiah Chaplin, *Memoir of William Carey, D, D., Late Missionary to Bengal, Professor of Oriental Languages in the College of Fort William, Calcutta* (Hartford,: Canfield and Robins, 1837), 50.

[373] Carey, *An Enquiry into the Obligations of Christians to Use Means for the Conversion of the Heathens*, 11.11 Carey praises the Moravians in several other writings; these have been collected by David A. Schattschneider, "William Carey, Modern Missions, and the Moravian Influence," *International Bulletin of Missionary Research* 22, no. 1 (1998): 10. Schattschneider suggests that Carey was familiar with the Moravian congregations in Yorkshire, Manchester, or Nottingham.

the Catholic mission in Brazil, Chili, Peru, and other countries in the New World[374] to make his Protestant readers jealous, but in a manner that we find rude, "Have not the popish missionaries surmounted all those difficulties generally thought to be insurmountable?"[375] In the spirit of modern civility pejoratives such as "popish" is unacceptable.

But it is the modern for-profit trading company that provides the model for which Carey is most exuberant. We will explain what it was about the private trading company that provided Carey with his most important analogy in section 4.5.2. In his *Enquiry*, Carey uses the word "company" twice in reference to the Dutch East-India Company and once again, referring to private trading companies in general;[376] such companies are clearly what Carey has in mind when he makes his famous proposal:

> Suppose a company of serious Christians, ministers and private persons, were to form themselves into a society, and make a number of rules respecting the regulation of the plan, and the persons who are to be employed as missionaries, the means of defraying the expense, etc., etc. This society must consist of persons

---

[374] Carey, *An Enquiry into the Obligations of Christians to Use Means for the Conversion of the Heathens*, 55-56.

[375] Ibid., 11. Today we must ask pardon of our Catholic brethren for Carey's insult. In humility we can restate Carey's appeal with respect. We can say with Richard H. Bliese and Horst Rzepkowski that "a historical consideration of Catholic missions reveals that to a great extent they were carried on my monks, religious orders, and congregations," and that, according to Vatican II, these "have up to this time played and still play, the greatest part in the evangelization of the world." Richard H. Bliese and Horst Rzepkowski, eds., *Missionary Societies*, ed. Karl Muller SVD, Dictionary of Mission: Theology, History, Perspectives (Maryknoll, NY: Orbis Books, 1997), 114. The authors further say that with the increase of missionary awareness in the Protestant world "a similar phenomenon developed: more and more missionary societies came to carry on missionary work, even if their origin, relationship to the church, and motivation were quite varied." This development, the authors write, is "due to the initiative of W. Carey" and his founding of the Baptist Missionary Society from which time "mission became the responsibility of well-organized and structured groups." 322

[376] Carey, *An Enquiry into the Obligations of Christians to Use Means for the Conversion of the Heathens*, 36, 37, 81, 82.

whose hearts are in the work, men of serious religion, and possessing a spirit of perseverance; there must be a determination not to admit any person who is not of this description, or to retain him longer than he answers to it.[377]

Carey then stated boldly, "We must not be contented with praying, without exerting ourselves in the use of means for the obtaining of those things we pray for."[378] This phrase, "the use of means," can be said to contain the essence of Carey's *Enquiry*.

Following its publication, fourteen persons met in the home of Mrs. Beeby Wallis of Kettering, England on October 2, 1792. They organized themselves as the "Particular Baptist Society for the Propagation of the Gospel Amongst the Heathen." The Society was soon renamed the Baptist Mission Society (BMS). The BMS Board accepted Carey's application to become a missionary and the Careys sailed to Serampore, India in April, 1793.[379] Carey never saw his homeland again.

Other "social scientists" began experimenting with Carey's theory soon after he departed for India. Dozens of mission enthusiasts began organizing themselves into special-purpose associations. William Carey's proposal to "use means" caught on in America even more rapidly than it had in England.[380] In a short time, Americans organized the New York Missionary Society (1796), the Northern Missionary Society

---

[377] Ibid., 81-82. Note that a member could be ousted from the society for failing to qualify, even after he had joined. In other words Carey foresees a screening process to get in, and if a member fails to keep his pledge, he or she can be removed from the group. All mission societies organize themselves in this way.
[378] Ibid., 80.
[379] For a fascinating account of Carey's contribution to India, see Vishal and Ruth Mangalwadi, *Who Was William Carey?*, ed. Ralph D. Winter and Steven C. Hawthorne, 3rd ed., Perspectives on the World Christian Movement (Pasadena: William Carey Library, 1999), 525ff.
[380] The Anglican Church Mission Society, formed in 1799, sent many German Lutherans but few Anglicans during its first fifty years. J. F. A. Ajayi, "From Mission to Church: The Heritage of the Church Mission Society," *International Bulletin of Missionary Research* 23, no. 2 (1999): 50.

and the Berkshire and Columbia Missionary Society (1797), the Missionary Society of Connecticut (1798), the Massachusetts Missionary Society (1799), and the Boston Female Society for Missionary Purposes (1800).[381] A number of students from Williams College in Massachusetts organized themselves as the "Society of the Brethren" in 1808. Its object was to "effect in the persons of its members a mission or missions to the heathen."[382] Members took an oath "to keep absolutely free from every engagement, which, after his prayerful attention, and after consultation with the brethren, shall be deemed incompatible with the object of this society,"[383] and "to solemnly promise to keep inviolably secret the existence of this society."[384] This society evolved into the American Board of Commissioners for Foreign Mission (ABCFM). The ABCFM sent its first five workers to India in 1812. The Board eventually opened work in 34 fields.[385] The remarkable story of how one Hawaiian man, Obookiah, came to New Haven, Connecticut on a trading ship and moved into Samuel Mills' home in 1810, and how the two of them studied theology at Andover in 1811 is told in Larue W. Piercy's book, *Hawaii's*

---

[381] Arthur Judson Brown, *One Hundred Years: A History of the Foreign Missionary Work of the Presbyterian Church in the USA* (New York: Revell, 1936), 14. Brown was a secretary of the Board of Foreign Missions of the Presbyterian Church in the U.S. A. from 1895 until his retirement at the age of seventy-two in 1929. He lived 34 more years, until 1963, when he died at the age of 106. See R. Park Johnson, "The Legacy of Arthur Judson Brown," *International Bulletin of Missionary Research* 10, no. 2 (1986): 71ff.

[382] Clarence Prouty Shedd, *Two Centuries of Student Christian Movements, Their Origin and Intercollegiate Life* (New York: Association press, 1934), 52.

[383] Timothy Clarke Wallstrom, *The Creation of a Student Movement to Evangelize the World* (Pasadena, CA: William Carey International University Press, 1980), 26.

[384] Shedd. 52. The records of the society were written in cipher. Shedd tells why: "The primary reason for secrecy was the indifferent and hostile attitude of a Church which could see in foreign missions only overheated religious zeal and fanaticism." 52.

[385] Pierson, "American Board of Commissioners for Foreign Mission," 54.

Missionary Saga.[386] Inspired by Obookiah's plea to bring the gospel to his people, the first missionaries to Hawaii in 1820.

Resistance to Carey's Paradigm. Thomas Kuhn, it will be remembered, theorized that a paradigm shift may occur when a scientist is bothered by the anomalies he finds in a time-honored paradigm.[387] As he considered the Reformed mission paradigm, Carey identified four anomalies that distressed him:

1. The first anomaly was the apparent failure of the Reformed and Lutheran churches to advance their mission cause outside of northern Europe.

2. The second anomaly was the success of Catholic religious orders to advance their mission to North and South America, Africa, and Asia.[388]

3. The third anomaly was the fact that English citizens were forming themselves into trading companies and were, by bending every effort, going to the ends of the earth to achieve their desired outcome.

4. The fourth anomaly was what Carey called "the success of former undertakings"[389] by missionaries sent out by organized mission agencies, especially (for Carey) the

---

[386] LaRue W. Piercy, *Hawaii's Missionary Saga: Sacrifice and Godliness in Paradise* (Honolulu: Mutual Publishing, 1992), 2-6.

[387] Kuhn, 53.

[388] Ironically, the Catholic era of missions was in decline at the time Carey wrote *An Enquiry*. The Franciscan and Dominican missions were no longer expanding, and the Pope had suppressed the Jesuit mission in 1773. "The importance of Carey's book and of the challenge posed for Catholics by the modern Protestant missionary movement cannot be overstated . . . Catholics realized that they needed to develop similar organizations to implement their own missionary ideals." William R. Burrows, "Catholics, Carey's "Means," and Twenty-First Century Mission," *International Bulletin of Missionary Research* 34, no. 3 (2010): 131.

Moravians. The Moravians succeeded where "we" have not, Carey observes; must the privilege of beginning such expeditions be retained only to Moravians? What can we learn from them?[390]

After Carey describes these four anomalies, he proposes a new paradigm, a new operating system, one that was incompatible with *sola synodica*. Readers of his *Enquiry* would have to choose between the two. If Thomas Kuhn's "resistance" theory is correct, we should anticipate a reaction to Carey's paradigm. Indeed, in 1796 the Presbyterian General Assembly of the Church of Scotland passed a resolution criticizing the nascent mission efforts: "To spread abroad among barbarians and heathen natives the knowledge of the Gospel seems to be highly preposterous, in so far as it anticipates, even reverses, the order of Nature."[391] This resolution provoked the friends of mission in the Church of Scotland to organize the Glasgow and Edinburgh (later the Scottish) Missionary Societies.[392] Other Scots from Baptist churches and from the Anglican Scottish Church began forming missionary societies "in the wake of the Evangelical Revival in the 1790s and especially William Carey's departure to India in 1793."[393] In 1829 the Church of

---

[389] Carey, *An Enquiry into the Obligations of Christians to Use Means for the Conversion of the Heathens*. His elaborate title includes the phrase "in which the religious state of the different nations of the world, the success of former undertakings, and the practicability of further undertakings are considered."

[390] The Moravians can teach us how voluntary mission structures might sustain themselves financially. See William J. Danker, *Profit for the Lord; Economic Activities in Moravian Missions and the Basel Mission Trading Company* (Grand Rapids: Eerdmans, 1971).

[391] Fletcher, 1. It would be twenty-eight years after the 1796 declaration before the Church of Scotland commissioned its first missionary, Alexander Duff.

[392] Andrew F. Walls, "Societies for Mission," in *The History of Christianity* (Berkhamsted, England: Lion Publishing, 1977), 551.

[393] Donald E. Meek, "Protestant Missions and the Evangelization of the Scottish Highlands, 1700-1850," *International Bulletin of Missionary Research* 21, no. 2 (1997): 68.

Scotland itself organized an official mission effort.[394] Andrew Walls would comment later, "After 1829 the Church of Scotland might claim to have integrated church and mission; but a glance at the origins of the various missionary operations of the Scottish churches reveals a patchwork of private initiatives."[395] What changed to bring about this new social contract between Church of Scotland (and Reformed Churches elsewhere) and independent mission agencies? David Bosch writes,

> The Reformation principle of the right of private judgment in interpreting Scripture was rekindled. An extension of this was that like-minded individuals could band together in order to promote a common cause. A plethora of new societies was the result.[396]

Thus, one principle from Reformed theology, freedom of conscience, set to work against the Reformed ideal that viewed the synod as the single divine instrument for the mission to the world.

4.5.1 The Appearance of Voluntary Societies after 1792 Enabled Protestants to Begin Achieving Their Mission Goals

In this section we are going to do a lot of counting and comparing. The reason we count, sociologist Rodney Stark states in his book, *The Cities of God,* is because "many of the really significant historical questions *demand* quantitative answers [emphasis is in original]."[397] To become confident of one's beliefs, Stark says, one has to do the math.[398]

---

[394] "The kingdom of God goes forth by jealousy," Ralph D. Winter often said.

[395] Andrew F. Walls, "The Missionary Movement: A Lay Fiefdom?," in *The Cross-Cultural Process in Christian History* (Maryknoll: Orbis, 2002), 223.

[396] Bosch, 328.

[397] Stark, 209.

[398] "The opinions of those who wouldn't count, shouldn't count," Stark says. Ibid., 222.

Therefore I counted the relevant data in two standard mission reference books, A. Scott Moreau's *Evangelical Dictionary of World Mission* (*EDWM*) and Gerald H. Anderson's *Biographical Dictionary of Christian Missions (BDCM)*. *EDWM* contains 292 missionary biographies[399] and *BDCM* contains 1100.[400] The findings indicate that following Carey's publishing of *An Enquiry* the Protestant mission era commenced. Whether Carey was the "father of modern missions" is irrelevant; he is important because he proposed "the use of Means" by which he meant a new missions operating system that was easily organized and widely adopted.

---

[399] See Appendix 1.
[400] See Appendix 2.

In the timeline below I compared the number of biographies in *EDWM* of Protestant missionaries who went overseas between two forty year periods, 1752-1792 (the year of Carey's *Enquiry)*, and 1792-1832 (Figure 2):

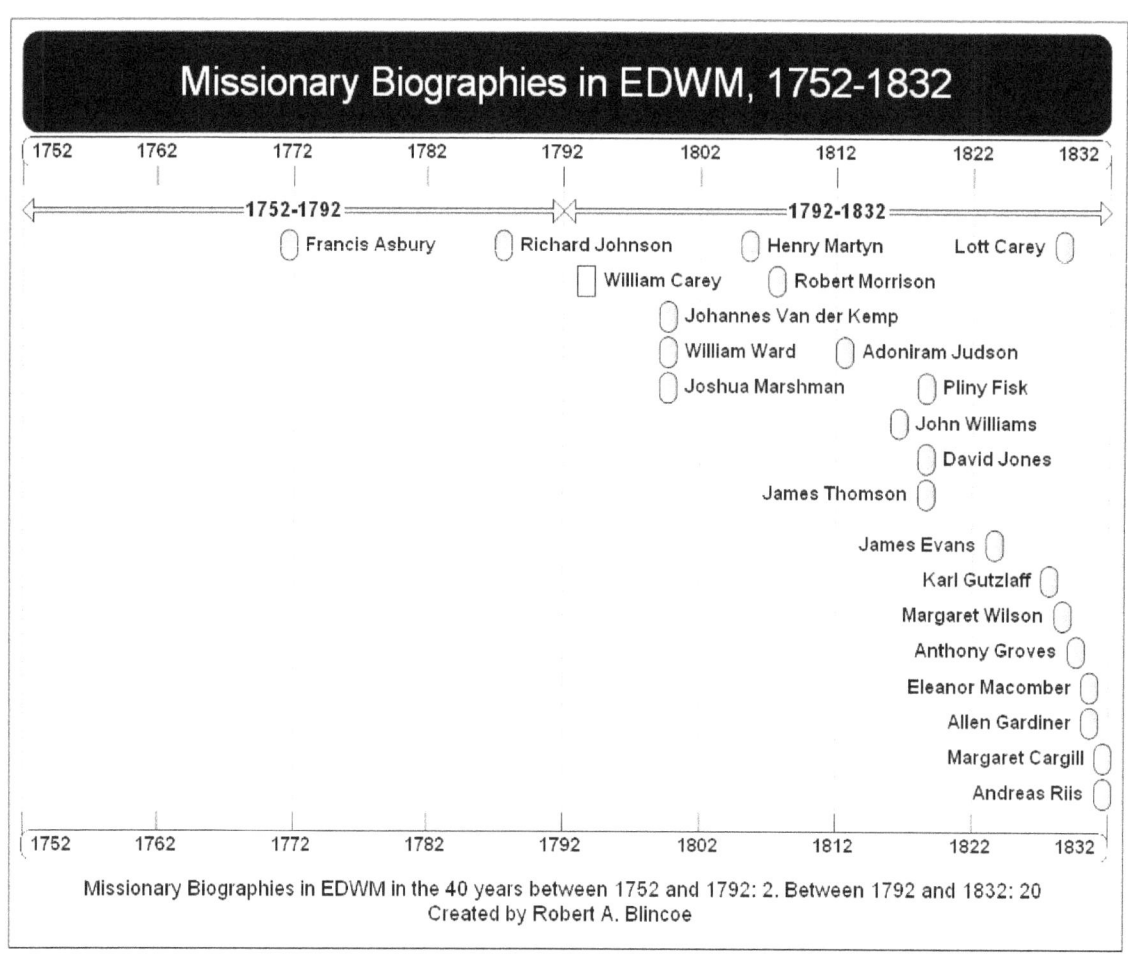

Figure 2. Timeline: Mission Biographies in EDWM 1752-1832

There are only two *EDWM* biographies of missionaries who went out in the forty year span prior to William Carey, but there are 20 in the forty year span that follows him. Here is the data represented in a graph (Figure 3):

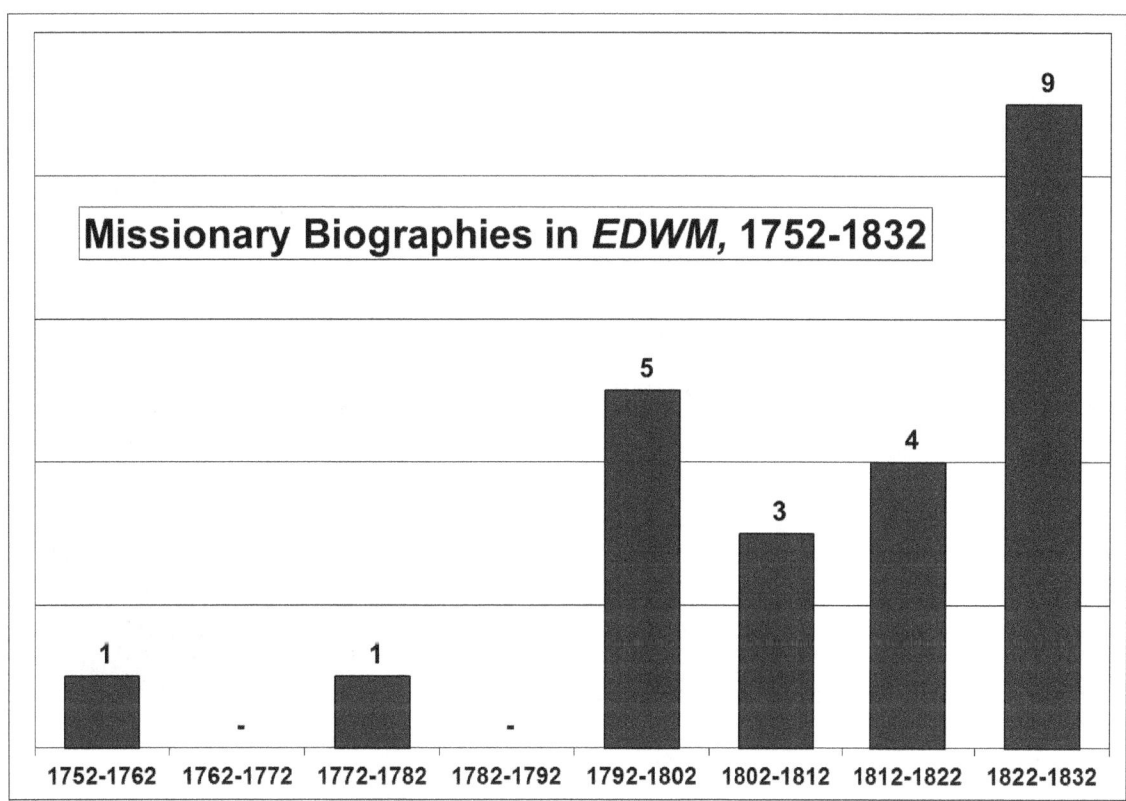

Figure 3. Mission Biographies in EDWM, 1752-1832 (2)

There are a total of 292 missionary biographies in *EDWM*; thirteen are biographies of missionaries who went out before William Carey, and 279 are biographies of missionaries who went out after him (Figure 4):

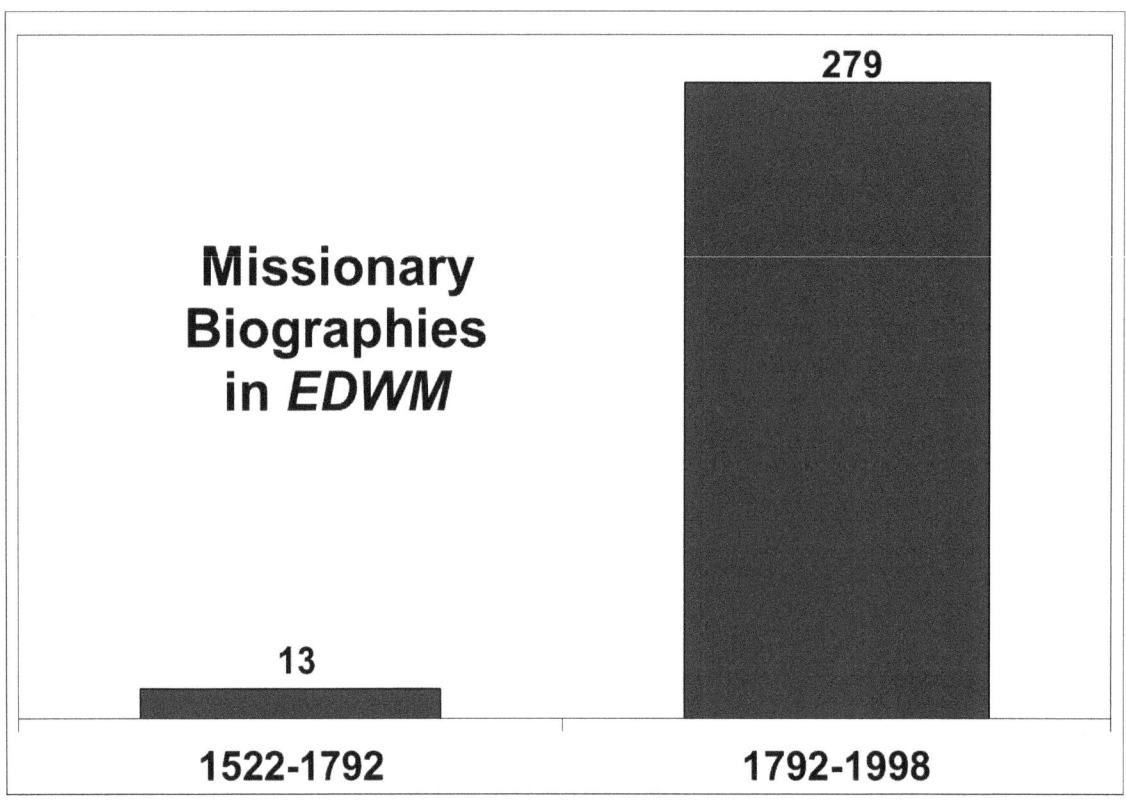

Figure 4. Timeline: Biographies in EDWM: 1522-1792, 1792-1998--A Comparison

Next I compared the number of *EDWM* articles on mission agencies that began in the 80 year period between 1752 and 1832. *EDWM* described zero mission agencies that formed in the 40 years preceding the publication of Carey's *Enquiry*, compared to 11 in the 40 years following (Figure 5):

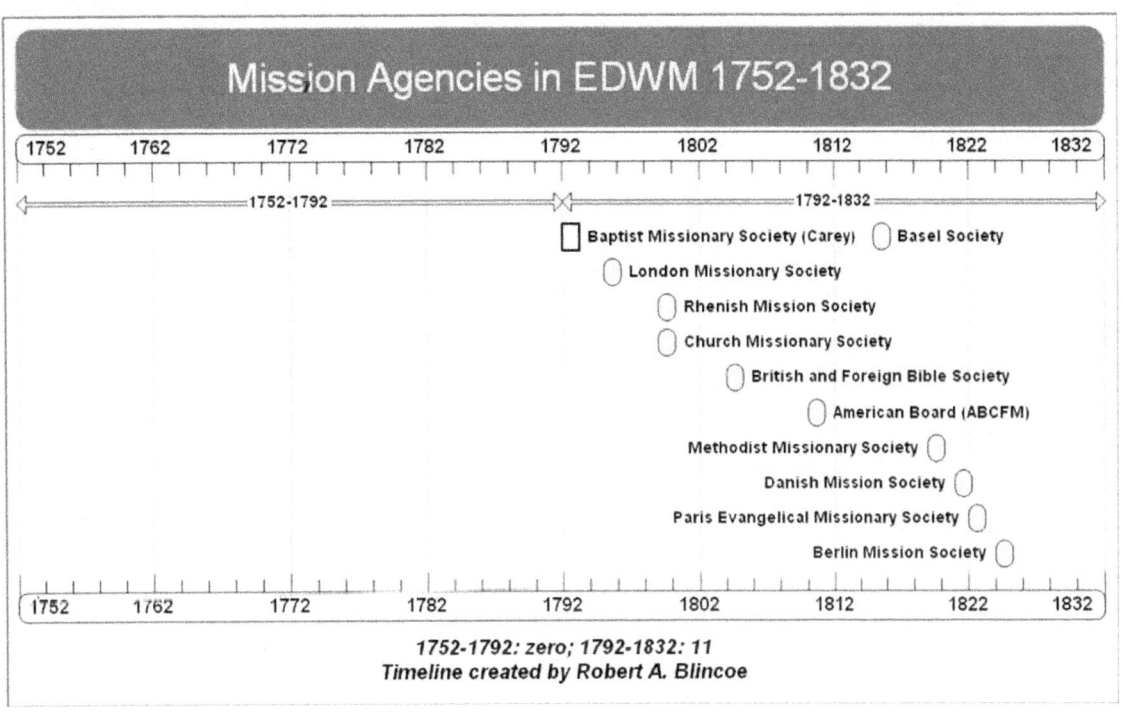

Figure 5. Timeline: Mission Agencies in EDWM, 1752-1832

William Carey's impact becomes obvious when looking at a timeline showing all the mission agency articles in EDWM from the Reformation age to 1822, that is, including the 30 years that followed Carey's publication (Figure 6):[401]

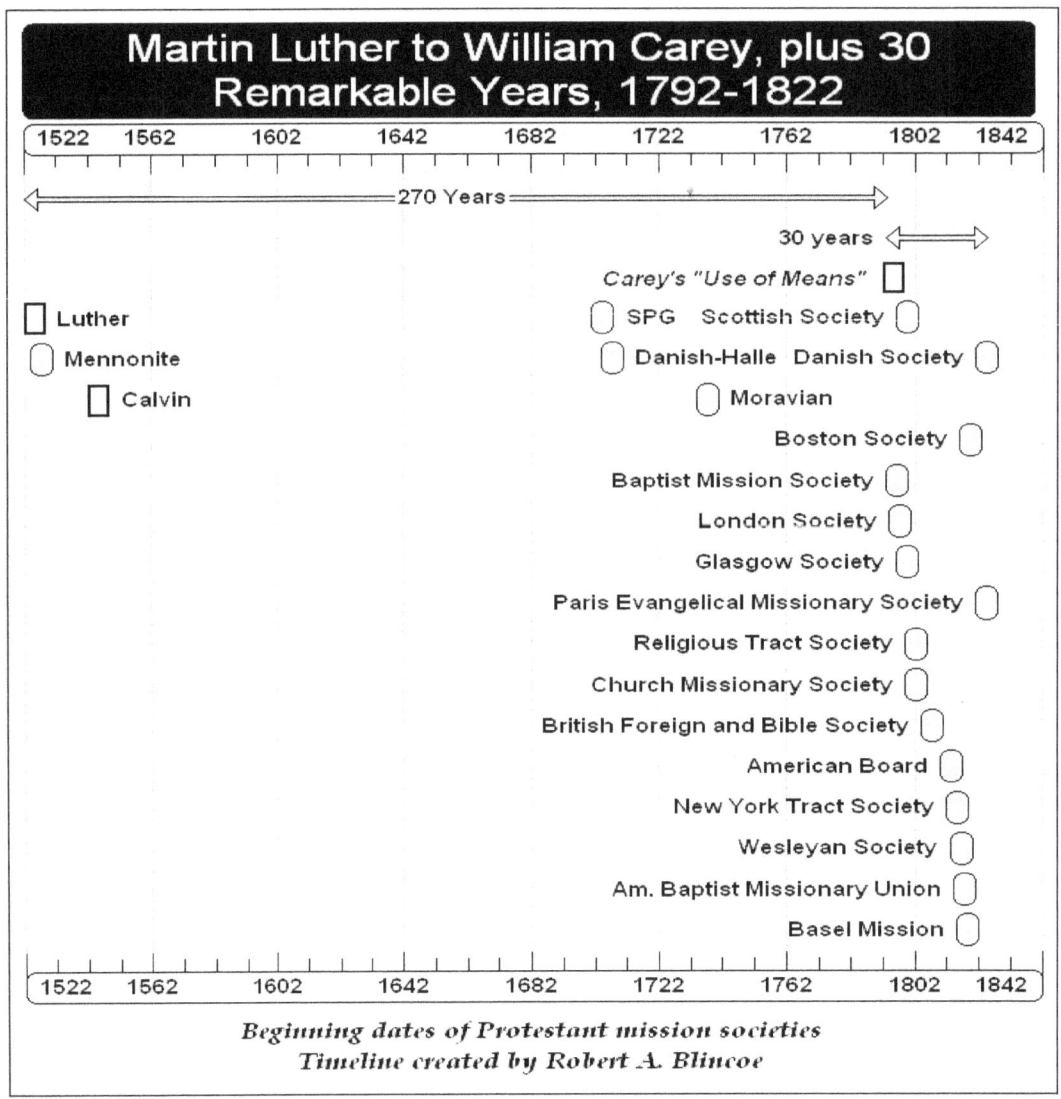

Figure 6. Timeline: Luther to Carey, plus 30 Remarkable Years

---

[401] There are 29 additional *EDWM* articles describing overseas mission agencies, with titles such as "Brazilian Mission Boards and Societies" and "Korean Mission Boards and Societies." All 29 overseas mission boards and societies described in *EDWM* formed in the 20th century, well after William Carey wrote his *Enquiry*.

To the extent the missionary biographies in *EDWM* allow a fair comparison between the actual number of missionaries who sailed before and after William Carey, we can reliably conclude that more than twenty times as many missionaries sailed in the 206 years between 1792 and 1998 (the date of *EDWM's* publication) as sailed in the 275 year between 1517 and 1792. Carey's "enabling technology" became the means of mission effort on every continent. David Bosch was correct when he wrote that "very little happened by way of missionary outreach during the first two centuries after the Reformation."[402] The data confirms what Donald Treadgold (d. 1994), author of *The History of Christianity*, wrote:

> The Protestant churches never did take the initiative in foreign missions. However, just before 1800 pietists or evangelicals did begin a massive effort, working not through ecclesiastical structures by through voluntary societies . . . Noteworthy among the individuals who gave impetus to the Pietist missionaries was William Carey, whose pamphlet *An Enquiry* (1792) led directly to the formation of the Baptist society, the very first of them.[403]

Data from Gerald Anderson's Biographies of Christian Missions. Next I counted missionary biographies from Gerald Anderson's *Biographical Dictionary of Christian Missions*[404] (*BDCM*). The results seem to confirm what I found in *EDWM*.

---

[402] Bosch, 245.
[403] Donald W. Treadgold, *A History of Christianity* (Belmont, MA: Nordland, 1979), 180.
[404] Gerald H. Anderson, *Biographical Dictionary of Christian Missions* (New York: Macmillan, 1998).

BDCM offers 13 biographies of missionaries that went out between the years 1752-1792, but 103 biographies for the years 1792-1832, eight times as many: (Figure 7)

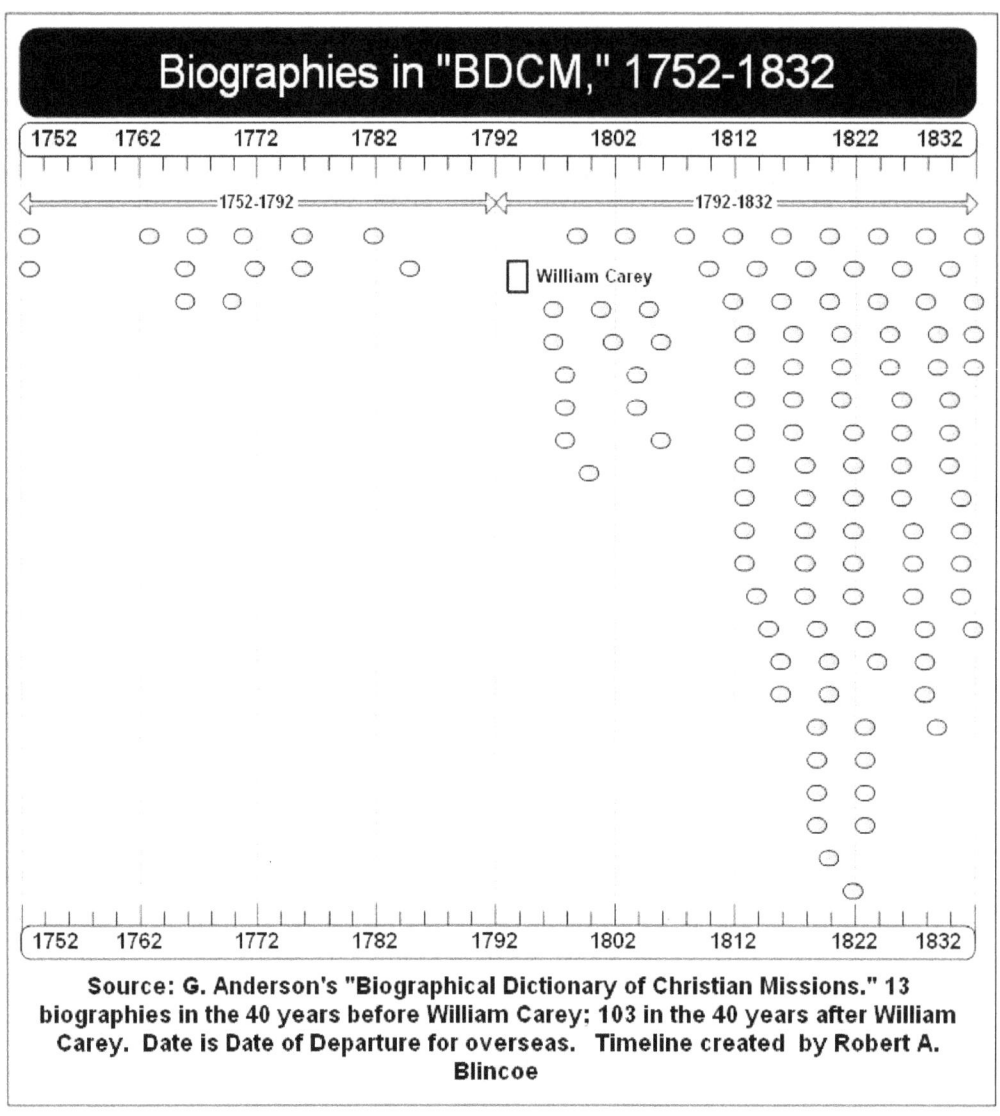

Figure 7. Timeline: Biographies in BDCM 1752-1832

Here is the same information presented in a different figure (Figure 8):

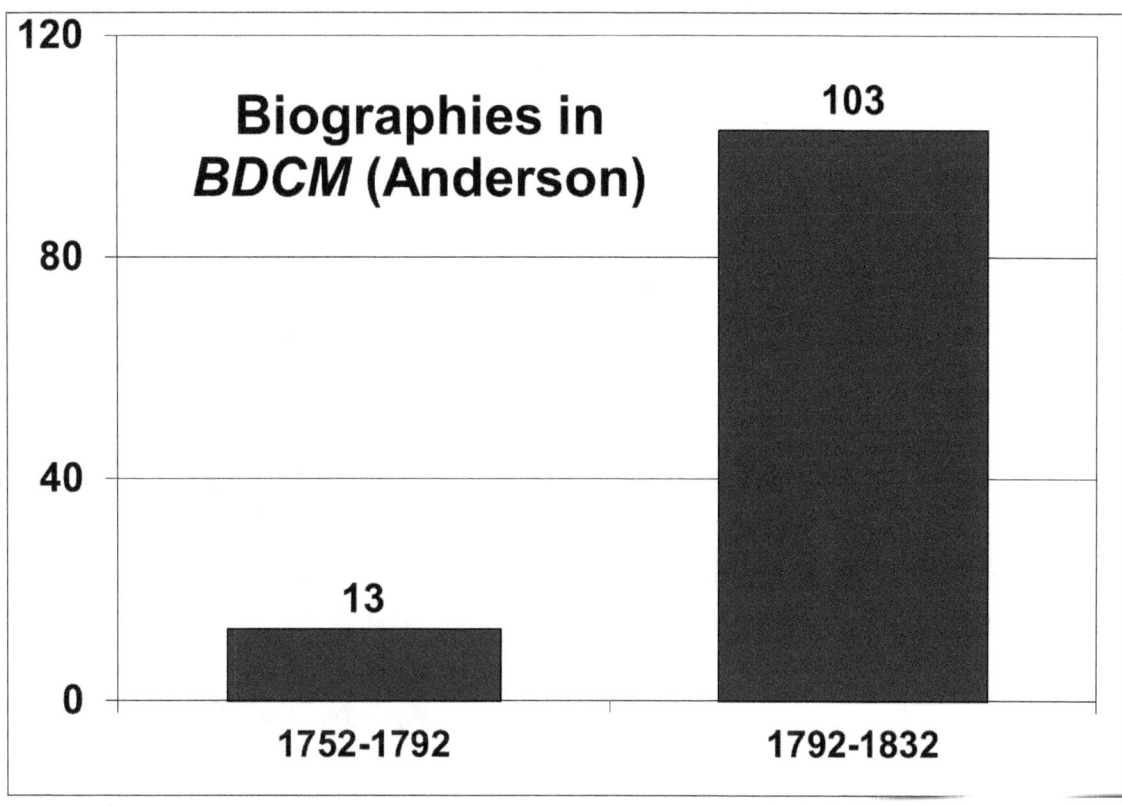

Figure 8. Timeline: Mission Biographies in BDCM 1752-1832 (2)

Many of the 13 Protestant missionaries in *BDCM* who went out between 1752 and 1792 were "early adopters" of what Carey proposed.[405]

- [405] Early adopters included 1) John Brainerd (David's younger brother) was financed and administered by the Society in Scotland for Propagating Christian Knowledge. Meek: 67. 2) Thomas Thompson joined the Society for the Propagation of the Gospel which assigned him to what is today Ghana. 3) Georg Schmidt was a Moravian missionary. 4) John Wesley, of course, formed a Holy Club at Oxford, and subsequently joined the SPCK and later established the Fetter Lane Society, which evolved into the Methodist movement. Basil Miller, *John Wesley: The World His Parish*, 3d ed. (Grand Rapids: Zondervan, 1943), 31, 79. Voluntary societies were essential for the spread of Methodism. Methodism began "not as church or a sect, but as a society . . . Wesley assumed that Methodists would attend Anglican services and sacraments." Tim Dowley, *The History of Christianity*, A Lion Handbook

In the 275 year period of the Reformation prior to Carey, *BDCM* includes 51 missionary biographies; but during the 208 year period between 1792 and 2000 there are 1049 missionary biographies, or 21 times as many[406] (Figure 9)

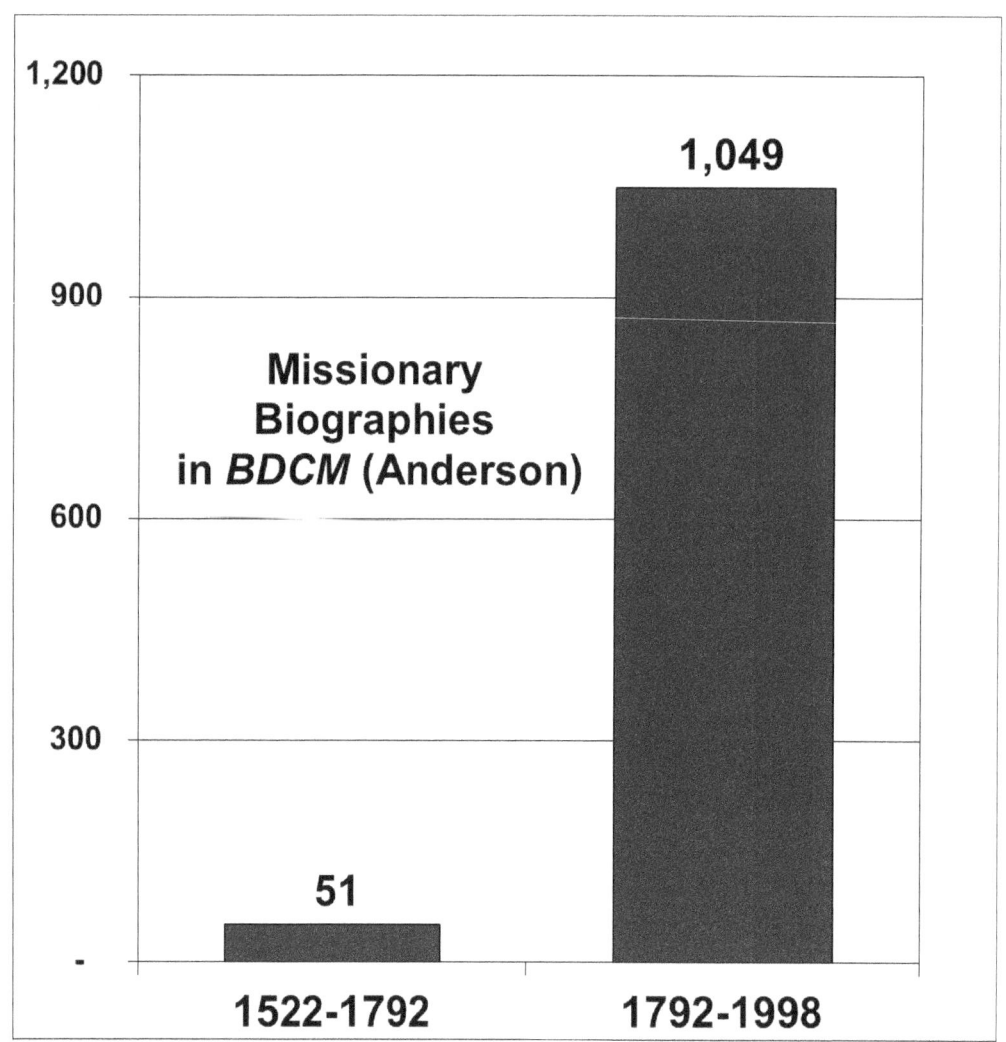

Figure 9. Timeline: Biographies in BDCM 1522-1792, 1792-1998--A Comparison

---

(Berkhamsted, England: Lion Publishing, 1977), 450. 5) Francis Asbury was the leading organizer of Wesleyan bands in America.
- Christian Friedrich Schwartz was sent out by the Danish-Halle mission, which the king of Denmark formed in order to send Lutheran missionaries to India.

[406] Anderson, *Biographical Dictionary of Christian Missions*. See Appendix 2.

In the timeline below the Protestant mission era is presented in fifty year segments. The data indicates that just before 1800 the Protestant mission era began (Figure 10):

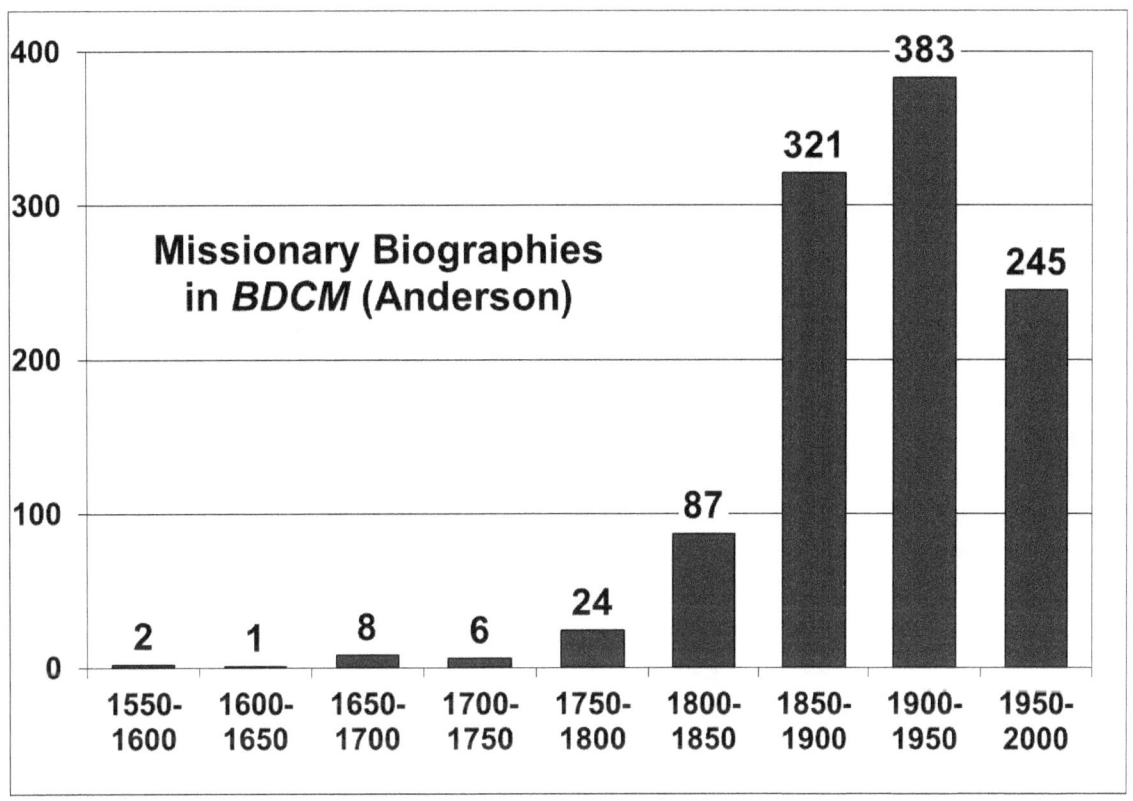

Figure 10. Timeline: Biographies in BDCM 1522-1998

William Carey's innovative mission operating system was a simple model that dozens and then hundreds of activists have copied. "The Protestant missionary movement that arose," Andrew Walls wrote, "became possible only by means of these new structures."[407] These structures made possible what Kenneth Scott Latourette described as

---

[407] Andrew F. Walls, *The Cross-Cultural Process in Christian History: Studies in the Transmission and Appropriation of Faith* (Maryknoll, NY: Orbis Books, 2002), 17.

"The Great Century" of Protestant missions, 1810-1914.[408] It is true that any number of books has been written about the failures, sometimes the mortifying failures, of some missionaries to maintain the standards of their cause; our libraries are lined with criticisms laid against the work missionaries have done. But hundreds of like-minded Christian who want to change the world and who are "driven to invent new forms of organizations" can pay tribute to the enduring influence of the shoemaker, William Carey. His "use of means" theory enabled others to multiply the number of agencies, something that could not be said for the Danish-Halle mission of the early 18th century.[409] On account of Carey a long era of immobility came to a close. The Pietists at last hoisted their sails. In his reference book, *The British Missionary Enterprise Since 1700*, Jeffrey Cox made this statement:

> The distinctive contribution of evangelicals in Britain was *organizational* rather than ideological or theological. Evangelicals did not invent the characteristic institution of modern Protestant missions, that is, the nongovernmental (or quasi-governmental) voluntary society. Pietists, Anglicans, Moravians, and Scottish Presbyterians experimented with such a form in the eighteenth century. In the 1790s evangelicals perfected this institution in a way that led to the creation of a new ecclesiastical profession, that of the modern missionary [emphasis added].[410]

---

[408] In fact, volumes 4, 5, and 6 of Latourette's seven volume masterpiece are devoted to this one century. Kenneth Scott Latourette, *A History of the Expansion of Christianity* (New York; London: Harper & Brothers, 1937).
[409] Mulholland: 94.
[410] Cox. Jeffrey, "What I Have Learned About Missions from Writing *the British Missionary Enterprise since 1700*," *International Bulletin of Missionary Research* 32 no. 2 (2008): 86.

Thus, we can validate R. Pierce Beaver's claim that Carey's Baptist Missionary Society "immediately stimulated new organizations."[411] Below we make some determinations from the data presented here.

Determinations Drawn from the Evidence. Pietists did not spring into action by (merely) proclaiming the importance of missions;[412] only by adopting Carey's operating system, the voluntary society did Pietists awaken from their reveries. This was what Vander Werff called "the great breakthrough."[413] This is why Arthur J. Brown could write, "In the last decade of the [18th] century, the deepening missionary interest found expression in *the organization of several local and independent societies* [emphasis added]."[414] This is why Ralph D. Winter hailed Carey's *Enquiry* as "probably the most influential single document in the history of Protestant missions"[415] and "the *Magna Carta* of the Protestant missions movement."[416] Carey "was only one of many similar figures from this period and as much a product as a shaper of the spirit of the time. Church renewal

---

[411] R. Pierce Beaver, *All Loves Excelling; American Protestant Women in World Mission* (Grand Rapids: Eerdmans, 1968), 16-17.

[412] In 1784 Jonathan Edwards had published *An Humble Attempt to Promote an Explicit Agreement and Visible Union of God's People, in Extraordinary Prayer for the Revival of Religion, and the Advancement of Christ's Kingdom in the Earth*. In that same year Baptists and other nonconformists throughout the English Midlands had begun meeting for one hour on the first Monday of very month to pray for a revival which would lead to the spread of the gospel "to the most distant parts of the habitable globe." Brian Stanley, "Winning the World: Carey and the Modern Missionary Movement," *Christian History* 5, no. 1 (1986 January): 9.

[413] Vander Werff, 25.

[414] Brown, 14.

[415] Winter, "Paul and the Regions Beyond," 6. Also Winter, "Protestant Mission Societies and the 'Other Protestant Schism'," 199.

[416] Ralph D. Winter, "Four Men, Three Eras," (1996). http://williamcareylibrary.com/ebooks/Four_Men_Three_Eras%20.pdf . Accessed December 2010.

and mission were simply in the air."[417] *In the air*, but the air began to fill the sails only when Carey "supposed" that a company of serious Christians could form themselves into a missionary society. The subsequent founding of overseas churches, orphanages, schools, dispensaries, and printing presses follows the publication of Carey's *Enquiry*, not the wishful thinking of the mission-minded Christians of his time. The difference was Carey's easy-to-assemble instruction booklet for ordinary people. It was Carey who proposed that the sails be gathered and hoisted to catch the wind.[418] But he was fortunate to make his propose after the year 1779, as the next section explains.

The Enabling Act of 1779. In 1779, Parliament passed an Enabling Act that authorized English citizens to organize public or private schools and associations apart from the authority of the Anglican Church. Robert Raikes (d. 1811) took advantage of this law in 1780 to organize a Sunday School. The Anglican Church disapproved; Raikes held his first classes in the kitchen of a Mrs. Meredith in his home town of Gloucester.[419] It is "unlikely that anything like the Sunday school could have arisen without the legal

---

[417] Bosch, 280. For example, in 1781 Andrew Fuller (d. 1815) wrote *The Gospel Worthy of all Acceptation*. Fuller published it in 1785 after he was able to apply to it the thought of American theologian Jonathan Edwards "in order to prove," Bosch wrote, "that Calvinism itself, as distinct from the false Calvinism was essentially a missionary theology." 280. Fuller's book influenced Baptist Church leaders in England to promote Christ's Great Commission, but did not result in any actual mission initiatives. Fuller ardently supported the Baptist Missionary Society from its founding subsequent to the publication of Carey's *Enquiry*; thus Fuller recognized the "enabling technology" by which "a serious company of Christians" would make *agenda* from *credenda*.

[418] Carey wrote his proposal, A. Christopher Smith notes, in "a rather inauspicious time for 'launching out into the deep,'" just three years after the French Revolution. A. Christopher Smith, "The Legacy of William Carey," *International Bulletin of Missionary Research* 16, no. 1 (1992): 4.

[419] See "History of Sunday School" in Elmer L. Towns, *Towns' Sunday School Encyclopedia* (Wheaton, Ill.: Tyndale House, 1993).

sanction of the Enabling Act."[420] In Raikes we see "the clear connection between a free society and the growth of independent religious organizations. Prior to 1779, "the philanthropy of Robert Raikes (or anyone else) would have been stifled by the laws of the country and the prejudice of those in ecclesiastical power."[421] English citizens began forming themselves into "little platoons"[422]—Edmund Burke's term for voluntary societies. Members of these societies devoted themselves to certain causes (e.g. abolition of slavery, prison reform, temperance, Christian overseas missions). These "voluntary forms of operation," M. J. D. Roberts wrote, "once accepted as 'safe' by civil and ecclesiastical authority, were accessible by any who had the will to adopt them."[423] Working class people were transformed into activists through the instrument of voluntary associations.[424] Too, English women organized moral reform societies, which "became the means by which women made a successful claim for recognition as legitimate participants in rational-critical debate."[425] An Age of Reform had begun. My findings

---

[420] Wesley Kenneth Willmer, J. David Schmidt, and Martyn Smith, *The Prospering Parachurch: Enlarging the Boundaries of God's Work*, 1st ed. (San Francisco, CA: Jossey-Bass, 1998), 37.

[421] Ibid. Today, of course, a pastor is expected to manage a Sunday school, the New Testament basis for which has become somehow obvious to most members of the church.

[422] Edmund Burke and J. C. D. Clark, *Reflections on the Revolution in France* (Stanford, CA: Stanford University Press, 2001), 202.

[423] M. J. D. Roberts, *Making English Morals: Voluntary Association and Moral Reform in England, 1787-1886*, Cambridge Social and Cultural Histories (Cambridge University Press, 2004), 294.

[424] Ibid. Gordon Wood, considered by some the most influential historian on the early years of the United States, said that what was going on in America in the early 1800s was "the rise of ordinary people into dominance." Quoted in Robert William Fogel, *The Fourth Great Awakening & the Future of Egalitarianism* (University of Chicago Press, 2000), 29.

[425] Roberts, 296.

indicate that when governments and ecclesiastical hierarchies validate the right of their citizens to organize for missions, their citizens are empowered to change the world.[426]

Today, more than four centuries after the establishment of the Virginia Company one may forget that *the government had to act* before citizens could form themselves into private companies:

> No matter how much modern businessmen may presume to the contrary, the company was a political creation. . . . Businessmen might see the joint company as a convenient form; from many politicians' viewpoint, it existed because it had been given a license to do so, and granted the privilege of limited liability. In the Anglo-Saxon world, the state might decide that it wanted relatively little in return: "these little republics," as Robert Lowe called [the corporations], were to be left alone.[427]

The legislation that allowed Raikes and Carey and others to form themselves into societies despite opposition from ecclesiastical administrations.

4.5.2 Voluntary Societies Resemble Trading Companies, Carey Observed

The most important similarity to what he was proposing, Carey said, was the private trading company. "There was something businesslike, something distinctly modern, about the launching of the new societies,"[428] David Bosch wrote. "Carey took his analogy," Bosch added, "neither from Scripture nor from theological tradition,"

---

[426] Karl Marx said, "The philosophers have only interpreted the world, in various ways; the point is to change it." Quoted in Merold Westphal, *Suspicion and Faith: The Religious Uses of Modern Atheism* (Grand Rapids: Eerdmans, 1993), 131.

[427] Micklethwait and Wooldridge, 54.

[428] Bosch, 330. See also Dwight P. Baker, "William Carey and the Business Model for Mission: Reflections on the Conduct of Mission at the Opening of the 21st Century," (Pasadena, CA: William Carey International University, 2001). Baker writes, "Carey's proposal to recast mission endeavor according to the pattern of a joint stock commercial business venture came just as the commercial company was undergoing significant change with introduction of what was to become the modern corporation. Modern

but from the contemporary commercial world—the organization of an overseas trading company, which carefully studied all the relevant information, selected its stock, ships and crews, and was willing to brave dangerous seas and unfriendly climates in order to achieve its objective. Carey proposed that, in similar fashion, a company of serious Christians might be formed with the objective of evangelizing distant peoples. It should be an "instrumental" society, that is, a society established with a clearly defined purpose along explicitly formulated lines.[429]

Beginning with the creation of the East India Company (chartered in 1600), the Company of Virginia (1606), the Plymouth Company (1606), and the Hudson Bay Company (1670)—private trading companies with which Carey would have been familiar—the British government passed several laws simplifying the process by which men could form companies for the purpose of creating wealth. The British crown would regulate and tax, but not manage, these businesses. No one could foresee how influential these companies would become; Micklethwait and Wooldridge, in their book *The Company*, aptly wrote:

> Hegel predicted that the most influential unit of the modern society would be the government, Marx predicted it would be the commune, Lenin and Hitler that it would be the political party. Before that, a succession of saints and sages claimed the same for the parish church, the feudal manor, and the monarchy. The big contention of this small book is that they have all been proved wrong. The most important organization in the world is the company. The company is the basis of the prosperity of the West and the best hope for the future of the rest of the world.[430]

Protestant missions and the modern corporation grew up together. The structure of the business corporation provided a mechanism and a model for organization of the mission enterpris" ibid., 1.

[429] Bosch, 330.
[430] Micklethwait and Wooldridge, xiv-xv.

Private trading companies evolved into limited-liability joint-stock companies, a distinct legal entity endowed by liberal governments with certain rights and responsibilities.[431] The British Parliament enacted laws entitling private companies with three rights:[432] 1) It would be an "artificial person," with the ability to do business as a real person; 2) It would issue tradable shares to any number of investors, and 3) those investors could have limited liability (so they could lose only the money they had committed to the firm). Starting a business or a not-for profit association no longer required special sanction from Parliament; citizens could set up a general-purpose corporation simply by filing the forms.

Free world governments everywhere have legalized the right of their citizens to form corporations. The private trading company was, Peter Drucker said, "the first autonomous institution in hundreds of years, the first to create a power center that was within society yet independent of the central government of the national state."[433] The private initiative and control has resulted in all manner of enterprise and achievement. "By contrast," write Micklethwait and Wooldridge, "civilizations that once outstripped the West failed to

---

[431] The principles of a joint stock company are used to organize many contemporary corporate entities in free market countries, such the French *société anonyme*, the German *Aktiengesellschaft*, the Italian *Società per Azioni* (S.p.A.), the Polish *Spółka Akcyjna* (SA), the Japanese *kabushiki kaisha*, and the South Korean *jushik hoesa*.

[432] The U.S. government grants these same rights: "When legally organized, the corporation, in a limited way, becomes a person and a citizen. The advantages of incorporation are these: It combines capital, knowledge and enterprise with limited pecuniary responsibility, which is generally the amount of stock owned by a person. The legislature of each State enjoys the right to regulate the organization of business and other corporations, religious, literary charitable and miscellaneous, within its own borders." Thomas E. Hill, *Hill's Manual of Business and Social Information* (Chicago: W. B. Conkey, 1915), 215. 215

[433] Quoted in Micklethwait and Wooldridge, 54.

develop private-sector companies"—the authors mention the Islamic world—"fell farther and farther behind."[434] The advantages of the private company are "conquering such obstinate refuseniks as the Chinese Communist Party and the partners of Goldman Sachs."[435] The US had 5 ½ million corporations in 2001; North Korea apparently has none. "Today the number of private-sector companies that a country boasts is a better guide to its status than the number of battleships it can muster. It is also not a bad guide to its political freedom."[436] In their description of a totalitarian regime Carl Friedrich and Zbigniew Brzezinski include as one of six distinguishing traits the prohibition of private, non-government organizations.[437] The enduring relevance of economist F. A. Hayek's warning against centralized control, sounded in his 1944 classic *Road to Serfdom*, demonstrates the need for citizens to guard their freedom to form special-purpose associations. Hayek's main point is "that coordination of activities through central direction and through voluntary cooperation are roads going in very different directions: the first to serfdom, the second to freedom."[438] For a government to authorize its citizens to organize themselves into causes that are interesting to only a few people, a single condition—monitoring by the government—is necessary to guarantee that two values important to the general population, namely, safety and truth-telling, will be maintained.

---

[434] Ibid., xxi.
[435] Ibid., xvi.
[436] Ibid., xx.
[437] Cited in Constance E. Smith and Anne E. Freedman, *Voluntary Associations: Perspectives on the Literature* (Cambridge, MA: Harvard University Press, 1972), 33.
[438] Friedrich A. von Hayek, *The Road to Serfdom*, 50th anniversary ed. (University of Chicago Press, 1994), xiii-xiv.

Percy Barnevik's wonderful phrase—"Decentralization goes hand in hand with central monitoring"[439]—is a perfect summary statement of the desired outcome of this dissertation.

The authors of *The Prospering Parachurch* comment, "The freedom that allowed Robert Raikes to begin his first Sunday school in a rented kitchen is still with us. This freedom is the necessary environment for the parachurch."[440] Today's ecclesiastical leaders should give "a license" to their church citizens to organize themselves for mission. This topic and its resolution will be a proposal, "A New Social Contract for Presbyterians," in Chapter Five.

Tension between Government and Trading Companies. "Throughout the twentieth century," write Micklethwait and Wooldridge, "the company jostled with the state that spawned it."[441] Read that with the church in mind, and it says, "Throughout the century mission agencies have existed in tension with church governments." This tension is normative; or, more precisely, can be normalized. Bosch describes the relations in New Testament Antioch between "the settled ministry" of elders and "the mobile ministry" of apostles, prophets and evangelists as "creative tension."[442] Mission agencies—Habitat for

---

[439] Percy Barnevik, CEO of Asea, Brown and Bovari. Quoted in Skreslet. 3. Skreslet pulled the quote by Percy Barnevik from Robert Kaplan's December 1997 *Atlantic Monthly* article, "Was Democracy Just a Moment?" 72.
[440] Willmer, Schmidt, and Smith, 37-38.
[441] Micklethwait and Wooldridge, xix.
[442] Bosch, 51. Bosch laments the waning of this creative tension, as the Antioch church became institutionalized "and less concerned with the world outside their walls. Soon they had to design rules for

Humanity, the American Bible Society, Young Life—turn out a "product," while church administrations—Presbyterian, Baptist, Calvary Chapel—retain the task of requiring a mission agency to maintain fiscal and doctrinal "quality control."[443] Normally this quality control is demonstrated when a mission agency's finances are independently audited if maintains membership in a certifying body, such as Missio Nexus.

The Company itself was an "Enabling Technology." "The limited liability corporation is the greatest single discovery of modern times,"[444] proclaimed Nicholas Murray Butler (d. 1947), president of Columbia University and recipient of the 1931 Nobel Peace Prize. Butler added, "Even steam and electricity would be reduced to comparative impotence without it."[445] This praise is warranted because, as Micklethwait and Wooldridge wrote, "the company itself was an enabling technology."[446] Peter Drucker agreed: "This new 'corporation,' this new *Societe Anonyme*, this new *Aktiengesellschaft*, could not be explained away as a reform . . . It clearly was an innovation."[447] It was a paradigm shift. Carey suggested that voluntary mission agencies be organized in the same way and be regulated in the same way, "obtaining their charter" and being "regulated, as to be likely

---

guaranteeing the decorum of their worship meetings (1 Cor 11:2-33; 1 Tim 2:1-15), for establishing criteria for the ideal clergyman and his wife (1 Tim 2:1-13)." 51

[443] Of course, the mission agencies are responsible to monitor themselves as well; hence their membership in the Interdenominational Foreign Mission Association (now CrossGlobal Link) or the Evangelical Foreign Mission Association (now Mission Exchange) as well as the Evangelical Council for Financial Accountability (ECFA).

[444] Micklethwait and Wooldridge, xx-xxi.

[445] Ibid.

[446] Ibid.

[447] Ibid. 54

to answer for their purpose."[448] But the resemblance does not stop here, "for," Carey wrote, "encouraged by the prospect of success, [the trading companies] use every effort, cast their bread upon the waters, cultivate friendship with everyone from whose information they expect the least advantage."[449] Passionate for profit, "they cross the widest and most tempestuous seas, and encounter the most unfavourable climates; they introduce themselves into the most barbarous nations, and sometimes undergo the most affecting hardships."[450] The owner's minds are, Carey realizes,

> in a state of anxiety and suspense, and a longer delay than usual in the arrival of their vessels agitates them with a thousand changeful thoughts, and foreboding apprehensions, which continue till the rich returns are safe arrived [sic] in port. But why these fears? Whence all these disquietudes, and this labour? Is it not because their souls enter into the spirit of the project, and their happiness in a manner depends on its success?[451]

As the perils of a for-profit enterprise are only bearable when the owners are sure that they are concentrating every strategy for the purpose of ensuring, so far as mortals may, the outcome that they desire, so also the "glorious outcome" which Carey wished to achieve forces the members of the special-purpose association to take the utmost care in their plans, lest by dispersing their energies the achievement they desire most be lost. In James Bryce's book *The American Commonwealth*, which was first printed in 1888, and

---

[448] Carey, *An Enquiry into the Obligations of Christians to Use Means for the Conversion of the Heathens*, 80.
[449] Ibid., 80-81.
[450] Ibid.
[451] Ibid., 81.

most recently in 2008, the author lauds the voluntary associations because they concentrate all their resources to achieve their stated ends:

> Associations are created, extended, and worked in the United States more quickly and effectively than in any other country. In nothing does the executive talent of the people better shine than in the promptitude wherewith the idea of an organization for common object is taken up, in the instinctive discipline that makes everyone who joins in starting it fall into his place, in the practical, business-like turn which the discussions forthwith take.[452]

Carey's paradigm enables a mission agency to lay hold of this organizational advantage, by which "everyone takes up a common object" and develops "an instinctive discipline" in order to achieve the agency's goals.

4.5.3 Voluntary Societies as "The Fortunate Subversion of the Church"—Observations of Andrew Walls

The Catholic [mission] movement had been able to develop on the basis of the religious orders, but, writes Andrew Walls, "the Reformation had slain the goose that laid that particular golden egg."[453] Fortunately Carey finally came along, Walls says, to invent "the organizational and the logistical" technology, that "most potent instrument of the Protestant missionary movement: the voluntary society."[454]

But reading church histories from cover to cover one discovers that some histories do not contain more than a passing reference to voluntary societies. Thus, Owen Chadwick's *The Victorian Church*, which, Walls calls "a noteworthy, many-sided study, of two

---

[452] quoted in Smith and Freedman, *Voluntary Associations: Perspectives on the Literature*, 35.
[453] Walls, "The Missionary Movement: A Lay Fiefdom?," 220.
[454] Ibid., 222.

volumes and 1,116 pages" contains "no chapter or section on the Victorian missionary movement . . . Chadwick's work reveals that the British missionary movement at its height was only peripheral to the Victorian church."[455] Chadwick does not mention Carey in his *History of Christianity*; in fact, the only references Chadwick makes to any Protestant missionaries that I found are to John Wesley and David Livingstone.[456] In Robert Glover's 380 page *History of World-Wide Missions* (1953) the chapter on the mission of the Reformers, titled "From Luther to the Halle Missionaries" fills only six pages, and all six pages describe Catholic missions.[457] Historic references to William Carey usually mention his missionary work in India or credit him with founding the Baptist Mission Society, as in, for example, *The Westminster Dictionary of Church History*.[458] In *Christianity* Roland Bainton allows one mention of William Carey, and a reference to his printing press in India.[459] Similar examples abound.[460]

---

[455] Andrew F. Walls, "Structural Problems in Mission Studies," in *The Missionary Movement in Christian History* (Maryknoll: Orbis, 1996), 146. "No doubt," adds Walls, "a history of Christianity composed in Jerusalem about AD 66 would have shown the Gentile mission as rather peripheral to Christian development. It is our possession of the 'mission studies' documents by Paul and Luke that makes possible another interpretation."

[456] Owen Chadwick, *A History of Christianity*, 1st U.S. ed. (New York: St. Martin's Press, 1996), 241, 274.

[457] Glover.

[458] Brauer and Gerrish, 160.

[459] Roland Herbert Bainton, *Christianity* (New York: American Heritage; Distributed by Houghton Mifflin, 1964), 352. 352

[460] In addition, there are at least 86 articles in the *Christian History* magazine that refer to Carey, but the references to Carey's *Enquiry* or to his proposal to organize mission societies are few. Some church histories make no mention of Carey's "Use of Means" as though it were not there, although they may mention Carey as being a missionary, including these:

- Carey is mentioned as "useful in the training of the [East India] Company's officials"—John McManners, *The Oxford Illustrated History of Christianity* (New York: Oxford University Press, 1990), 491.

Such faint praise somewhat understates an event I am portraying as the most consequential Christian milestone that has occurred in church history since the Reformation. Ernst Benz fittingly wrote that "the religious and theological conflicts on the European continent and the beginnings of the church in North America have claimed all the interest of the historians so that the history of mission has appeared to be a kind of subordinate subject."[461] Latourette's seven volume *History of Christianity* is the magnificent exception, for it arranges, as Benz notes, "a total picture of the life and growth of Christian Churches in which the history of missions is considered to be the most important expression of the life of the Church."[462] But issue 36 of *Christian History*, "The Missions Manifesto: An Excerpt from the *Magna Carta* of the Protestant Mission Movement"[463] carries a three page excerpt of Carey's *Enquiry* that inexplicably contains no reference to the central paragraph to which all of Carey's spread sheets and facts were directed, "Suppose a company of serious Christians were to form themselves into a society." Nor is Carey's major analogy, to the private trading company, by which his readers were meant to understand his proposal, mentioned in the article. Fortunately Paul

---

- "The Baptist Missionary Society was founded at his pleading in 1792; a year later, Carey sailed to India as its first missionary."—Brian Moynahan, *The Faith : A History of Christianity*, 1st ed. (New York: Doubleday, 2002), 627.
- Carey as the missionary who helped organize the Baptist Missionary Society.—Michael Collins and Matthew Arlen Price, *The Story of Christianity*, 1st American ed. (New York: DK Press, 1999), 182.
- William Carey "organized the first Baptist missionary society and in 1793 he and his family sailed for India."—B. K. Kuiper, *The Church in History* (Grand Rapids: National Union of Christian Schools, 1951), 320.

[461] Ernst Benz, "Pietist and Puritan Sources of Early Protestant World Missions (Cotton Mather and H. Francke)," *Church History*, (1951): 28.
[462] Ibid.
[463] http://www.christianitytoday.com/ch/1992/issue36/3618.html

Pierson's article in the same issue, "Why Did the 19th Century Explode with Missions?" credits Carey for what happened next:

> In 1792, Carey sparked the creation of the Particular Baptist Society for the Propagation of the Gospel Amongst the Heathen. There soon followed an explosion of mission agencies: London Missionary Society (1795), Scottish and Glasgow Missionary Societies (1796), Church Mission Society (1799), Religious Tract Society (1799), and the British and Foreign Bible Society (1804). Similar groups formed in continental Europe and America, including the American Board of Commissioners for Foreign Missions (1810) and, among Baptists, the General Convention for Foreign Missions (1814).[464]

The "instrumental nature" of the voluntary societies. After Carey, ordinary church members began forming "little republics" to change the world. Walls writes, "A new type of church government was growing up alongside the old . . . It altered the power base. It was the voluntary society which first made the laymen of real significance in the church."[465] The novel contribution of the missionary societies, for Walls, is their "instrumental nature."[466] An *instrument* is "a means whereby something is achieved, performed, or furthered."[467] Problems of all kinds, including the root problems of the world are addressed and sometimes solved, as people of goodwill band themselves together in voluntary societies. Walls writes, "In a voluntary association, individuals, churches, and congregations freely act together for an object of common interest. It is essentially a pragmatic approach, the design of *an instrument for a specific purpose*

---

[464] Paul E. Pierson, "Why Did the 1800s Explode with Missions?," *Christian History* 11, no. 4 (1992): 21.
[465] Walls, "The Fortunate Subversion of the Church," 249.
[466] Ibid., 242.
[467] Merriam-Webster Inc. s.v. "Instrument."

[emphasis added]."[468] Walls credits William Carey for showing the Protestant church this way forward: "Carey's crucial words are 'the obligation to *use means.*' At the heart of it lies the responsibility of Christians to invent the appropriate instrument, to accomplish a task which God has laid upon them."[469] Before Carey, "the Church structures could only do what they had always done; a new concept needed a new instrument."[470] And "in Europe and America alike, effective overseas missions began not with the official machinery of the churches, but with voluntary societies."[471] Those relatively few Churchmen, Walls wrote, who thought seriously about evangelization outside the Church of England, "realized that nothing could be done without a new structure."[472] Stanley H. Skreslet agrees: "Mission structures are critical tools, therefore, not least because without them no theory of mission has a chance of ever becoming more than unincarnated mutterings, words without effect in a world that expects action."[473]

But most church leaders were suspicious of special-purpose associations. Walls says they complained: "Why were the meetings necessary? Were the Church services not good enough for them? Against the background of the times any sectional meetings took on the

---

[468] Walls, "The Fortunate Subversion of the Church," 242.
[469] Ibid., 244. Emphasis is in original.
[470] Ibid., 245.
[471] Walls, "The American Dimension of the Missionary Movement," 229. Not only Europe and America: Ralph Winter had globalized this thought in the opening sentence in "Two Structures," stating that the mission of the church begins with the sodalities, "whether Christianity takes on Western or Asian form." Preface.
[472] Walls, "The Fortunate Subversion of the Church," 243.
[473] Skreslet: 2.

appearance of political disaffection or ecclesiastical discontent."[474] Church and denominational officers were alert to every threat to their control; they asked whether donations that should be going to the church were being siphoned off by mission groups. "The simple fact," Walls states, "was that the Church as then organized, whether episcopal, or presbyterian, or congregational, *could not* effectively operate mission overseas. Christians had accordingly to 'use means' to do so."[475] The voluntary society "subverted all the classical forms of Church government, while fitting comfortably into none of them."[476] We have to remember, writes Walls,

> how fixed and immutable these forms appeared to eighteenth-century men. They had been argued out for centuries, each on the basis of Scripture and reason—and still three forms remained . . . People had spent themselves for the sake of the purity of these forms, had shed their blood for them, and been on occasion ready to shed the blood of others for them.[477]

And then it suddenly became clear "that there were things—and not small things, but big things, things like the evangelization of the world—which were beyond the capacities of these splendid systems of gospel truth."[478] Walls continues,

> The men of high theological and ecclesiastical principle were often the enemies of the missionary movement. When (or rather, if) the elder Ryland barked out at Carey, "Young man, sit down; when God wants to convert the heathens, He'll do it without your help or mine" (one of those stories which is probably not true but which *ought* to be true), he was simply expressing a standard form of Protestant doctrine [emphasis is in original].[479]

---

[474] Walls, "The Fortunate Subversion of the Church," 243.
[475] Ibid., 247. Emphasis is in original.
[476] Ibid.
[477] Ibid.
[478] Ibid.
[479] Ibid., 246.

Hence church leaders suspected that William Carey and all who follow his pattern—which is to say the New Testament pattern—had swept away the authority of the local church. So there is tension between the governing ecclesiastical structures, which value order, and the founders and members of mission agencies, which value autonomy. Max Warren said we must accept "the inevitability of tension," but added that "too much tension makes administration impossible."[480] Bauer adds that leaders of mission structures and leaders of congregational structures would do well to accept the difference in task between the two kinds of structures:

> If mission structure leaders could understand and accept the fact that the congregational structure is an organ of coordination that is primarily concerned with organization, unity, worship, nurture and service for existing members, and if congregational leaders could understand that the mission structures largely consists of action and mobility in order to fulfill their specific tasks, then perhaps each structure could be more accepting of the other. With acceptance and understanding would also come a favorable reduction in tension between the two.[481]

Sociological research indicates that voluntary associations exist naturally within most and perhaps all general populations. This adds support to my thesis that the relationship between Protestant hierarchies and voluntary societies should be normalized, as I attempt to demonstrate in the next section.

4.6. Sodalities Everywhere: Special-Purpose Associations Among all Peoples

---

[480] Max Warren, *Crowded Canvas: Some Experiences of a Life-Time* (London: Hodder & Stoughton, 1974), 157.
[481] Bauer, Chapter 2, page 11.

Social contracts relating special-purpose associations to general populations apparently exist everywhere. "It would appear," Ralph D. Winter wrote, "that every human society, whether secular or religious, needs *both* modalities (i.e., overall *governing structures*) and sodalities (i.e., other structures, decentralized, especially *voluntary initiatives*) [emphasis is in original]."[482] In this section I describe a number of references to sociological studies of voluntary societies that are found among populations in Europe and Asia, and also in Islam and Judaism, that we might know that sodalities exist in many, perhaps all, cultures and religions. I will explain the origin of the term "sodality," how it was first used by Catholics, then by anthropologists. Ralph D. Winter uses it in its anthropological sense. He was the first person to pair the term "sodality" with a new term that he coined, "modality."[483]

Sodality and Modality: A Symbiotic Pairing. Roman Catholic academics were apparently the first to use the term *sodality*, referring to religious orders, convents, monasteries and other "pious associations."[484] Later, anthropologist Elman R. Service (d. 1996) applied a non-religious meaning to *sodality*; Service used it to describe "an association" that has

---

[482] Winter, "Protestant Mission Societies and the 'Other Protestant Schism'," 196.
[483] Ibid., 197.
[484] http://www.newadvent.org/cathen/14120a.htm. From the Latin *sodalitatem* (nom. *sodalitas*) "companionship, a brotherhood," from *sodalis* "companion."

"some corporate functions or purposes . . . Sodality is close in spirit to . . . 'special purpose group'."[485] Service described them thus:

> They cross-cut the residential segments of the society, such as households, neighborhoods, and villages, and unite them socially and politically in a new way. . . . For example, age grades . . . secret societies, and clubs for such single special purposes as the curing of illness or the performing of particular ceremonies. These all serve to unite persons who are members of different residential units.[486]

For the anthropologist, then, in every society there are some or maybe hundreds of *sodalities*. The Veterans of Foreign Wars, a *Star Trek* fan club, or the American Academy of Pediatrics are examples of sodalities. A high school student body is a modality, while the voluntary associations into which students form themselves are sodalities.[487] Members decide whether and for how long persons can belong to a sodality.

---

[485] Service. 13. Robert Wuthnow also uses the term "special purpose groups." Robert Wuthnow, "The Growth of Special Purpose Groups," in *The Restructuring of American Religion: Society and Faith since World War 2*(Princeton, NJ: Princeton University Press, 1988), 181-182.

[486] Elman Rogers Service, *Profiles in Ethnology*, 3d ed. (New York: Harper & Row, 1978), 5-6. 5-6

[487] Lou L. Fuller, in an article called "Two Principles of Human Association" illustrated the point by recalling that his friends formed a sodality in elementary school:

> When I was in the fourth grade of grammar school a group of some five or six of us formed a modest "voluntary association" of our own. We met at our recess in the corner of the school lot farthest from the school building. We sat about the ground and talked. We were by way of being a literary society. We shared in common a very special interest in *The Idylls of the King* and *Treasure Island*.
>
> Shortly after we started holding our meetings we became aware of a figure hovering in the background. It turned out to be a somewhat prepossessing classmate named Wilber. We told him to go away; we were having a meeting. But day after day he continued to haunt our little group. Finally we called him before us and asked him what he was up to. It turned out he was desperately lonesome and wanted to join our company. He was, with some misgivings, admitted to formal membership.
>
> Though Wilber became at once a faithful attendant of our meetings, it soon became apparent that we had made a serious mistake. Though he tried valiantly to take part in our discussions, it was clear that his interests, and in our opinion, his capacities did not move with ours. We decided to expel Wilber. The deed had to be accomplished in a manner befitting the literary dedication of our society. It was decided he should be given the Black Spot. Lon L. Fuller, "Two Principles of Human Association " in *Voluntary Associations* (New York: Atherton Press, 1969), 3-4.

Anne Freedman wrote that members of sodalities "are not born into such associations as they are into the family or the church."[488]

4.6.1 Ralph D. Winter's "Two Structures" Thesis as a Sociological Paradigm

Ralph D. Winter uses *sodality* in the same sense as Elman Service, that is, "any coherent sub-group within a community which does not include entire families but only teams, task forces, or social groups of some kind."[489] Sodalities are "substructures within the community that have an autonomy within and under the tribal government."[490] (Figure 11)

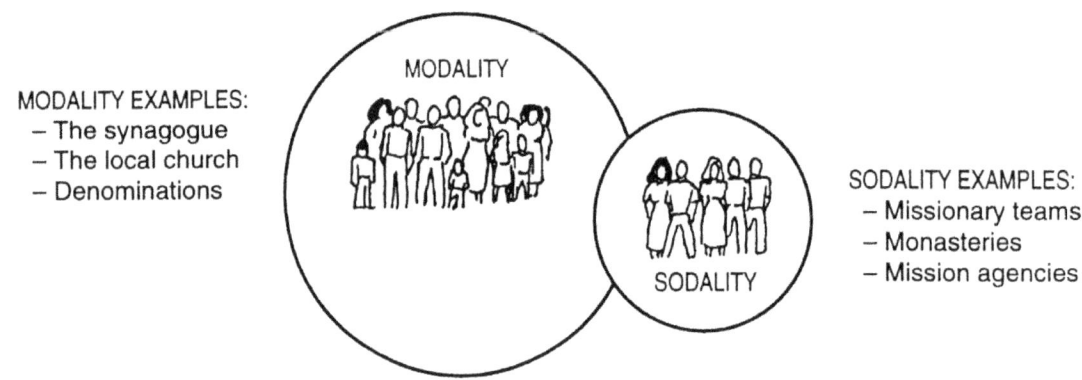

Figure 11. Modality and Sodality[491]

---

[488] Smith and Freedman, *Voluntary Associations: Perspectives on the Literature*, viii.

[489] Ralph D. Winter, "Sodality and Modality," in *Evangelical Dictionary of World Missions* (Grand Rapids: Baker Books, 2000), 894.

[490] Winter, "Protestant Mission Societies and the 'Other Protestant Schism'," 196-197.

[491] Jonathan Lewis, "Modality and Sodality," in *World Mission: An Analysis of the World Christian Movement.* (Pasadena, CA: William Carey Library, 1994).

I believe Winter first paired the term modality with sodality in his 1970 article, "The Warp and the Woof."[492] However, the German sociologist Ferdinand Tönnies (d. 1936) previously described (in 1887) these two kinds of communities as *Gemeinschaft*—the kinship relationships, or the neighborhood, or the community as a whole, or what Winter calls the modality; and *Gesellschaft*—the voluntary association or the private trading company that Winter calls the sodality.[493] *Gesellschaften* "must be held together by deliberately formulated prescriptions"[494]—that is, conditions which only a part of the population would be able to meet.[495] Winter writes that in a modality "there is no distinction of sex or age," while members of a sodality make "an adult second decision beyond modality membership."[496] "At the risk of stating the obvious," Winter writes,

---

[492] Ralph D. Winter and R. Pierce Beaver, *The Warp and the Woof; Organizing for Mission* (South Pasadena, CA: William Carey Library, 1970). Winter further explained sodality and modality in: 1) Winter, "Churches Need Missions Because Modalities Need Sodalities." And 2) Winter, "The Two Structures of God's Redemptive Mission." And 3) Ralph D. Winter, "Protestant Mission Societies: The American Experience," *Missiology* 7, no. 2 (1979). See also 4) Winter, "Sodality and Modality." *Evangelical Dictionary of World Missions*.

[493] Ferdinand Tönnies and Charles Price Loomis, *Community & Society (Gemeinschaft Und Gesellschaft)* (East Lansing,: Michigan State University Press, 1957).

[494] "Tönnies, Ferdinand," in *The New Encyclopedia Britannica* (University of Chicago Press, 1991), s. v. "Gesellshchaft".

[495] Like employees in a private business, members "are useful in mission structures," C. Peter Wagner said, "to the extent that they can help get the job done. When they cease to be useful they are dismissed." Quoted in Bauer, Chapter 2, page 6. Carey agreed: "There must be a determination not to admit any person who is not of this description, or to retain him longer than he answers to it." Carey, *An Enquiry into the Obligations of Christians to Use Means for the Conversion of the Heathens*, 83. Thus, a member of a mission society should be made to resign when he or she is no longer contributing to the outcome for which the society is held accountable by its board of directors. This is quite unlike congregational structures, as C. Peter Wagner points out:

> The maimed, the lame and the blind are welcomed by the congregational structure, but not by the mission structures, unless their handicap is overcome. The two mission structures I served with, for example, required strict medical exams for membership. No congregation that I have ever joined has asked me for my medical history. Each procedure is appropriate for the structure. In Bauer, 6-7.

[496] Winter, "Sodality and Modality," 894.

one of the important characteristics of a church as contrasted to a Rotary Club, an Inter-Varsity chapter, a mission agency, a men's Bible study, or a Christian Businessmen's Committee is that a church (whether Baptist or Episcopalian) includes whole families; membership in these other groups has some age or sex limitation. Anthropologists call such fellowships *sodalities*. The differences between sodalities we may call *sodal* differences. (Other structured groupings which have no age or sex limitations between them are *modal*.) Church governments, whose territorial bounds overlap those of other churches (as in the U.S.) ordinarily ignore or oppose those sodalities they do not themselves institute. In the case of the United Presbyterians, for example, the National Mariners organization could die and probably denominational officials would not weep too much [emphasis is in original].[497]

Winter's "Warp and Woof" analogy refers, of course, to the horizontal and vertical strands of fabric in cloth and carpet.[498] "Just as it is impossible to make cloth without threads going both crosswise and also up and down," Winter wrote, "it is crucially important to regard these *two* structures working together as *the warp and the woof* of the fabric, the fabric being the Christian movement—the people of God, the ecclesia of the New Testament [emphasis is in original]."[499]

---

[497] Winter, "Churches Need Missions Because Modalities Need Sodalities," 195. Members of First Presbyterian Church of Pomona, California started The Mariners, a club for married couples, in the mid-1950s. Its popularity spread quickly until thousands of Presbyterian churches had Mariners clubs. The clubs met every month for fellowship and for carrying out a mission that each club identified. Their popularity waned in the late 1970s.

[498] The dictionary describes *woof* as "the widthwise, or horizontal, yarns, in woven fabrics, carried over and under the warp, or lengthwise, yarns and running from selvage to selvage." Merriam-Webster Inc. s.v. "woof." The word "woof" or *weft* derives from the Old English word *wefan*, to weave. The word selvage means "self edge."

[499] Winter, "Protestant Mission Societies and the 'Other Protestant Schism'," 198.

(Figure 12)

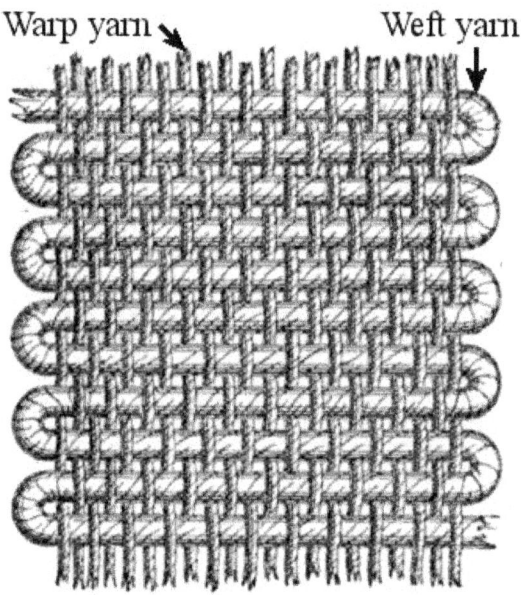

Figure 12. Warp and Woof[500]

In his 1982 dissertation *Congregational and Mission Structures* Bruce L. Bauer's term "mission structure" corresponds to Winter's "sodality" while "modality" is called the "congregational structure."[501] Bauer's pair of terms helps the student remember which structure is the "sodality" and which "modality."[502] However, the genius of Winter's pair of terms is to understand voluntary structures and congregations in terms of *sodalities among populations everywhere*. The social scientist sees *sodal* and *modal* structures in

---

[500] http://www.sarkisian.com/images/warpweft.jpg
[501] Bauer, Chapter 2, page 5.
[502] The Lausanne Committee report on church-mission relationships says that the meaning of the terms "modality" and "sodality" is "neither widespread nor consistent," so "it seems wise to employ the more traditional vocabulary." Lausanne, *Cooperating in World Evangelization: A Handbook on Church/Parachurch Relationships* (Pattaya: Lausanne Movement, 1980). Occasional Paper 24, Church and Parachurch, Theological Preamble. See http://www.lausanne.org/en/documents/lops/67-lop-24.html#1.

every society, and, thanks to Winter's thesis, these familiar structures can be seen occurring naturally in the church (and in Jewish society, as we observed in section 2.1). Therefore, while Bauer's terms help us understand the church as a pairing of congregational and mission structures, we must keep in mind the important parallel to social science and to private companies that Carey had in mind when he proposed organizing mission societies.

4.6.2 The Voluntary Nature of the American People

\ The voluntary nature of the American people impressed, among others, three careful observers: Rufus Anderson, Alexis de Tocqueville and George Marsden.[503] They found that in a free society, citizens form themselves into all manner of voluntary associations.

Observations of Rufus Anderson. Rufus Anderson (1796-1880) was the general secretary of the American Board of Commissioners for Foreign Mission, beginning in 1832. Anderson's father, a Congregationalist pastor also named Rufus Anderson, belonged to the school of New England theology known as "Hopkinsian" after Samuel Hopkins, the brother-in-law of Jonathan Edwards, thus assuring, wrote R. Pierce Beaver, "a missionary

---

[503] Other observers concur with these three men. In his book *American Protestantism*, Winthrop Hudson wrote, "Essentially a technique devised by British churchmen, the voluntary society was seized upon by American Protestants as a perfect instrument by which they could pool their efforts to influence public opinion, effect reforms, meet humanitarian needs, establish colleges, provide religious instruction, organize publishing ventures, and carry on extensive and wide-ranging missionary activities." Winthrop Still Hudson, *American Protestantism*, The Chicago History of American Civilization (University of Chicago Press, 1961), 15. *U.S News and World Report* recently devoted an entire issue to America's volunteer tradition; see "Giving Back," *US News and World Report* November 2010.

concern in the theological atmosphere of the home." [504] When Anderson retired in 1866 more than 1200 missionaries were serving under the American board, and only six had not been appointed under him and upon his recommendation[505]

In 1837 Anderson wrote a pamphlet, later called *The Time for the World's Conversion Has Come*. Listing the indicators favorable to this outcome, Rufus Anderson was especially optimistic because of the appearance of voluntary associations. In a section titled "The Churches Never Before Organized for the Conversion of the World" he wrote:

> It was not until the present century that the evangelical churches of Christendom were ever really organized with a view to the conversion of the world. What are called voluntary associations for religious purposes, as distinct from local churches, are not indeed a new thing on the earth. They have existed, in some form, from an early period of the Christian church. It was probably through such that the gospel has ever been propagated by the church beyond the voices of its own immediate pastors. Monasteries were voluntary societies; and so were the different orders of monks. It was by means of associations such as these that the gospel was originally propagated among our ancestors and over Europe. These are the Papal forms of missionary societies and missions.[506]

Anderson stated that "Missionary, Bible, Tract and other kindred societies" were "the Protestant form" of associations that "have existed from an early period of the Christian Church."[507] Members "freely act together" and are "free to give, and to determine what

---

[504] Beaver, *To Advance the Gospel; Selections from the Writings of Rufus Anderson*, 10.
[505] Ibid., 12.
[506] Ibid., 64-65. Elsewhere, Rufus Anderson wrote that there were no mission societies in the New Testament. (ibid., 15.). I have tried to explain otherwise in section 2.1.2. Had Anderson learned of the Jewish mission structure and Paul's familiarity with it, Anderson would have further strengthened his own case.
[507] Ibid., 65.

they shall give for what objects, in order to be cheerful and accepted givers."[508] A more elegant summary of voluntaryism's particular advantage would be hard to imagine.

"Our age is singular and remarkable," Anderson went on to write, "for its disposition to associate in action . . . It associates for the accomplishment of almost every object."[509] And "this Protestant form of association—free, open, responsible—embracing all classes, both sexes, all ages, the masses of the people—is peculiar to modern times, and almost to our age."[510] Anderson gives the crucial explanation as to why this age has been made possible:

> Such great and extended associations could not possibly have been worked, they could not have been created, or kept in existence, without the present degree of civil and religious liberty and social security, or without the present extended habits of reading and the consequently wide-spread intelligence among the people; nor could they exist on a sufficiently broad scale, nor act with sufficient energy for the conversion of the world, under despotic governments, or without the present amazing facilities for communication on the land, and the world-wide commerce on the seas.[511]

"Like the New England Congregationalist he was," writes Andrew Walls, Anderson "states that such associations could only arise in countries which had an open, responsible form of government."[512] Rufus Anderson was bullish on voluntary societies. He was not alone, as historian George Marsden observes.

---

[508] Ibid.
[509] Ibid.
[510] Ibid.
[511] Ibid., 66.
[512] Walls, "The Fortunate Subversion of the Church," 242.

Observations of George Marsden. George Marsden has written the definitive history of the Presbyterian Schism of 1837. He interprets the schism as a breach between advocates of voluntary societies and their counterparts. "The voluntary principle," he writes,

> had been prominent since the Great Awakening and had prepared the way for disestablishment in 1818. Lyman Beecher later observed that the end of dependence on state support was "the best thing that ever happened to the State of Connecticut." The churches, said Beecher, thrown "on their own resources and on God," now increased their influence "by voluntary efforts, societies, missions, and revivals."[513]

"American evangelicals," Marsden continued, "had long recognized the principle dramatized in Connecticut: if Christians were to win victory in democratic America, their only recourse was to go to the people and lead them to respond voluntarily."[514] The upsurge in the number of voluntary societies in the first years of the 19th century "indicates again the evangelicals' increasing recognition that success would depend on persuasion of a free people."[515] Sermons in the newly-disestablished era became less doctrinal and more focused on the love of God, and church became, according to the

---

[513] George M. Marsden, *The Evangelical Mind and the New School Presbyterian Experience; a Case Study of Thought and Theology in Nineteenth-Century America*, Yale Publications in American Studies, 20 (New Haven,: Yale University Press, 1970), 12-13. 12-13. Canada, in contrast to the United States, maintained an established church for three centuries. "The concept of the church occupying an official place in society and having a primary responsibility for guiding the social order remained central to the Canadian understanding of the church up to the 1960s." Craig Van Gelder, "Understanding the Church in North America," in *Missional Church* (Grand Rapids: Eerdmans, 1998), 55.

[514] Marsden, xii-xiii. *The Westminster Dictionary of Church History* defines *voluntaryism* as "the principle of voluntary support of religious systems and institutions rather than state assistance for such purposes. Voluntaryism was the direct consequence of the establishment of religious liberty in the United States. It was something totally new in Christian history. From the time of Constantine in the early 4th century to the end of the 18th century the Christian church had been supported by and sustained by the state . . . Not only did the churches survive under voluntary support, but they flourished in a way unmatched by any church-state system . . . Activism became one of voluntaryism's special marks . . . Also, the laity came to play a special role in voluntaryism. It was difficult for clericalism to prevail long in such a system." Brauer and Gerrish, 852-853.

[515] Marsden, 15.

authors of *Habits of the Heart*, "a place of love and acceptance in an otherwise harsh and competitive society."[516] For the sake of unity most congregations in the early 19th century suppressed discussion of divisive issues such as temperance and slavery. But "religion did not cease to be concerned with moral order; it operated with a new emphasis on the individuality and the voluntary association."[517] Through societies and voluntary associations, "the Christian clergy and laity could bring their concerns about temperance and slavery without disturbing the warm intimacy and loving harmony of the local congregation."[518] For example, the 1836 Presbyterian General Assembly resolved "that this whole subject [slavery] be indefinitely postponed,"[519] even though in 1818 the General Assembly had voted its objection to slavery in the most vigorous terms.[520] Thus, the broadening Presbyterian Church seemed satisfied to leave to voluntary societies the moral assault against slavery. By the 1830s "almost every form of vice or oppression had a corresponding moral or benevolent society to stamp it out":

> This "benevolent empire" included not only societies for major reforms, as the American Colonization Society, the American Anti-Slavery Society, the American Temperance Society, and the American Peace Society, but also organizations dedicated to less well-known good causes, as the Seventh Commandment Society, the New York Anti-Tobacco Society, the American

---

[516] Robert Neelly Bellah, *Habits of the Heart: Individualism and Commitment in American Life* (Berkeley, CA: University of California Press, 1985), 223.

[517] Ibid., 222.

[518] Ibid., 224.

[519] Lefferts Augustine Loetscher, *A Brief History of the Presbyterians*, 4th ed. (Philadelphia: Westminster Press, 1958), 81.

[520] Ibid. The 1818 Presbyterian General Assembly adopted this resolution: "We consider the voluntary enslaving of one part of the human race by another . . . utterly inconsistent with the law of God . . . and . . . totally irreconcilable with the spirit and principles of the gospel of Christ."

Seamen's Friend Society, the Protestant Half Orphan Asylum Society, and the Society for the Encouragement of Faithful Domestic Servants in New York.[521]

In his book *Evangelicalism and Modern America,* Marsden explains evangelicalism not as a vast number of pulpits and denominations, but as a fleet of voluntary associations. "The evangelical denomination," he writes, is "essentially a transdenominational assemblage of unaffiliated agencies and their supporters, plus some denominationally sponsored seminaries and colleges which support such parachurch institutions."[522] Evangelicalism is "built around networks of parachurch agencies."[523] Pellowe cites other scholars who agree with Marsden, including Richard Quebedeaux,[524] Mark Ellingsen[525] and Princeton University sociologist Robert Wuthnow.[526] Parachurch organizations, Wuthnow wrote, "have grown to such a large proportion that they now appear to cast their imprint heavily on the character of American religion."[527] They "have enjoyed a long history, alongside churches and denominations, as ways of advancing and

---

[521] Marsden, 15. Marsden states that in 1826 the six most prosperous agencies were the American Education Society, which supported divinity students; the American Board of Comissioners for Foreign Missions; the American Home Missionary Society; the American Bible Society; the American Sunday-School Union; and the American Tract Society. "The combined budgets of these major evangelical organizations easily rivaled the major expenditures of the federal government, and in some respects, their influence seemed as great." 16

[522] George M. Marsden, *Evangelicalism and Modern America* (Grand Rapids: Eerdmans, 1984), xiv.

[523] Ibid.

[524] Richard Quebedeaux, *The Young Evangelicals: Revolution in Orthodoxy*, 1st ed. (New York: Harper & Row, 1974).

[525] Mark Ellingsen, *The Evangelical Movement: Growth, Impact, Controversy, Dialog* (Minneapolis: Augsburg, 1988).

[526] Wuthnow, *The Restructuring of American Religion: Society and Faith since World War 2*, 121.

[527] Ibid.

renewing Western religion."[528] One 19th century writer who remarked enthusiastically about advance and renewal in the American scene was Alexis de Tocqueville.

Observations of Alexis de Tocqueville. Alexis de Tocqueville (d. 1859) toured the young United States for nine months in 1831 and 1832. He praised its government for guaranteeing the right of her citizens to freely from voluntary societies.[529] "Decentralization," de Tocqueville observed, "has been carried to a degree that no European nation can tolerate, I think, without profound unrest, and which even produces distressing effects in America."[530] But the alternative—centralization—bears the full weight of his criticism:

> Centralization, it is true, easily succeeds in subjecting the external actions of man to a certain uniformity. Centralization succeeds without difficulty in impressing a regular style on current affairs; in skillfully regimenting the details of social orderliness; in repressing slight disorders and small offenses; in maintaining society in a status quo that is properly neither decadence nor progress; in keeping in the social body a sort of administrative somnolence that administrators are accustomed to calling good order and public tranquility. It excels, at a word, at preventing, not doing. [But] when it is a question of moving society profoundly or pressing it to a rapid advance, its force abandons it. If its measures need the concurrence of individuals, one is then wholly surprised at the weakness of that immense machine; it finds itself suddenly reduced to impotence.[531]

---

[528] Wuthnow, "The Growth of Special Purpose Groups."

[529] Alexis de Tocqueville, *Democracy in America / Translated, Edited, and with an Introduction by Harvey C. Mansfield and Delba Winthrop* (University of Chicago Press, 1833), 281. He contrasted the American experience with what he knew from Europe. "Everywhere that at the head of a new undertaking, you see the government in France and a great lord in England, count on it that you will perceive an association in the United States." Ibid., 489.

[530] Ibid., 84.

[531] Ibid., 86.

De Tocqueville then enthuses that Americans form voluntary associations "to attain the different ends they propose for themselves."[532] Each new social problem "immediately awakens the idea of it. The art of association then becomes, as I have said, the mother science; all study it and apply it."[533] De Tocqueville went on to say,

> Americans of all ages, all conditions, all minds, constantly unite. Not only do they have commercial and industrial associations in which all take part, but they also have a thousand other kinds; religious, moral, grave, futile, very general, very particular, immense and very small; Americans use associations to give fetes, to found seminaries, to build inns, to raise churches, to distribute books, to send missionaries to the antipodes; in this manner they create hospitals, prisons, schools. Finally, if it is a question of bringing to light a truth or developing a sentiment with the support of a great example, they associate.[534]

One would think from reading de Alexis de Tocqueville, George Marsden and Rufus Anderson that everyone in America was forming voluntary associations. But that was not so; the leaders of the Presbyterian Church persuaded themselves that its central office was the only missionary society with which the congregations and pastors and members ought to have anything to do. In a chapter titled "The Triumph of Denominationalism, 1852-1861," Marsden recounts the efforts before the Civil War by church officers to enforce a uniform, centralized expression of mission.[535] But top-down control was out of step with the wishes of the American people.[536]

---

[532] Ibid., 496.
[533] Ibid.
[534] Ibid., 489.
[535] Marsden, *The Evangelical Mind and the New School Presbyterian Experience; a Case Study of Thought and Theology in Nineteenth-Century America*, 128ff.
[536] In their valuable reference book, *Voluntary Associations: Perspectives on the Literature,* Constance E. Smith and Anne E. Freedman determined that "the American penchant for turning to voluntary action as a solution to social, political, and personal problems has, if anything, probably intensified since Tocqueville

4.6.3 A Brief Study of Foreign Voluntary Societies

The existence of voluntary societies in many cultures gives evidence that likeminded people from among most or all general populations form themselves into special-interest associations. This finding will help church populations normalize a relationship between administrations and voluntary societies. We begin with the populations of Europe.

Voluntary Societies in Europe: England and France. In *Voluntary Associations, A Study of Groups in Free Societies* D. B. Robertson refers to a "great proliferation" of voluntary societies in 17th century England.[537] So does Anne Freedman.[538] The French Revolution of 1789 awakened English philosopher Edmund Burke to his affection for "the little platoons,"[539] voluntary associations. Burke "was one of the first writers to realise the importance of the spontaneous social groupings that people create for themselves as bulwarks defending civil society against despots and revolutionaries."[540] Between 1780 and 1844, according to Richard V. Pierard, British Christians "founded at least 223

---

made his observations." Smith and Freedman, *Voluntary Associations: Perspectives on the Literature*, Preface. Smith and Freedman undertook the monumental project of citing all the research on voluntary associations up to that time (the year was 1972). They took up this effort after discovering the research on voluntary societies to be "in great disarray," such that scholars were "proceeding in ignorance of each other's efforts." Ibid., vi. The authors list hundreds of books and articles on sociological topics at the end of each chapter.

[537] D. B. Robertson and James Luther Adams, *Voluntary Associations, a Study of Groups in Free Societies; Essays in Honor of James Luther Adams* (Richmond, VA: John Knox Press, 1966), 8.
[538] Smith and Freedman, *Voluntary Associations: Perspectives on the Literature*, 134.
[539] Burke and Clark, 202.
[540] http://www.igreens.org.uk/little_platoons.htm

national religious, moral, educational, and philanthropic institutions and societies to alleviate child abuse, poverty, illiteracy, and other social ills."[541]

In contrast to England, French law makes the organizing of voluntary associations "relatively difficult."[542] In *The Social Contract* French philosopher Jacques Rousseau (d. 1778) criticized voluntary associations, which he called "partial societies" or partial associations. "Partial associations are formed at the expense of the great associations. . . . If the general will is to be able to express itself there should be no partial society within the State."[543] Rousseau's influence on political thinking deterred the development of voluntary associations in France, much as the influence of John Locke (d. 1797) and John Stuart Mill (d. 1873) promoted their development in England.[544]

Denmark. Sociologists Robert and Barbara Gallatin Anderson reached a conclusion that in Denmark the voluntary association is "easily founded: it is free to adjust with amoeba-like fluidity to a flood of problems beyond the scope or ken of other institutions

---

[541] Pierard adds, "Among the religious and benevolent societies for impoverished or exploited women were Forlorn Females Fund of Mercy; Maritime Female Penitent Refuge for Poor, Degraded Females; Society for Returning Young Women to Their Friends in the Country; Friendly Female Society for the Relief of Poor, Infirm, Aged Widows, and Single Women of Good Character Who Have Seen Better Days." Richard V. Pierard, "William Wilberforce and the Abolition of the Slave Trade," *Christian History* 16, no. 1 (1997): 2.

[542] Smith and Freedman, *Voluntary Associations: Perspectives on the Literature*, 131.

[543] Jean-Jacques Rousseau, *The Social Contract, and Discourses* (New York: Dutton, 1950), 27.

[544] John Locke and J. W. Gough, *The Second Treatise of Civil Government, and, a Letter Concerning Toleration* (Oxford: Basil Blackwell, 1948), 164; John Stuart Mill, *Utilitarianism, Liberty, and Representative Government* (London, New York: J.M. Dent & sons E.P. Dutton & Co., 1931).

or in combinations of them. Its job done, it can go out of business without consequences beyond projects at hand."[545]

Voluntary Associations in Asia. In Japan members of voluntary societies—*buraku*—serve a wide range of purposes, described by Edward Norbeck.[546] Other studies conducted in Mexico, Ireland, Sierra Leone, Germany, Mali, Israel, and Greece have been collected by Constance Smith and Anne Freedman.[547]

In Malaysia voluntary associations have proliferated, but along kinship lines. That is, Malay Chinese, Malay Muslims, South Asians and Europeans form clubs based on native or clan relationships.[548] These clubs bind like with like, defining who is "in" and who is "out" of business deals and social dealings. Indonesians form voluntary societies called *yayasan* to address long-standing social problems. For example, Randy and Wendy H. in Indonesia have registered a *yayasan* with the government. It's called "Loving the Poor."[549] By this structure they have started businesses for the poor who live near the garbage dumps.

Overseas Chinese form business organizations, *kongsi* (Chinese: 公司; pinyin: *gōngsī*) or "clan halls" whose members share the same Chinese surname. Diaspora Chinese utilize the system of *kongsi* to overcome economic difficulty and social

---

[545] Robert and Barbara Gallatin Anderson, "Voluntary Associations and Urbanization," *American Journal of Sociology* 65, (1959): 272.
[546] Smith and Freedman, *Voluntary Associations: Perspectives on the Literature*, 134.
[547] Ibid., 135ff.
[548] Stephen A. Douglas and Paul Pedersen, *Blood, Believer, and Brother: The Development of Voluntary Associations in Malaysia* (Athens: Ohio University, 1973), 4.
[549] Personal interview August 2005

ostracism. Thus, the *kongsi* is similar to modern business partnerships, but also draws on a deeper spirit of cooperation and consideration of mutual welfare.[550]

Voluntary Societies in Islam. The general Muslim population is the *dar al-Islam* ("house of Islam"); the *dar* is a citizenship into which all Muslims are born.[551] An Islamic voluntary agency (*waqf*) addresses two social needs: 1) education and 2) direct aid to the poor. But Islamic governments, especially in Asia, permit their citizens to form non-government organizations. Thousands of NGOs in Bangladesh implement most of that country's development work, a phenomenon without equal anywhere else in the world. Most of these NGOs were established in the past thirty-five years.[552] After the Soviet Union invaded Afghanistan in 1979, Afghanistan became the object of considerable mobilization in the Muslim world: different Muslim agencies worked to make this war an "Islamic cause" (*qadiiya islamiya*). After 2002, with the coming of US and European funding in Afghanistan, many local NGOs (*bonyad*) were created to implement development programs. I interviewed an American development worker, TJ, who was employed by a Muslim non-government organization in Afghanistan, the Sanayee Development Foundation.[553] An Afghan businessman founded Sanayee in 1986 in order to build an English language school in Peshawar. Sanayee trains teachers in Afghan

---

[550] http://en.wikipedia.org/wiki/Kongsi. In China the term *kongsi* refers to a private business.
[551] This citizenship resembles the church citizenship of medieval Europe during the thousand years when there was no church membership; everyone except the Jews, from London to Lithuania, was Catholic.
[552] Bornstein, 4.
[553] Robert A. Blincoe, *Interview with T.J.: My Experience Working for an Afghan N.G.O.* (Mesa, Arizona, August 2007).

villages; it pays teachers for a short while to prime the process. A second Sanayee program teaches conflict resolution to village elders, and to government officials and teachers and mullahs. It teaches how conflicts develop, how a conflict grows, and how to communicate in ways that move a conflict towards resolution. Sanayee is funded by Canadian and European organizations. It has a board of directors and by-laws and is registered with the Afghan government and submits to an external audit, though Sanayee met this condition only when required by the western donor agencies.

By contrast, the governments of Turkey and most Arab countries do not permit non-government organizations to operate because they perceive NGOs to be fronts for anti-government activities. The royal family of Jordan, for example, operates its own government aid agencies in order to render voluntary agencies, ostensibly, redundant. Thus, Jordan's royal family eliminates the threat that opposition groups will foment sedition through pretend aid agencies. Other Arab countries do the same.[554] In southern Lebanon during the 1980s when the state collapsed, Hezbollah stepped in to provide a wide range of social, educational and health services for the Shi'ite community. Research of voluntary societies providing relief services in Arab Israeli villages and in Egypt testify that, relatively speaking, Islamist voluntary associations are capable of delivering effective services in certain contexts where the state has been unable or unwilling to provide them.[555] For example, after a serious earthquake in Cairo killed some 500 people

---

[554] For more on Islamic charities see: Jonathan Benthall and Jérôme Bellion-Jourdan, *The Charitable Crescent: Politics of Aid in the Muslim World* (London ; New York: I.B. Tauris, 2003).
[555] Ibid., 88.

in 1992, the Muslim Brotherhood took a leading humanitarian role. When Egypt was hit by serious floods in November 1994, the government's response was slow and ineffective; but the Muslim Brotherhood and similar organizations which gave refuge in the mosques to families who had lost their roofs. In the late 1990s, at least half of all welfare associations in Egypt were Islamic in character, often based in mosques built and controlled by the Muslim brotherhood rather than the state, providing services to millions. [556]

Free-world Governments (Modalities) Regulate Private Companies (Sodalities)

Free world governments regulate private companies and non-profit corporation. As indicated in the news story about Detroit ("Private Groups Push Detroit Ahead"),[557] the symbiosis between City Hall and private groups requires a social contract that respects both partners.

---

[556] Ibid.
[557] Gallagher, 1.

In Figure 13 a sampling of free-world government agencies regulate various non-profit and for-profit organizations. Once licensed, a for-profit company is free to make every effort to make a profit; similarly, a non-profit agency is free to achieve the goals set by its board of directors.[558] (Figure 13)

Regulatory agency	Non-Profit Corporations
Detroit City Hall	River Front Conservancy, Detroit
State of Arizona Corporation Commission	Kurdish Literature Association
American Dental Association	Society of American Indian Dentists
--	For-Profit Corporations
Federal Aviation Administration	Southwest Airlines, etc.
Arizona State Board of Barbers and Cosmetology	Joe's Barber Shop, Mesa AZ
Los Angeles County Dept. of Public Health	Los Angeles Restaurants

Figure 13. Free-World Governments Respond to the Interests of their Citizens by Regulating Corporations

Free-world governments monitor and license, but do not administer, such for-profit corporations as airlines, restaurants, and barber shops; they do the same for non-profit organizations.[559] Church governing boards should recognize and regulate voluntary

---

[558] I recommend John Carver and Miriam Mayhew Carver, *Reinventing Your Board: A Step-by-Step Guide to Implementing Policy Governance*, Rev. ed. (San Francisco: John Wiley, 2006).

[559] There was a day when citizens formed themselves into associations for the purpose of starting public libraries. For example, in the library where I am studying today a framed copy of a notice from the *Mesa Free Press* dated March 24, 1906 hangs on the wall. It reads:

associations in this same way. "Neither structure," Pellowe wrote, "is more central than the other, although the church structure regulates the specialized structure, on the principle that the specialized reports to the more general."[560] This is the new social contract proposed in this dissertation.

4.6.4 Illustrating the Sodality-Modality Pairing as a Double Helix

It will be helpful, I believe, to explain the relationship between sodality and modality by suggesting its resemblance to something more familiar to us. The relationship between the two helices of a double helix molecule resembles the desired relationship of sodality to modality. What is a double helix? It is "the coiled structure of a double-stranded DNA molecule[561] . . . a pair of parallel helices intertwined about a common axis."[562]

Mesa is to have a free reading room and library. The ladies of the town have taken the matter up, affected an organization and will push the good work along. Officers were elected as follows: President, Mrs. J. G. Spangler; vice-president, Mrs. Fanny Dana; second vice-president, Mrs. Dr. J.E. Drane; secretary, Miss Nora Smith; treasurer, Mrs. P.E. Fuller.

[560] Pellowe, *A Practical Theology for Relations between Churches and Self-Governing Agencies*, 80-81.

[561] *The American Heritage® Dictionary of the English Language, Fourth Edition.* Houghton Mifflin Company, 2004. s.v. "Double helix." After using this metaphor, I was gratified to read Craig Van Gelder's essay, "An Ecclesiastical Geno-Project: Unpacking the DNA of Denominations and Denominationalism" in Craig Van Gelder, *The Missional Church and Denominations : Helping Congregations Develop a Missional Identity*, Missional Church Series (Grand Rapids, Mich.: William B. Eerdmans Pub., 2008), 12-45. Van Gelder references William Carey's conception of the mission society and "the hundreds of such religious societies that were formed locally or regionally" (29-30). "The formation of mission societies deeply impacted the genetic code of the emerging denominational church" (30). My own understanding of the church as a double helix of a DNA molecule occurred independently from Van Gelder's, and goes in a different direction.

[562] www.diclib.com

These two strands are coactive, harmonious, and symbiotic. The double helix illustrates the pairing of sodality and modality (Figure 14):

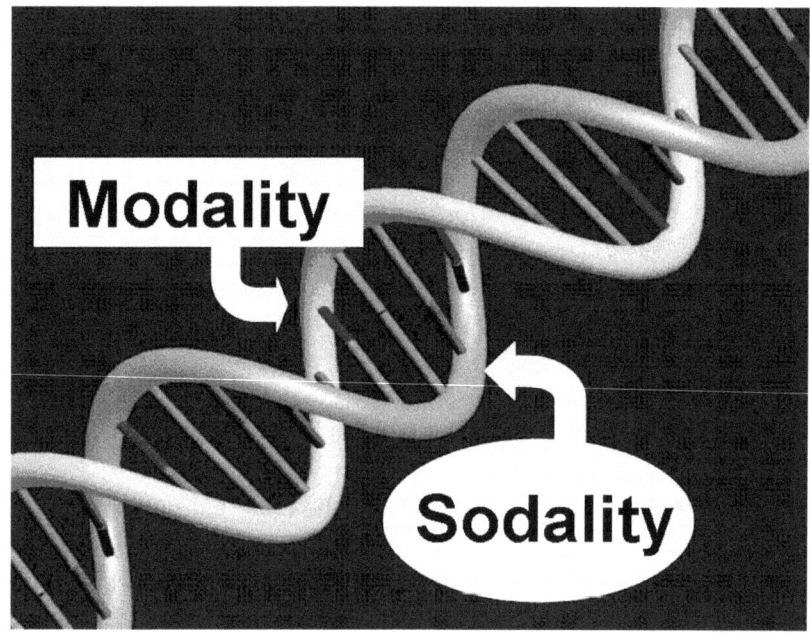

Figure 14. Double Helix: Sodality and Modality

Until 1953, when James Watson and Francis Crick suggested the double helix, the structure of the DNA molecule was unexplainable, or more accurately, was explained by a paradigm plagued with anomalies. Their article in *Nature* magazine began with these famously understated words: "The structure of the DNA molecule is a double helix. This structure has novel features which are of considerable biological interest."[563] The science community was suddenly pushed to choose one or the other paradigms, and to be persuaded that Watson and Crick's explained nature better than the other. Today, scientists assume that every living cell consists of a binary relationship between two

---

[563] Francis Crick and James Watson, "Letter," *Nature*, April 25 1953, 737.

coiled strands, double helix. We may consider a church board or a denominational board to be one strand: the other is the voluntary society. For example, William Carey was a member of both a Baptist denomination and also a member of a mission agency: (Figure 15):

Figure 15. Double Helix: Carey's Baptist Church and Carey's Baptist Mission Society

The resemblance of the relationship between church governments and special-interest mission groups to a double helix encourages an attitude of mutual respect between these two structures.

Two Structures in New Testament Israel. The double helix serves to demonstrate the relationship between two structures in the Jewish experience during the first century. We explained the Jewish pairing of these "two structures" in Section 2.1. (Figure 16)

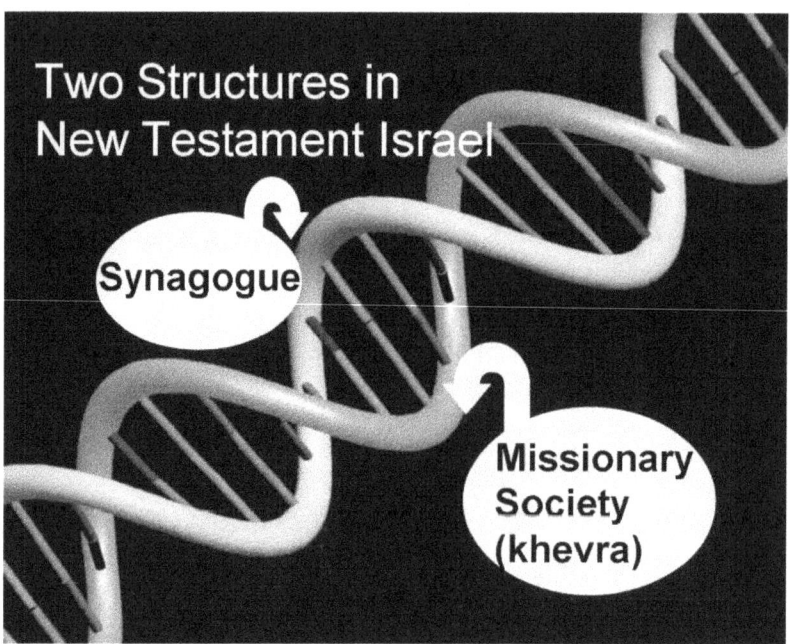

Figure 16. Double Helix Representation of Synagogue and Khevra

Two Structures in Islam. A pairing of modality and sodality in Islam can be represented by a double helix. (Figure 17)

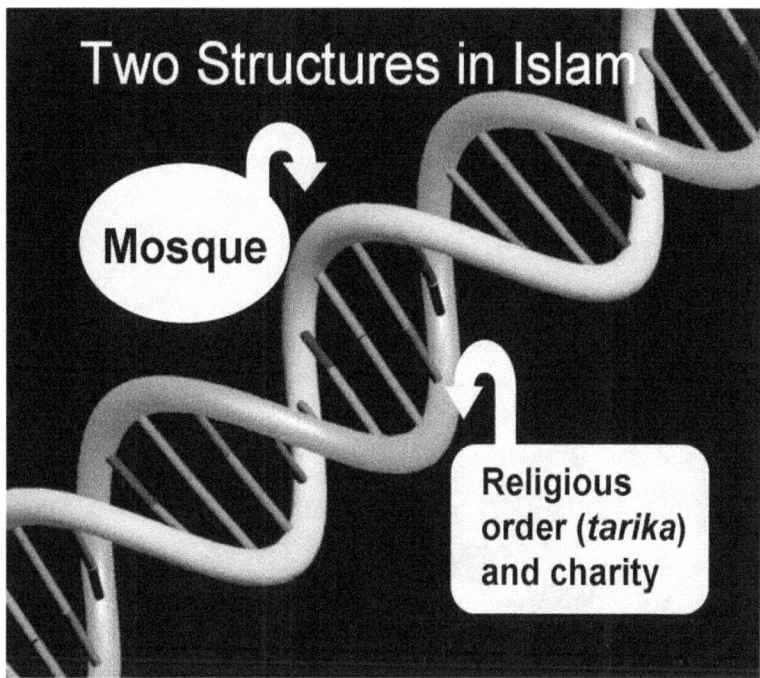

Figure 17. Double Helix: Two Structures in Islam

Every Muslim is a "member" or citizen in the "house of Islam," the modality structure. The second structure is the religious order (*tarika*) or charity (*waqf*).

One Structure in the Reformed and Lutheran Churches. When Martin Luther and John Calvin and especially the Reformers who followed them prohibited voluntary mission structures from forming, the double helix nature of the church was damaged: (Figure 18)

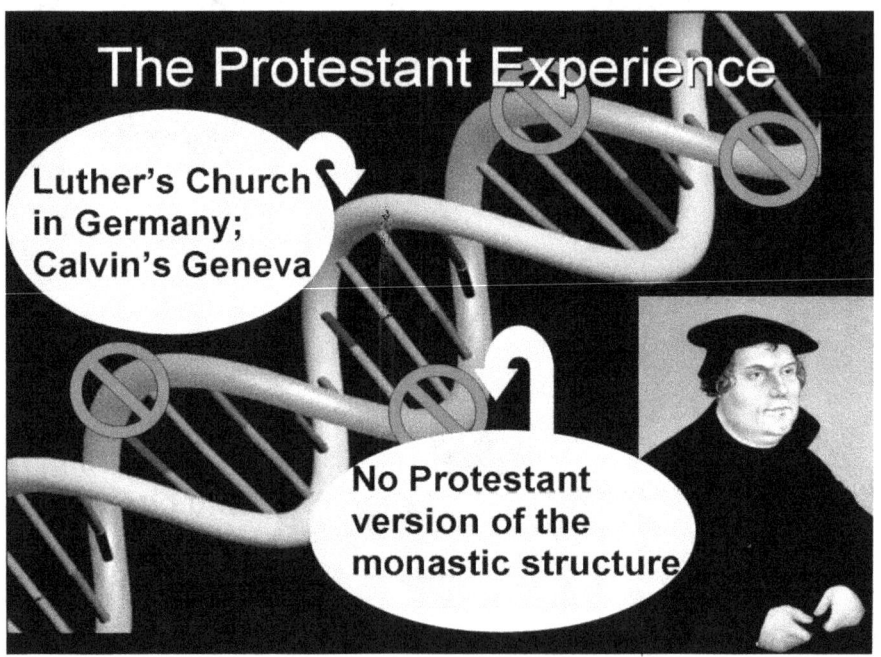

Figure 18. Double Helix Representation of Protestant "Sola Synodica"

Historical data presented in this dissertation indicates that this damage was the reason for the Protestant inability to follow the Catholic example in carrying out its mission ideals.

4.6.5 The Term "Parachurch" in Light of the "Two Structures" Paradigm

Though there have always been "two structures," and though special purpose associations occur naturally in all populations, supporters of the *sola synodica* paradigm sometimes use the term "parachurch"[564] to describe mission agencies in a slightly negative way. As Stephen Board wrote, "It is widely held that 'if the churches were really doing their job the parachurch groups wouldn't be necessary.'"[565] "Unlike the relative acceptance such structures have in the case of the orders in the Roman Catholic tradition," writes Winter, "the same thing within Protestantism is ignored, despised or denigrated by such phrases as *parachurch structures* [emphasis is in original]."[566] Winter continues, "In truth, modern American congregations are so far removed from the *ecclesias* of the New Testament that it would just as reasonable to refer to our contemporary congregations as 'paramission' structures."[567] Parachurch, when used as a pejorative, is a distortion of the demonstrated "two structures" New Testament paradigm. We err, Winter says, when we "refer to the congregation and its denominational superstructure "as the church *as if there were no other structure making up the church*

---

[564] The term *parachurch* was coined in the late 1960s. See Willmer, Schmidt, and Smith, 12. John Nyquist is helpful in placing the parachurch organizations in the historical context:

> Parachurch agencies appear at first glance to be a relatively recent phenomenon, by many accounts beginning their ministries shortly after the Second World War. But a closer look at the history of the church and its missionary enterprise will reveal a longer and deeper background. John Nyquist, "Parachurch Agencies and Mission," in *Evangelical Dictionary of World Missions* (Grand Rapids: Baker Books, 2000), 722.

[565] Stephen Board, "The Great Evangelical Power Shift," *Eternity* 30:6, (1979): 19.

[566] Ralph D. Winter, "Global Cross-Cultural Mission Collaboration: 1910 to 2010," (Pasadena: William Carey International University, 2008), 2.

[567] Ibid. Louis B. Weeks offers a remarkable history of the broadening bureaucratic growth of American denominations, beginning in the 1890s. 42ff. Similarly, Alex Rattray Hay laments the appearance of "highly organized, modern Denominations with culture, wealth and beautiful buildings" in his book, *The New Testament Order for Church and Missionary*. Hay, 21. "We do wonder about the assumption," Winter writes, "that the denomination was a divinely instituted structure, while the societies were merely human creations." Winter, "Protestant Mission Societies and the 'Other Protestant Schism'," 200-01.

[emphasis is in original]."[568] Eugene Teselle agrees, pointing out that "before there was a 'local' ministry in the churches, there was an 'itinerant' ministry by which churches were founded and by which they were edified in an ongoing way . . . Mission has an *original authority* in the Christian church." [569]

Darrell L. Guder, in his essay "Para-parochial Movements: The Religious Order Revisited" corrects a perception implied by the term "parachurch," that perception being "almost a church, resembling a church."[570] He asks that we start, again, with a missiological approach to understanding the purpose of the church:

> The view of the church which emerges from this missiological approach is, then, *highly instrumental*. The church is God's instrument for the accomplishment of God's purposes. The way in which the church is to be structured to do that is defined by the mission, nature and purposes of God. Such a missiological approach obviously places in question any attempt to restrict the forms of Christian mission to a particular tradition, or structure, or hierarchy. The church is emphatically for the sake of mission. The organizational implication of this missiological position is to relativize the question of forms and structures. It makes a term like "para-church" with its "first class church" and "second class church" implications ultimately impossible [emphasis added].[571]

"The fundamental question, then," Guder continues, "is not one of structure as much as it is a question of mission: What is the mission of the church and how does that

---

[568] Winter, "The Two Structures of God's Redemptive Mission," 129.

[569] Eugene TeSelle, "Church and Parachurch: Christian Freedom, Ecclesiastical Order, and the Problem of Voluntary Organizations (Unpublished)," (Nashville: Vanderbilt University, 1994). This essay was originally prepared for a research project on "the church and the groups," initiated and conducted by Eugene TeSelle, Professor of Systematic Theology in the Divinity School, Vanderbilt University; the consultation at which this essay and the essay by Darrell L. Guder, referenced in the next paragraph, were presented and discussed took place at Vanderbilt in September 1994.

[570] Darrell L. Guder, "Para-Parochial Movements: The Religious Order Revisited," (Vanderbilt University: September, 1994), Manuscript.

[571] Ibid., 7.

mission define its forms?"⁵⁷² Particularly instructive in framing a theology of (first) mission and (second) forms was Karl Barth's After developing his theology of the *mission Dei* Barth turns his attention to the validity of organizing effective structures for the carrying out of that mission.

4.6.6 Karl Barth's "Special Working Fellowships"

Guder introduces Karl Barth's theology of "special working fellowships of the Church" (*Besondere Arbeitsgemeinschaften der Kirche*), which Barth locates in section 72 of his *Dogmatics*, "The Holy Spirit and the Sending of the Christian Community."⁵⁷³ Barth sees the role of sodalities, Waldron Scott has pointed out, as "proper and even indispensable to Christian ministry."⁵⁷⁴ Barth's theology of special working fellowships is "thoroughly missional,"⁵⁷⁵ Guder writes. Barth "understands that the one unifying mission of the church can express itself in a number of organizational ways"⁵⁷⁶ "Not all Christians," Barth wrote, "will belong in the same way to the same kind of community. There will be a vast variety of special working fellowships, all going about the 'activity demanded of all Christians.'"⁵⁷⁷ But, under the empowerment of the Holy Spirit, they will do so "in a particular form of thought, speech and action, Christian witness being given in

---

⁵⁷² Ibid., 5.
⁵⁷³ Karl Barth, *Church Dogmatics*, vol. IV/3 (Edinburgh: T. & T. Clark, 1957), Section 72. No. 4. 830ff. Guder adds that "No. 4, is translated 'The Ministry of the Community,' but should be translated 'The Service of the Community.' This translation in the English edition is unnecessarily clericalizing and out of touch with Barth's whole argument!" Private correspondence, July 31, 2010.
⁵⁷⁴ Waldron Scott, "Karl Barth's Theology of Mission," *Missiology* 3, no. 2 (1975): 221.
⁵⁷⁵ Guder, *The Continuing Conversion of the Church*, 184.
⁵⁷⁶ Ibid.
⁵⁷⁷ Barth, 856.

a particular way."[578] For Barth a "multiplicity of the ministry of witness" is "normal and legitimate":[579]

> The Holy Spirit does not enforce a flat uniformity. Hence the Christian community, quite apart from the natural individuality of its members and the consequent dangers, cannot be a barracks, nor can its members be the uniformed inhabitants, nor can their activity be the execution of a well-drilled maneuver. Their divine calling and endowment are as such manifold. They are always new and different.[580]

For Barth, the communion of the Holy Spirit, "which constitutes the whole community," will always "express itself concretely *in the form of specific communions* which within the sphere of the one action of the community *are called and equipped in detail for the same or similar action*. It can and *should develop special working fellowships* to which *all Christians cannot and will not necessarily belong* [emphasis added]."[581] In performing the duties commanded of all Christians, Barth says, a particular set of Christians may render "a particular service" in "a particular way."[582] The "multiplicity of the ministry" has "nothing whatever to do with the sinful corruption of the Christians."[583] The groups they form are not schisms, for schisms "cannot arise if everything is in order in this matter."[584] "Care must be taken," Barth continues, "to assure that the aim of these

---

[578] Ibid.

[579] Ibid., 856. There is another kind of multiplicity of ministries that is abnormal, and "from below," Barth writes. This kind "jeopardizes and perhaps to a large degree actually hampers this ministry," that is, the ministry of the Holy Spirit in granting to the church different services of calling. 855

[580] Ibid., 855.

[581] Ibid., 856.

[582] Ibid.

[583] Ibid., 855.

[584] Ibid., 856. Winter approved of Barth's comment that schisms will not arise where there is a proper perspective on "special groups" Barth's perspective, Winter said, was "crucially important." But he wrote

"genuine working fellowships" is

> simply to achieve in closer fellowship the ministry and witness of the community in the world. Where these presuppositions are present, no objection need be raised; we may welcome and encourage the rise and continuation of particular fellowships of the few or the many within the general fellowship of all Christians. In the plurality of such fellowships of work and service and witness the unity of the living community of the living Jesus Christ will be the more powerful and visible, speaking the more clearly for that which it has to express with its existence in the world.[585]

Guder suggests that Ralph Winter's "Two Structures" is similar to Barth's special working fellowships: "Without using the terms," Guder points out, "Barth was, in fact, approaching the question of the forms of ministry communities in ways close to the modality/sodality schematic proposed by Winter."[586]

Summary. God assembles His people to hear His word, "I will be your God." At the close of worship the Lord *dismisses* His people "in order to perform a task."[587] "Above all," Guder writes, "the public worship of the mission community always leads to the pivotal act of sending."[588] But there is a problem—an anomaly—because, Guder states, "neither

---

that he had "a bit of difficulty with the word *special* in Barth's analysis." Ralph D. Winter, *The Story of the P.C.M.S., P.U.M.A., P.O.W.E., and the P.F.F.* (Worldwide Ministries Division of the P.C.U.S.A., Louisville, KY, October 26, 1995), Manuscript, 6. Winter then explained, "What is so special about the vital mass of Christian energies which we classify as 'parachurch?' Are private enterprises like General Motors 'special?' Are not such initiatives which are regulated by the civil government, but not administered by them, normal rather than special?" Ibid.

[585] Barth. 856

[586] Guder, "Para-Parochial Movements: The Religious Order Revisited," 16.

[587] Guder, "Missional Structures: The Particular Community," 44.

[588] Ibid., 243. Guder adds, "The community that is called together is the community that is sent. Every occasion of public worship is a sending event."

the structures nor the theology of our established Western traditional churches is missional."[589] "Organizational constraints," Guder goes on to say,

> quickly eclipse the theological assumption that particular communities exist for their mission. The community owns property, has staff, makes commitments, and must therefore ensure that the budget is raised and the program continued. Maintenance replaces mission as the guiding principle of the community's life. The challenge facing the church in North America today is a radical one. It is that neither maintenance nor survival is an adequate purpose for any particular community or ecclesial structure.[590]

"Our challenge today," Guder writes, "is to move from church with mission to missional church."[591] This challenge remains unresolved in many Protestant denominations and churches because the relationship between ecclesiastical hierarchies and mission societies has yet to be normalized. The church's future effectiveness in bringing the ideals of Jesus to bear on our fallen world depends on making a paradigm shift. Members of voluntary structures can have confidence in their organizations are adapted from patterns practiced by Jesus Christ and Paul the apostle. Sodalities apparently exist among all peoples and all cultures. Their members are eradicating root problems everywhere. As Carey said, there is a "glorious prize" that "stretches our every nerve" and we should never imagine "that it was to be obtained in any other way"[592] than forming voluntary associations.

---

[589] Darrell L. Guder and Lois Barrett, *Missional Church: A Vision for the Sending of the Church in North America*, ed. Darrell L. Guder (Grand Rapids: Eerdmans, 1998), 5.
[590] Guder, "Missional Structures: The Particular Community," 240.
[591] Guder and Barrett, *Missional Church: A Vision for the Sending of the Church in North America*, 6.
[592] Carey, *An Enquiry into the Obligations of Christians to Use Means for the Conversion of the Heathens*, 80.

4.7. Presbyterian Mission History: Initiative, Reaction, and Desired Symbiosis

In previous sections I have explained 1) the significance of the Jewish and Pauline mission structures in supporting the "two structures" paradigm; 2) the Celtic Church governance model by which bishops were subordinate to abbots for centuries. 3) how religious orders gave Catholics an advantage; 4) how the Reformers deterred their members from forming anything like Catholic orders; 5) that William Carey's most important analogy—comparing mission societies to a private trading companies—enables us to understand how mission societies should be regulated; 6) how the "two structures" paradigm occurs naturally in every culture. In this section I give reasons to persuade the reader to adopt the "two structures" paradigm after drawing lessons from Presbyterian mission history in the United States.

Early Support for Mission Societies. In 1802, the Presbyterian General Assembly appointed a "Standing Committee of Missions." And at its meeting on March 31, 1803 the Standing Committee wrote to various "missionary associations in Europe and America" to inquire into "the measures and successes of others engaged in Missionary undertakings."[593] The General Assembly then authorized two mission programs to

---

[593] Clifford Merrill Drury, *Presbyterian Panorama; One Hundred and Fifty Years of National Missions History* (Philadelphia,: Board of Christian Education, Presbyterian Church in the United States of America, 1952), 4. In its letter, the Standing Committee stated that "since its beginning early in the 18th century the practice has existed among us, of sending ministers of the gospel to preach to those who had not its institutions regularly established among them." 7. The names of those early missionaries are collected in Clifford Drury's 1952 book *Presbyterian Panorama*. It is noteworthy that Drury credits mission societies for the sending and care of the pioneer missionaries. For example, The Society for the Propagation of the Gospel published John Eliot's translation of the Bible into the language of the Algonquin Indians; one Azariah Horton was "the first officially commissioned Presbyterian missionary in colonial days," but

provide salaries for pastors on the Western frontiers (Kentucky, Ohio, western Pennsylvania). The first was a "circuit rider" plan administrated directly by the General Assembly. The second was a cooperative effort between Presbyterian, Congregationalist, Dutch Reformed and Associate Reformed churches organized as the American Home Missionary Society. This made for "keen competition", Clifford Drury wrote,[594] and Presbyterian donors soon showed their preference for the American Home Missionary Society plan to fund settled pastors over of circuit riders favored by the Presbyterian Standing Committee in Philadelphia.[595] From its first year, 1816, Drury continues:

> The American Home Missionary Society experienced rapid growth. At the end of its first year's operations, it reported receipts of $18,130.76 and a force of 169 missionaries and agents. In its eleventh annual report the Society stated that it had receive during the previous year $85,701.59 [an annual growth rate of 16 per cent], and that it had aided 810 missionaries.[596]

This success, Drury adds, was "phenomenal as compared with the contemporary activities of the Presbyterian Board of Missions."[597] "It is evident," he observed, "that the larger part of Presbyterian benevolences was being channeled through the voluntary societies."[598] A short time later, in 1837, Presbyterian leaders would close ranks to expel

---

"Horton's support came from the Scottish Society for Propagation of Christian Knowledge." 7. Drury also mentions David Brainerd, and his brother John, whose ministries among the Indians were supported by the Scottish Society. 7, 8

[594] Ibid., 52.
[595] Ibid., 30-31.
[596] Ibid., 67.
[597] Ibid.
[598] Ibid., 80.

Presbyterians for donating to The AHMS and other interdenominational mission societies.[599]

4.7.1 The Presbyterian Schism of 1837

The 1837 General Assembly of the Presbyterian Church was a scene of "bitter debates and disorders with few parallels in American church history."[600] The majority, holding that the Presbyterian Church was the only "missionary society" to which Presbyterians needed to belong, expelled 60,000 dissenting communicants from membership in the church. Here is what happened.

The New School Position. Presbyterians who supported the American Home Mission Society and other voluntary societies were called New School Presbyterians. "On general principles . . . as well as from all past experience," argued Absalom Peters (1793-1869), a New School champion,

> we are constrained to believe that the voluntary associated action of evangelical Christians, as far as it is practicable, is much better suited to the object of the world's conversion, than any form of church organization for this purpose, ever has been or can be.[601]

---

[599] The continued quarrel in the Presbyterian Church over three great issues that were deepening the chasm between the two parties—slavery, doctrinal questions, and mission polity—began to have a negative effect upon church membership. The denomination reported having 247,964 members in 1834. No report was made for 1835. Only 219,943 were reported in 1836, showing a net loss of about 12 per cent in the two-year period. Thousands of members, sick of the quarrel, were changing their affiliations to other denominations. Ibid., 84.

[600] Marsden, *The Evangelical Mind and the New School Presbyterian Experience; a Case Study of Thought and Theology in Nineteenth-Century America*, 59.

[601] Ibid., 72. Peters' tract was titled "A Plea for Voluntary Societies."

The New School paradigm was not new; the Philadelphia Presbytery, in the very earliest years of American Presbyterianism, had asked its pastors to "encourage the formation of private Christian societies for doing good."[602] It was no novelty, then, when General Assemblies in the early 19th century recommended voluntary societies to their constituencies. Earl MacCormac writes,

> Among those recommended were the American Bible Society, the American Colonization Society, and the American Tract Society. In addition, Presbyterians participated in the Young Men's Society of New York, the New York Evangelical Missionary Society, the Northern Missionary Society in the State of New York, and, in 1807, the General Convention of Congregational and Presbyterian Ministers of Vermont had resolved itself into a missionary society.[603]

But by the early 1830s Presbyterian Church leaders had grown uneasy with these cooperative efforts. "The question of cooperation with voluntary societies was an explosive issue in the Presbyterian Assembly in the years preceding the division,"[604] wrote George Marsden.

The Old School Position. Ecclesiastical leaders took the position, known as Old School, that "the Presbyterian Church is a missionary society"[605] and the only missionary society with which Presbyterians should have anything to do. Dramatically, Reverend John Holt

---

[602] David G. Dawson, "The Evolving Role of Presbytery after Christendom," Unpublished, (2005, March 23): 2. According to Dawson, the Philadelphia Presbytery passed an overture in 1707, the year after Francis Makemie and others founded it, admonishing pastors to "encourage the formation of private Christian societies for doing good." The recent phenomenon of presbyteries acting as mission boards is, in Dawson's perspective, a trend away from the role held by presbyteries in their earliest days.

[603] Earl R. MacCormac, "Missions and the Presbyterian Schism of 1837," *Church History* 32, no. 1 (1963): 34.

[604] Marsden, *The Evangelical Mind and the New School Presbyterian Experience; a Case Study of Thought and Theology in Nineteenth-Century America*, 74.

[605] David G. Dawson, "A Recurring Issue of Mission Administration," *Missiology* 25, no. 4 (1997): 457.

Rice dictated a letter on his deathbed on March 4, 1831, "to the upcoming General Assembly of the Presbyterian Church in the United States of America."[606] Knowing he would not live to make the plea in person, Holt implored the General Assembly to withdraw its support of voluntary mission societies, and to resolve "that the Presbyterian Church in the United States is a Missionary Society; the object of which is to assist in the conversion of the world; and that every member of the Church is a member for life of said Society."[607] The General Assembly did not enact Holt's death-bed plea in 1831, but over the next six years many more Presbyterians came to share his opinion. Joshua L. Wilson, an Old School pastor from Cincinnati, advanced four reasons why the Presbyterian Church and its members should disassociate from the voluntary societies.[608] They were:

1. The Lord Jesus Christ has committed the management of Christian missions to his church.
2. The Presbyterian Church, being one great family of the church of Jesus Christ, is by her form of government, organized into a Christian Missionary Society.
3. The American Home Missionary Society is not an ecclesiastical, but a civil institution.
4. By interference and importunity, she disturbs the peace, and injures the prosperity of the Presbyterian Church.

The implication, MacCormac writes, was "that the Presbyterian Church already possessed the structure of a missionary organization and, as an ecclesiastical body upon

---

[606] Ibid.
[607] Ibid.
[608] MacCormac: 37.

which Christ's missionary imperative was binding, should conduct her own missions."[609] Dr. Samuel Miller, of Princeton, who in 1833 had been favorably disposed to the voluntary societies,[610] now favored the Old School position regarding the American Home Missionary Society:

> Yet we all know that they have no public standards to which they conform. They have no confession of faith; no ecclesiastical responsibility. They may deviate greatly and grievously from the purity of the Gospel; and if this should ever occur, there will be no [other] power than the vague and ever varying power of public sentiment to call them to account or to arrest their wayward career.[611]

From this premise it followed that, since the Presbyterian Church did not administrate the AHMS, it was out of order. The *sola synodica* paradigm could not co-exist with the "two structures" paradigm; like tectonic plates, one had to give way to the other.

The Old School Votes for Schism.[612] The General Assembly of 1837, after clamorous debate and the dismissal of the New School members from its rolls the General Assembly passed the following resolution:

> We believe that facts too familiar to need repetition here warrant us in affirming that *the organization and operations of* the so-called American Home Missionary Society and American Education Society, and its branches of whatever name, are exceedingly injurious to the peace and purity of the Presbyterian Church. We recommend, accordingly, that they should cease to operate within any of our churches [emphasis added].[613]

---

[609] Ibid.

[610] In 1833 Miller wrote favorably of the New School position in his "Letters to Presbyterians on the Present Crisis in the Presbyterian Church." Drury, 85.

[611] Ibid.

[612] For a day-by-day account of the 1837 General Assembly proceedings see ibid., 87-90.

[613] MacCormac: 32.

The Old School majority followed this resolution by expelling the four synods which favored the "New School" synods, and dissolving the Presbytery of Wilmington and the Third Presbytery of Philadelphia. Just under half of the 2400 Presbyterian congregations was thus removed from the rolls of the church.[614] The remaining delegates of the 1837 Assembly voted to censure the American Home Missionary and American Education Societies. "Then," George Marsden writes, "to complete the victory, it established its own Board of Foreign Missions as well."[615] The new board immediately took over the administration of 44 Presbyterian missionaries who were serving overseas with the ABCFM at that time.[616]

The 1837 General Assembly took these drastic steps, it explained, because of the harm being done to the peace and purity of the Church by "*the organization and operations of*" special-interest mission agencies. Cooperation with voluntary mission agencies had come to be perceived as "exceedingly injurious" to the unity of the church. Dissolving relations with the mission agencies would correct, it was supposed, a theological error.

A pattern had been established—a few Presbyterians would initiate a mission effort by forming a voluntary society. Many would begin funding it. Ecclesiastical leaders

---

[614] In 1838, two rival Presbyterian General Assemblies met in Philadelphia, Marsden writes, "each claiming to be the General Assembly of the Presbyterian Church in the United States of America. The New School body, with approximately 100,000 communicant members, 85 presbyteries and 1,200 churches and ministers, represented slightly less than half the Presbyterian Church in the United States of America." Marsden, *The Evangelical Mind and the New School Presbyterian Experience; a Case Study of Thought and Theology in Nineteenth-Century America*, 65-66.
[615] Ibid., 74.
[616] Pierson, "Presbyterian Missions," 784.

would criticize the effort, then act to deter members from further involvement on the grounds of maintaining the peace and unity of the church. For example, in August 1839 Robert J. Breckinridge published "Facts and Considerations in Regard to Ecclesiastical Control in Benevolent Operations." His objection to independent boards represents the Old School position. "These boards divest the Church of its proper control over the particular subject, in the guise of a real delegation of power" he wrote, "and vest this divested power in a few critical hands, at the seat of the operations."[617]

David Dawson has pulled together the pertinent historical data for the period following the 1837 schism. He recounts how James Henley Thornwell, professor and president of South Carolina College, defended his Old School position in an 1840 position paper. "Boards," he wrote, "are directly subversive of the form of government embodied in the Constitution of our own church. They involve a practical renunciation of Presbyterianism."[618] For Thornwell, even the Foreign Mission Board and Domestic Mission Board created by the 1837 General Assembly were out of order. Charles Hodge countered that this was "hyper-hyper-hyper High Church Presbyterianism."[619] Writes Dawson of Hodge, "He contended that the presbytery could not handle the logistics for such responsibility and that there is a Christian liberty that allows the use of means

---

[617] Robert J. Breckenridge, "Facts and Considerations in Regard to Ecclesiastical Control in Benevolent Operations," *The Baltimore Literary and Religious Magazine*, no. 5 (1839). quoted in Dawson, "A Recurring Issue of Mission Administration," 459.

[618] James Henley Thornwell, "A Memorial to the Synod of South Carolina and Georgia on the Subject of Ecclesiastical Boards.," *The Baltimore Literary and Religious Magazine*, no. 4 (1840): 147. Quoted in Dawson, "A Recurring Issue of Mission Administration," 462.

[619] Dawson, "A Recurring Issue of Mission Administration," 462. Dawson is quoting from J. B. Adger, "The General Assembly of 1860," *The Southern Presbyterian Review*, no. 13 (1861): 370.

appropriate to the situation."⁶²⁰ Thornwall's proposal was identical to that of the 17th century Dutch theological Voetius; from the historical evidence I believe we could predict that, had presbyteries retained the sole authority to initiate Presbyterian mission the 19th century would have resembled the cautionary tale of 16th and 17th when the sails of Reformed mission remained unhoisted.

Some Official Presbyterian Histories of Mission were Redacted to Begin in 1837. Many official Presbyterian histories identify the creation of the Foreign Mission Board in 1837 with the beginning of the Presbyterian mission era.⁶²¹ "In 1837," wrote Donald Black, "the PCUSA started its journey."⁶²² One would not know from Black's version of history that Presbyterians had been forming themselves into mission societies before 1837, or that they have been ever since. The 1934 General Assembly declared that before 1837 the Presbyterian Church had attempted to outsource its mission efforts to voluntary agencies but that experience "had clearly demonstrated the inefficacy of such agencies under a Presbyterian form of government."⁶²³ An exception was made for "certain

---

[620] Dawson, "A Recurring Issue of Mission Administration," 462.

[621] These five histories of the Presbyterian Church state that the history of Presbyterian mission began in 1837: 1) Brown.; 2) G. Thompson and Donald T. Black Brown, "Structures for a Changing Church," in *A History of Presbyterian Missions 1944-2007*(Louisville: Geneva Press, 2008).; 3) Drury.; 4) James H. Smylie and others, *Go Therefore: 150 Years of Presbyterians in Global Mission* (Atlanta: Produced for the General Assembly Mission Board, Presbyterian Church (U.S.A.), by the Presbyterian Publishing House, 1987).; 5) Sherron George, "Faithfulness through the Storm: Changing Theology of Mission," in *A History of Presbyterian Mission, 1944-2007* (Louisville: Geneva Press, 2008), 24.

[622] Brown, "Structures for a Changing Church," 58.

[623] Quoted in William J. Weston, *Presbyterian Pluralism: Competition in a Protestant House*, 1st ed. (Knoxville, TN: University of Tennessee Press, 1997), 42.

interdenominational work which the church could not do alone" and which the General Assembly had "approved in specific deliverances."[624]

Yet the tendency of 19th century Americans to form voluntary societies was strong, as Marsden, de Tocqueville, and Rufus Anderson concluded. For example, during the Civil War Presbyterian women "were active in such relief organizations as the Christian Commission."[625] That experience, Drury writes, "opened up the possibilities of organized efforts to thousands of women. Following the war, these women cast about for some outlet for their newly realized potentialities. Many of them found that opening in the churches."[626] In a short time, women organized themselves into 10,000 mission societies in congregations across the country. "No other form of American intervention overseas has made a more powerful cultural impact," R. Pierce Beaver wrote, "than this work for women and children."[627] "The first necessity," Beaver believed, in order to account for this remarkable and enduring legacy, "is a description of it in terms of the structures and institutions through which it developed."[628] Here is a brief history of the mission structures that Presbyterian women initiated and sustained in the decades following the Civil War.

4.7.2 Presbyterian Women's Societies from the Second Half of the 19th Century

---

[624] Ibid.
[625] Drury, 198.
[626] Ibid.
[627] Beaver, *All Loves Excelling; American Protestant Women in World Mission*, 11.
[628] Ibid.

The history of the relationship of Presbyterian women's societies to Presbyterian leadership can be divided into three parts: confrontation, commendation, and centralization, as I attempt to demonstrate in the next section.

Confrontation. In 1870 Presbyterian women in Philadelphia organized themselves into the Foreign Missionary Society and began publishing *Woman's Work for Woman.* Arthur J, Brown in his book *One Hundred Years*, published in 1936, wrote of the General Assembly's reaction:

> When, in 1870, the Assembly's Board of Foreign Missions heard that some women in Philadelphia wanted to organize themselves into a missionary society to help it in its work among women and children, one of its secretaries from New York came to talk it over with a meeting of pastors and women convened for the purpose. The minutes recorded that the propriety of an independent organization was questioned, and that the opinion was expressed that the work could be more easily, cheaply, and better done through the regular agencies of the Church.[629]

Commendation. But the furrowed brows on the faces of Presbyterian board executives brightened considerably when the women's societies proved themselves denominationally loyal—and financially generous. The General Assembly of 1875 authorized the Woman's Board "to represent and promote" the interests of the church while "using its own methods, independent of other control."[630] Soon there were seven regionally based women's boards, governed by women and independent of the General Assembly's Board of Foreign Missions. By 1879, women's societies were supporting

---

[629] Brown, *One Hundred Years: A History of the Foreign Missionary Work of the Presbyterian Church in the USA*, 114.

[630] *Minutes of the General Assembly of the Presbyterian Church of the United States of America*, ed. Stated Clerk (Philadelphia: 1875).

Presbyterian missionaries in Syria, Persia, India, China, Thailand (Siam), Japan, Africa and Mexico, as well as missionaries to Native Americans.[631] The General Assembly of 1880 noted approvingly:

> Of the $585,844 that have come into the treasury of our Board, the women have sent in $176,000, an advance of $40,000 over the previous year. This amount is 30% of the whole amount, or if the legacies be left out, then 40%. These efforts of the women of our church are worthy of all praise.[632]

History credits Presbyterian women's societies with initiating mission work among Chinese immigrants arriving in the United States. This happened in 1881 when the North Pacific Branch of the Woman's Foreign Missionary Society organized a mission to Chinese women in Portland. The California Branch of the Philadelphia Woman's Foreign Missionary Society had been organized in 1873; in 1889 it became the Woman's Occidental Board of Foreign Missions, being active in the mission to Chinese women in San Francisco.[633] By 1883 the Board of Foreign Missions reported enthusiastically: "We have enrolled 1284 women's societies and bands in 49 presbyteries."[634] This extraordinary growth—in just thirteen years—paralleled the burst of newly-organized mission societies that appeared in the first years after Carey published *An Enquiry*. W.

---

[631] Brown, *One Hundred Years: A History of the Foreign Missionary Work of the Presbyterian Church in the USA*, 117.

[632] *Minutes of the General Assembly of the Presbyterian Church of the United States of America*, ed. Stated Clerk (Philadelphia: 1880).

[633] Brown, *One Hundred Years: A History of the Foreign Missionary Work of the Presbyterian Church in the USA*, 124.

[634] *Minutes of the General Assembly of the Presbyterian Church of the United States of America*, ed. Stated Clerk (Philadelphia: 1883).

Stanley Rycroft writes of a particular offering which became popular among women's societies:

> The most dramatic and effective way of raising money was by way of what came to be known as a Thank Offering. The idea was outlined in the April, 1888 issue of the *Women's Missionary Magazine*; each woman in the church would provide herself with a "mite box" in which to deposit her offerings during the year. Over the years, this practice became immensely popular among the women of the church, and produced a large part of the funds for missionary work.[635]

The General Assembly of 1889 agreed to transfer the support of all medical work abroad to the Women's General Missionary Society,[636] though later the Board of Foreign Missions undertook its own medical missions. In 1890 the PCUSA women's societies gave more to home missions than all the congregations combined.[637] In addition, the Women's General Missionary Society assumed support of all unmarried women in the foreign fields—a responsibility that it continued until the General Assembly dissolved it in 1922.[638]

There is more commendation. The 1893 General Assembly stated that "The Women's Societies have exceeded any figure hitherto attained, reaching the handsome total of $329,889. In 1897 when the General Assembly reported:

> that in view of the financial outlook it did not feel justified in sending new missionaries to the field. A number of noble men and women had been appointed

---

[635] W. Stanley Rycroft, *The Ecumenical Witness of the United Presbyterian Church in the U.S.A* (New York: Commission on Ecumenical Mission and Relations, United Presbyterian Church in the U.S.A., 1968), 81.

[636] Ibid.

[637] Milton J. Coalter, John M. Mulder, and Louis B. Weeks, "Introduction," in *The Organizational Revolution: Presbyterians and American Denominationalism* (Louisville, KY: Westminster/John Knox, 1992), 29.

[638] Rycroft, 81.

in the hope that they might be sent, but the crushing debt with which the Board closed the fiscal year made it impossible to send them unless special funds were provided for the purpose. In the providence of God, however, the church rallied grandly to the rescue, and 38 new missionaries, including wives, were sent, *the means being provided by individuals, churches, women's societies, young people's societies, and by the Synod of Missouri's Committee on Foreign Missions* [emphasis added]."[639]

Latourette wrote that "although much opposition was voiced by the church members and indifference characterized the majority, in the aggregate, by the latter part of the [19th] century, the contributors to these societies numbered several hundred thousands.[640] Arthur J. Brown marvels that between 1870 and 1920, 30% of the total receipts of the Presbyterian Board of Foreign Mission were credited to the women's boards and societies:

> The total receipts for the 50 years from Presbyterian women for Foreign Missions, were reported to be $17,154,630, an almost unbelievable sum when one realizes that the gifts did not represent large plate collections, but the tithing of small sums and gifts of self-denial and sacrifice. Prayers were the secret of this magnificent giving.[641]

Centralization. But after 1923 most of the women's agencies were merged into the general denominational boards, where they came under more ecclesiastical control and were administrated by men. Robert Speer defended this action:

> If we have in our churches women's organizations, what have we got? Haven't

---

[639] *Minutes of the General Assembly of the Presbyterian Church of the United States of America*, ed. Stated Clerk (Philadelphia: 1897), 11.

[640] Latourette, *A History of the Expansion of Christianity*, Vol. IV. 100.

[641] Brown, *One Hundred Years: A History of the Foreign Missionary Work of the Presbyterian Church in the USA*, 135. See also Drury, "The Women's Missionary Boards," 197-219. Giving by Presbyterian Women Boards contributed 30% of the entire Foreign Mission Board budget for fifty years, 1870 to 1920. Women's Boards contributed 2.27 percent of the Worldwide Ministries Division 2005 budget.[641]

we got two churches? We have one church made up of men and women, with a social program, an educational program, and a religious program. Then we have a separation of women, with identical programs except for worship. We do not want to divide what is spoken of as "the church" and "the women." The great danger is that the women will think that their society is the only thing they have to work over.[642]

In 1923 the General Assembly voted to gather the funds of thousands of women's societies into a central budget and manage a single fund from New York City. After that year the General Assembly minutes stop reporting the activities and giving of individual women's mission societies. My own attempts to uncover the record of donations by women's societies after 1923, in order to know if giving declined, have been fruitless: the director of the Presbyterian Historical Society told me that the General Assembly changed the way financial records were recorded after 1923, making any comparisons to prior years impossible.[643] David Dawson discovered the same difficulty:

> Within the history of a particular board the annual reports have changed their overall format and nomenclature for reporting and classifying data. Consequently it is difficult to precisely track the numbers involved so that accurate comparisons can be drawn.[644]

---

[642]Lois A. Boyd, R. Douglas Brackenridge, and The Presbyterian Historical Society., *Presbyterian Women in America: Two Centuries of a Quest for Status*, 2nd ed., Contributions to the Study of Religion (Westport, CT: Greenwood Press, 1996), 60-61.

[643] Bridget Arthur Clancy of the Presbyterian Historical Society wrote to me April 24, 2003: "Re: Women's giving. Dear Mr. Blincoe: Thank you for your phone call and follow-up email to the Presbyterian Historical Society for information about the history of giving by women's mission groups in the Presbyterian Church in the U.S.A. As you mentioned during our telephone conversation, the contribution amounts from women's groups began to be reported along with youth societies' offerings in 1921. However, during the 1923 reorganization, the work of the various women's boards was subsumed under the other agencies of the church. You were hoping to find someplace that still listed the contributory amounts broken down by the individual groups. I have done a check of the 'Minutes' of the General Assembly from 1930 through 2000, and I have not been able to locate any separate tables with these details. Sincerely, Bridget Arthur Clancy," Reference Librarian Presbyterian Historical Society. 425 Lombard St. Philadelphia, PA 19147. www.history.pcusa.org

[644] David G. Dawson, "Counting the Cost," in *A History of Presbyterian Missions, 1944-2007* (Louisville: Geneva Press, 2008), 36. In the PCUS, the General Assembly continued to report giving by women's

Joan C. LaFollette's research indicates that giving by Presbyterian women's associations trended upward until 1935, but admits that "comparing financial data over an eighty-five year period is difficult because of periodic changes in reporting methods."[645]

R. Pierce Beaver said that "centralization" led eventually to "the destruction of the women's foreign mission movement."[646] He elaborated:

> It was frequently alleged that the women were competing as rivals with the official church organizations. Money was supposedly deflected from the denominational budget. Pastors and higher central officials disliked their inability to control such funds, and this second line of giving went against the trend toward centralization . . . Some declared that the women always had plenty of money for their projects, while the general work starved. It was frequently stated that if there were only one organization everything might then be kept in proper balance.[647]

Paralleling the experience of the Presbyterian Church, the National Council of the Congregational Churches in 1924 "politely but firmly" coerced the three Women's Boards of Mission "to merge with the American board by appointing a Committee on Missionary Organization to achieve organizational unity on the grounds of improving efficiency."[648] Methodist women held control of their mission societies for three more decades, until 1964, when reorganization of their societies was effected at the insistence

---

societies until 1957. Judy Theriault, "Presbyterian Women," (Pasadena: Presbyterian Center for Mission Studies, 1995), 13.

[645] Joan C. LaFollette, "Presbyterian Women's Organizations," in *The Organizational Revolution: Presbyterians and American Denominationalism* (Louisville, KY: Westminster Press, John Knox, 1992), 207.

[646] R. Pierce Beaver, *American Protestant Women in World Mission: A History of the First Feminist Movement in North America*, Rev. ed. (Grand Rapids: Eerdmans, 1980), 184ff.

[647] Beaver, *All Loves Excelling; American Protestant Women in World Mission*, 178.

[648] Ibid., 183. But the Baptist story is quite different, Beaver adds: "In some inexplicable manner there was adopted in 1929 a new basis of cooperation which recognized the sovereignty and independence of the WABFMS in women's work" (184-85).

of the bishops, "who were bent on integration."[649] In the official documents the intention of the bishops is "elimination of dual control,"[650] despite the math lesson of the ledger: women's missionary societies "incurred far less overhead than the general boards."[651] Still church leaders found reasons to complain:

> Arguments emerged that women were causing imbalance in the missionary effort, or that their successful fundraising was causing financial hardship for the general missionary board. But *not until the goal of efficiency reigned supreme in the 1920s did the centralization of denominational structures succeed in dismantling the movement*. The byproduct to the merger was that the male-controlled general boards took the money raised by the women. The male-run Board of Christian Education tried to seize women's missionary funds by misrepresenting itself as a mission organization. As the women of the church tried to defend the integrity of their missionary work, years of hostility between women and the church bureaucracy resulted [emphasis added].[652]

In 1931, the Presbyterian Church General Council re-directed the women's funds to make up a deficit in the Christian Education program.[653] Church women reacted vigorously. Their societies voted 2,001-1,669 to protest the General Council's decision. Stated Clerk Lewis Seymour Mudge proposed that a study group be formed to interpret the vote. But when Mudge addressed the biennial meeting of the women's societies in May, 1931 the audience confronted him:

---

[649] Ibid., 188.

[650] Ibid.

[651] Dana Lee Robert, *American Women in Mission: A Social History of Their Thought and Practice*, ed. Wilbert R. Shenk (Macon, Ga.: Mercer University Press, 1997), 303.

[652] Ibid., 305-06.

[653] The Board of Christian Education promoted this change with a series of advertisements in various church papers. One advertisement began with a question in bold type, "WHERE WILL OUR CHURCH GET ITS MINISTERS, HOME MISSIONARIES, AND FOREIGN MISSIONARIES IF THE FUTURE OF THE WORLD OF OUR Presbyterian Board of Christian Education is curtailed?" Quoted in Boyd, Brackenridge, and The Presbyterian Historical Society., 65.

> Every seat in the auditorium (was) filled; women were standing along the walls and the aisles. The full account of the meeting in *Women and Missions*, while factually accurate, does not convey the hostility that Mudge faced. They questioned Mudge on why the General Council did not accept the vote as the will of organized churchwomen. Notes taken by an eyewitness indicate that women uninhibitedly shouted their displeasure before Mudge could even formulate replies to questions. After Mudge left the auditorium, the women overwhelming (sic) voted to go on record to register "our earnest protest" against the creation of a committee to study the significance of the vote, because it would "continue to exaggerate the confusion and unrest which have hampered our work during the past year."[654]

By the late 1930s a growing number of church administrators called for a national organization of women that would appeal broadly to all the women in the church. In a remarkable book, *Presbyterian Women in America: Two Centuries of a Quest for Status*, Lois A. Boyd recounts what happened at the 1943 General Assembly:

> Council member Helen Weber assured commissioners that the proposed new organization *would represent all churchwomen, "not just the missionary-minded who form our present set-up and who constitute less than half of all Presbyterian women."* [emphasis added].[655]

By a unanimous vote the General Assembly brought into existence a National Council of Women's Organizations, representing all church women, and insuring that mission-minded women would become a minority, and that the minority would not be able to initiate any actions. No wonder Dana Robert could write that "the dismantling of the woman's missionary movement makes for depressing reading":

> In each case, women fought and resisted the mergers, but they were either powerless to defend themselves because they had no laity rights in the church, or else they were forced to accept compromises that slowed but could not stop the

---

[654] Ibid., 35.
[655] Ibid., 37.

ultimate dissolution of their organizations . . . Men argued against women's missionary societies throughout their history based on pretexts that women diverted the attention of the denomination from the primary missionary task, that women did not know how to handle money, and that single women missionaries caused trouble on the mission field.[656]

"Every woman is a member." From 1980 to 1986 I was pastor of a church—St. Andrews Presbyterian in Strathmore, California—with an active chapter of Presbyterian Women. Some Sundays one of the members would invite women to attend an upcoming meeting. "And remember," she would say, "every woman in the congregation is a member of Presbyterian Women."[657] Of course, when every woman is a member, then some women who are especially interested in achieving a particular mission outcome should start organizing themselves as a subset of the whole. Women who want to solve problems that are not interesting to most members need to form organizations appropriate for the issues that concerned women want to address.

4.7.3 Christian Endeavor and its Presbyterian Challenger, Westminster Fellowship

We have considered how Presbyterian officers took control of the women's societies' funds. There are other examples of hierarchical reaction to independent mission initiatives. In the early 20th century Presbyterian administrators became alarmed by the popularity of an interdenominational youth movement called Christian Endeavor. As a

---

[656] Robert, 303.

[657] In May 1978 at Skyline Presbyterian Church in Tacoma, Washington I was made an honorary lifetime member of the Presbyterian Women. How this happened I haven't a clue.

reaction, the Presbyterians created Westminster Fellowship for Presbyterian youth. Here is what happened.

The first Christian Endeavor society was organized on February 2, 1881.[658] Rev. Francis E. Clark, pastor of Williston Congregational Church in Portland, Maine, formed the society in the parlor of his home at 62 Neal Street—the parsonage of Church. During the first meeting, Clark framed a constitution for the society and called it "Williston Young People's Society of Christian Endeavor." It was to be, Clark wrote, "an out-and-out Christian society": and the activities "were to centre around the weekly young people's prayer meeting."[659] Most importantly it was led by the youth; the members held one another accountable to attend the weekly meetings and to daily read the Bible and to pray. By the time its founder Dr. Francis Clark wrote his autobiography in 1922, eighty thousand organizations bore the name Christian Endeavor, hundreds of them meeting in Presbyterian Churches,[660] the offerings collected at meetings going to their churches.[661] Nearly every year in the early 20th century the Presbyterian Women's Board reported the number of children enrolled in Junior Christian Endeavor Societies.[662] The Presbyterian Church Department of Young People's Work published *The Presbyterian Christian*

---

[658] Francis E. Clark, *Christian Endeavor in All Lands* (Boston: The United Society of Christian Endeavor, 1886), 35.

[659] Francis E. Clark, *Memories of Many Men in Many Lands: An Autobiography* (Boston: United Society of Christian Endeavor, 1922), 41.

[660] Ibid., 699.

[661] "The Women's Societies have exceeded any figure hitherto attained, reaching the handsome total of $329,889, while the Christian Endeavor Societies have nearly doubled their gifts." *Minutes of the General Assembly of the Presbyterian Church of the United States of America*, ed. Stated Clerk (Philadelphia: 1893).

[662] Drury, 205.

Endeavor Manual from 1912 through 1920.[663] The Presbyterian Historical Society (PHS) holds hundreds of volumes which record the proceedings of meetings of the Christian Endeavor Societies that were recognized by Presbyterian congregations and presbyteries in the sixty year period between 1880 and 1940.[664]

But the General Assembly created Westminster Fellowship (WF) in 1943,[665] the same year that the General Assembly created the National Council of Women's Organization. Ralph D. Winter writes, "My parents transferred to Lake Avenue Congregational Church when WF began scheduling regional meetings on the same date as the CE regionals."[666] Winter wrote, comparing the impact of Christian Endeavor to the combined impact of Young Life, Campus Crusade, Youth for Christ, Navigators and Intervarsity:

> I believe that all of these together do not equal the scope or momentum of the Christian Endeavor movement that swept this country (and the world) between 1890 and 1930. Ruth Rouse, in the second volume of the *History of the Ecumenical Movement* is the only ecumenical writer I know who gives credit to this movement . . . But it lost out when denominations pulled out of the movement in the 30s to found their own denominational versions of the movement.[667]

Humanitarian Relief Funds—Presbyterian Attempts to Retain Exclusive Control. There are more examples of church leaders deterring voluntary initiatives. We have referred to the 1960 of the Board of World Missions of the Presbyterian Church in the United States

---

[663] http://www.history.pcusa.org/dbtw-wpd/WebOPACmenu.htm. Type in "Christian Endeavor"
[664] Ibid.
[665] Email to Robert Blincoe, by Eileen Mayer Sklar, 24 November 2009, Westminster Fellowship, Presbyterian Historical Society. Philadelphia. *Manual* for the Westminster Fellowship (call no. MI 3.92 W52).
[666] Personal correspondence from Ralph D. Winter, November 25, 2008
[667] Winter, *The Story of the P.C.M.S., P.U.M.A., P.O.W.E., and the P.F.F.*, 5.

(PCUS) to adopt a statement critical of non-Presbyterian relief agencies, including CARE, Christian Children's Fund, and World Vision.[668] The Board went on to state:

> While it is not our function to evaluate the work of these agencies, it is pointed out that they are not related to our Church and are not recommended as the approved channel for the relief activities of our own people. All members of our Church are urgently requested to send their relief funds through their churches to the Treasurer of the Board of World Missions for administration by the Department of Overseas Relief and Inter-Church Aid. This, we believe, will assure the most effective and economical use of our relief funds and provide an avenue through which the Church can give a direct Christian witness in its ministry with human need.[669]

The history of Presbyterian mission is a kind of Hegelian case study: a few members form special-purpose associations, then church hierarchies start rival organizations and test the loyalty of church members on the basis of their support for church programs. Ralph Winter writes, "To this day, among Protestants, there continues to be deep confusion about the legitimacy and proper relationship of the two structures that have manifested themselves throughout the history of the Christian movement."[670] Though "the voluntary principle is essential to world mission," Beaver wrote, denominational and ecumenical structures continue to "frown upon spontaneous action and establishment of

---

[668] Weingartner, 112.

[669] Ibid. No church headquarters to issue to its constituent members a remonstrative letter like this today. To heal the breach church headquarters should respond to its pluralist constituency by listing the commendable, unrelated voluntary societies that the members are joining and contributing to. Moreover, the interest of Christians continues to "gravitate to the specific," as Ralph Winter said; for example, the *Mission Handbook* lists more than 1000 mission agencies under more than 100 headings such as agricultural assistance, aviation, services, Bible distribution, church construction, disability assistance programs, evangelism, translation, youth programs, etc.

[670] Winter, "The Two Structures of God's Redemptive Mission," 134.

direct relationships which they do not initiate or administer."[671] "We claimed," Beaver added, "that official commitment of denominational churches through official boards was a better way and better justified by Bible and theology." However, Beaver continued,

> Our boards were put into the straight-jacket of denominational structure and budget, became administratively rigid, were subjected to American business managerial principles and methods, and eventually deprived the local disciples and congregations of meaningful and conscious part in the sending operation. The whole thing became depersonalized. Now many members have been lost to the cause, alienated or discouraged. *Pioneering experimentation is the order of the day* [emphasis added].[672]

It is for the purpose of healing this breach that I ask the reader to consider the paradigm presented in Ralph D. Winter's articles, "The Two Structures of God's Redemptive Mission"[673] and "Protestant Missionary Societies."[674] A new reporting relationship between mission societies and local churches and denominations is the desired symbiosis. For nearly a century the Presbyterian Book of Order normalized a relationship between them, as described in the next section.

4.7.4 The Presbyterian Book of Order *Provision for "Special Organizations"*

For most of the 20th century the *Book of Order* provided a status for special-purpose associations and a statute by which the Presbyterian Church regulated them. In 1902 the 114th General Assembly added a chapter to the *Book of Order* (Chapter 23 in 1902, but

---

[671] Beaver, *American Protestant Women in World Mission: A History of the First Feminist Movement in North America*, 184ff.
[672] R. Pierce Beaver, "A Plea for a New Voluntarism," *Concordia Theological Monthly*, (June 1971): 4.
[673] Winter, "The Two Structures of God's Redemptive Mission."
[674] Winter, "Protestant Mission Societies: The American Experience."

retitled Chapter 28 soon afterward) called "Of the Organizations of the Church: Their Rights and Duties."[675] Here is the text that became part of the *Book of Order*:

> Section 1. The members of a particular church or particular churches may associate together and may associate with themselves other regular members of the congregation or congregations, under regular forms of association, for the conduct of a special work for missionary or other benevolent purposes, or for the purpose of instruction in religion and development in Christian nurture.
>
> Section 2. Where special organizations of the character above indicated exist in a particular church, they shall be under the immediate direction, control and oversight of the Session of said church; where they cover the territory included within a Presbytery or Synod, they shall be responsible to the judicatory having jurisdiction; and where they cover territory greater than a Synod, they shall be responsible to the General Assembly.
>
> Section 3. The names or titles of special organizations may be chosen by themselves, and the organizations shall have power to adopt each its own Constitution and to elect its own officers, subject always to the powers of review and control vested by the Constitution in the several judicatories of the Church.[676]

The Chapter 28 organizations, as they were called, annually reported to the General Assembly. The General Assembly regulated—but did not govern—these organizations. When the Northern and Southern churches reunited in 1983, the Northern Church provision recognizing special-interest mission groups was added to the new *Book of Order* (Chapter 28 was redesignated as Chapter 9.0601, "Right to Organize," in 1983). "This was a crucial decision," writes Gary Eller. "The Form of Government constitutionally legitimized organized advocacy groups within the [newly-formed]

---

[675] *Minutes of the General Assembly of the Presbyterian Church of the United States of America*, ed. Stated Clerk (Philadelphia: 1902), 164-65. Henry Van Dyke was Moderator of the 1902 General Assembly.
[676] Ibid.

PCUSA."[677] The *Book of Order* provided a way to regulate these groups ("Review and Control," G-9.0602) by 1) requiring a yearly report, and 2) making a determination every year as to whether an organization was "in compliance" or "not in compliance" with the witness of the Presbyterian Church. The term "in compliance" indicated "adherence to the Constitution of the Presbyterian Church (U.S.A.) and [the] guidelines, but does not imply the General Assembly's concurrence with, or endorsement of, the organization's position."[678] To be found "not in compliance" carried disciplinary consequences. Criteria for evaluating special organizations were developed along with a list of privileges for groups found "in compliance." In his article "The New Missions and the Mission of the Church," Ralph D. Winter reports on his discussion with church officials that led Winter to conclude that Chapter 28 / Chapter Nine "clearly provides for the spontaneous emergence of other organizations which organize first and ask approval later," an advantage that Winter interpreted as "highly significant."[679]

There were 19 "Chapter Nine" organizations at the time of the merger in 1983.[680] But the provocative agendas of a few of them, notably the Presbyterian Lay Committee and

---

[677] Gary S. Eller, "Special Interest Groups and American Presbyterianism," in *The Organizational Revolution: Presbyterians and American Denominationalism* (Louisville, KY: Westminster/John Knox, 1992), 259.

[678] *Book of Order*, (Louisville, KY: Office of the General Assembly, Presbyterian Church USA, 1992), G-9.0602.

[679] Ralph D. Winter, "The New Missions and the Mission of the Church," *International Review of Mission* 60, no. 1 (1971, January): 92-93.

[680] The Chapter Nine organizations were: Presbyterians for Democracy and Religious Freedom, The Outreach Foundation, The Presbyterian Lay Committee, The Witherspoon Society, The Presbyterian Network on Alcohol and Other Drug Abuse, Presbyterians for Biblical Sexuality, Presbyterian Peace Fellowship, Presbyterians Pro-Life Research, The New Earth Covenant Community, Covenant Fellowship of Presbyterians, Presbyterians for Biblical Concerns, Association of Presbyterians in Cross-Cultural

the Presbyterian Gay and Lesbian Caucus, seemed in the minds of many Presbyterians to enjoy the endorsement of the whole church, even though the *Book of Order* made it clear that special organizations "are not official agencies of the Presbyterian Church (U.S.A.)" and that "they bear alone responsibility for their views and actions."[681] Sadly, the 1991 General Assembly voted 422-104 to eliminate the provision recognizing special-purpose associations by the church. The Church expunged the chapter from the *Book of Order*, and the formal reporting relationship was dissolved.[682]

Presbyterian voluntary societies still exist,[683] enabled to do so by US non-profit corporation law, and they still represent Presbyterian constituencies; but the regulatory relationship previously maintained has ended. Gary Eller writes,

---

Mission, Literacy and Evangelism International, Presbyterian Center for Mission Studies, Presbyterian Frontier Fellowship, Presbyterian Order for World Evangelization, Presbyterian Elders in Prayer, Presbyterian Renewal Ministries, and Reformed Order of Discipleship. *Minutes of the General Assembly of the Presbyterian Church of the United States of America*, ed. Stated Clerk (Philadelphia: 1991). Most of the Chapter Nine organizations would identify themselves as "conservative," but not all, a point make in Richard G. Hutcheson, *Wheel within the Wheel: Confronting the Management Crisis of the Pluralistic Church* (Atlanta: John Knox Press, 1979), 115-16.

[681] *Book of Order*, G-9.0602.

[682] *The Special Commission of 1925*. But this dissolution was at variance with "the principle of toleration" described by Robert Speer in the Special Commission Report of 1925 (quoted in Weston, 79.) Speer and the other members of the Commission stated that the Presbyterian way of settling disputes was by the "union of hearts." The report stated, "Toleration as a principle application within the Presbyterian Church refers to an attitude and a practice . . . Presbyterianism is a great body of belief, but it is more than a belief; it is also a tradition, a controlling sentiment. The ties which bind us to it are not of the mind only; they are ties of the heart as well." Ibid., 80.

"More than defending toleration, though," William J. Weston adds, "the Special Commission report eloquently expressed the loyalists' devotion to the Presbyterian Church itself. When the General Assembly of 1926 embraced this tolerant and constitutional understanding of the Presbyterian Church, *the tide turned in favor of pluralism in the church*" [emphasis added]. Ibid., 81.

[683] I serve on the boards of the Presbyterian Center for Mission Studies and the Presbyterian Order for World Evangelization. These organizations reported annually to the General Assembly until 1991 when the General Assembly stopped giving oversight to them.

> Can special-purpose groups be agents of reconciliation within the Presbyterian Church? Respectful dialogue and concern for the whole Presbyterian family must bring opposites together in the pursuit of the mission of the church. "If this is done in the power of the Spirit," writes [David G.] Dawson, "the 'theological Balkanization' of the Presbyterian Church can end, and the identity of the new church can be firmly established, and authentic ministries of faithfulness can begin."[684]

Recognize and Regulate. As I write, the President of the United States has just flown over wildfires burning in Arizona's pine forests.[685] He declared the forests a disaster area. Meanwhile, down on the ground, highly motivated teams of elite volunteer firefighters known as "hot shots" have arrived from all over the country on a mission to save the forests. The government registers and funds hotshot crews and calls on their specialization to battle the blaze. These two structures—government above and specialized crews on the ground—need each other to identify and begin to eradicate more of the root problems in our world.

4.7.5 Trends in Mission Giving: The Presbyterian Experience

In this section I provide evidence that, in order to reverse the downward trend in Presbyterian giving, it is in the best interest of ecclesiastical hierarchies to recognize that their members prefer to designate their giving. Designated funding enjoys the advantage of satisfying the donors, which is to say, satisfying the owners, of voluntary associations. For the sake of retaining the good will of the members of churches and denominations,

---

[684] Eller, 278.
[685] June 2002; http://en.wikipedia.org/wiki/Hotshot_crew

church administrators must demonstrate their own good will by modifying the unified budget funding model. In his valuable study, *A Funding System for the 21st Century*, David G. Dawson describes "inherent systemic problems in the funding systems"[686] that go back to the 1837 schism:

> From these early years there were tensions between what the boards wanted, namely undesignated contributions, and how the people and churches were giving, namely designated. Board secretaries complained that contributions to "special objects" (as they were called) obligated the board to future work without guarantee of adequate support for present commitments.[687]

After 1837, writes Dawson, "the Presbyterian Church was, de facto, in the business of maintaining a *funding system* to receive the gifts of individuals and churches to support the mission boards under the purview of its General Assembly."[688] This system had all the inefficiencies of government without the necessary risks that new initiatives demand, risks that William Carey called "all these disquietudes and all these labours."[689] Despite the attempt by church leaders to control the disbursement of funds, "designated giving continued to prevail," Dawson writes, until "the highpoint in mission giving" came in about 1920.[690] In a section titled, "The Critical Years of the 1920's and Reorganization," Dawson writes,

---

[686] David G. Dawson, *A Mission Funding System for the 21st Century* (New College, University of Edinburgh, Scotland, 2004), 4.
[687] Ibid.
[688] Ibid.
[689] Carey, *An Enquiry into the Obligations of Christians to Use Means for the Conversion of the Heathens*, 81.
[690] Dawson, *A Mission Funding System for the 21st Century*, 5.

According to James E. Moorhead the "mystique of efficiency"[691] shaped the organizational life of the Presbyterian Church (and many other denominations) in the 1920's reorganization and centralization. Leaders employed scientific planning, business management, rational organization, professional expertise, and effective promotion techniques.[692]

In 1920 the General Assembly formed a Special Committee on the Reorganization of Boards and Agencies. Robert E. Speer, secretary of the Board of Foreign Missions, employed his extraordinary organizational skills to consolidate the thirteen boards into four (Foreign Missions, National Missions, Christian Education, and Ministerial Relief). The Special Committee accepted his proposal, but "the obsession with efficiency inherent in the 1923 reorganization came at a cost," Dawson writes. A new church age of "leadership by experts and managers whose wisdom was considered superior."[693] Experts and managers believed that the virtue of efficiency trumped the value of designated giving. But donors found ways to bypass the unified mission budget, and new, de-centralized streams formed a delta of donor-driven initiatives. Ralph Winter writes,

> By 1950, when the "unified budget" approach had gained widespread consensus among the denominations as a further step toward centralization, another vast new crop of powerful voluntary societies was being born, the money from individual church members somehow constantly gravitating to the specific.[694]

---

[691] James E. Moorhead, "Presbyterians and the Mystique of Organizational Efficiency," in *Reimagining Denominationalism* (New York: Oxford University Press, 1994), 265. Quoted in Dawson, *A Mission Funding System for the 21st Century*, 5.

[692] Moorhead, 265. Samuel Haber said that "efficient" and "good" came close to meaning the same thing in the 1920s. Ibid.

[693] Dawson, *A Mission Funding System for the 21st Century*, 5-6. See also Ronald B. Rice, "Congregational Giving to Denominational Mission within the United Presbyterian Church" (Doctoral of Ministry thesis, San Francisco Theological Seminary, 1978), 5.

[694] Winter, "Protestant Mission Societies: The American Experience," 210.

The inclination of donors to fund specific causes is the subject of D. Scott Cormode's 1992 study, "A Financial History of Presbyterian Congregations Since World War Two." Cormode believes that the reason for the upward trend in donor-driven giving lies "in a broader process of alienation from institutions that are seen as distant and remote."[695] Church members "overwhelmingly identify themselves with congregations, not denominations."[696] Yet in the last third of the 20th century the Presbyterian Church promoted a program called "One Mission." One Mission funneled all the mission offerings from the congregations up to church headquarters, then distributed some of it back to synods and presbyteries. The 1970 General Assembly undergirded this program with a dubious theological statement: "We affirm our conviction that the General Mission Program of the General Assembly is the central symbol of the unity of the whole Church in its collective response to mission."[697] ("That," Dawson adds, "I would contend, is really scary theology!"[698]

Also in 1970 the Presbyterian mission leadership began allowing church members to designate their giving by selecting from Extra Commitment Opportunities. By 1985 the annual total of giving through Extra Commitment Opportunities reached $819,000, with another $2,194,698 donated to "projects outside the budget."[699] The success of the Extra

---

[695] D. Scott Cormode, "A Financial History of Presbyterian Congregations since World War Two," in *The Organizational Revolution: Presbyterians and American Denominationalism* (Louisville, KY: Westminster/John Knox Press, 1992), 27.
[696] Ibid.
[697] Dawson, *A Mission Funding System for the 21st Century*, 9.
[698] Ibid.
[699] Dawson, "Counting the Cost," 49.

Commitment Opportunities indicates there was a "strong interest among churches and their members in having a say in where mission dollars were to be spent."[700] But Extra Commitment Opportunities giving did not fund the General Assembly mission program. The 1990 General Assembly reminded Presbyterian churches to support the unified mission budget, saying, "The support of Presbyterian mission through Unified Giving is a responsibility of church sessions, and should always be given priority."[701] Sherron George adds, "the lack of balance of unified or undesignated giving with designated giving is beginning to undermine much of the historic mission presence of the PC(USA). The trend has produced a financial crisis . . . We must be careful not to succumb to our consumer and individualistic culture."[702] The assumption here, Dawson says, is that "congregations are useful for raising funds, but from there they should leave mission to the experts."[703] This "encourages donors to believe that they can pay for Christian witness without any personal involvement or cost. This not only embraces an unbiblical elitism but also a problematic understanding of vocation and apostolic witness."[704] The estrangement of the donor from the apostolic witness is probably a contributing factor to the downward trend in giving, as the figure below demonstrates. From 1993 – 2000

---

[700] Ibid.
[701] Dawson, *A Mission Funding System for the 21st Century*, 9.
[702] George, 100.
[703] Dawson, *A Mission Funding System for the 21st Century*, 9.
[704] Ibid.

undesignated mission support declined more than 10% from $27.4 million to $24.5 million. During the same period designated giving increased 239%.[705] (Figure 19)

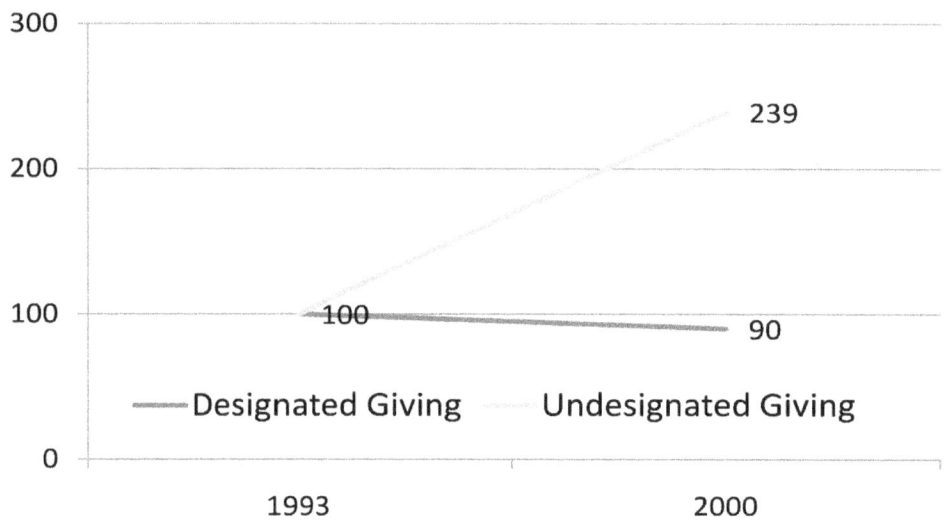

Figure 19. Trends in Presbyterian Giving, Designated and Undesignated

This trend led Dawson to suggest

> that the discouraging record in the number of missionaries and the amount of money given in support of Presbyterian international mission for the past sixty years is due in large part to, as Sanneh suggests, missiological confusion about missionary vocations *and the refusal to consider any change in the unified, centralized funding system.* In this same period, global mission in the world did not recede even though PCUSA missionary involvement did. In fact, it was a period of great growth and diversification [emphasis added].[706]

---

[705] Leslie Scanlon, "New Strategies for Raising Mission Dollars Considered by P.C.U.S.A. Officials," *The Presbyterian Outlook*, (February 25, 2002): 4.

[706] Dawson, "Counting the Cost," 57. Dawson's references Lamin O. Sanneh, "Christian Missions and the Western Guilt Complex," *The Christian Century* April 8, (1987): 331-34.

Max Warren and Hans-Werner Genischen were suggesting "twenty years ago," R. Pierce Beaver wrote in 1971, "that the voluntary principle is essential to mission."[707] Beaver went on to write,

> We claimed that official commitment of denominational churches through official boards was a better way and better justified by Bible and theology. But our boards were put into the straightjacket of denominational structure and budget, became administratively rigid, were subjected to American business management principles and methods, and eventually deprived the local disciples and congregations of a meaningful and conscious part in the sending operation. The whole thing became depersonalized.[708]

Beaver then lauds the voluntary societies of the 19th and 20th centuries. "It is time once again to look to voluntary association and action for rescue and to foster voluntarism among those who remain devoted."[709]

Trends in Centralized Giving and De-centralized Giving: a Contrast. Since the 1980s Presbyterian Church sessions have begun directing their giving to non-Presbyterian causes instead of sending it "up" and receiving some of it back:

> In 1976 the statistical reports began to ask for this information and from these reports we have discovered that gifts to non-Presbyterian mission amounted to 20% in the local community and 20% beyond the local community. That percent increased slowly through the 1980s and accelerated during the 1990s to the point where in 2003 churches gave almost three times as much to local mission as they did to the General Assembly ($150/60 million) and more to other mission beyond the local community ($66/60 million) than they gave to the General Assembly.[710]

---

[707] R. Pierce Beaver, "The Christian Mission, a Look into the Future," *Concordia Theological Monthly* 42, (1971): 348.
[708] Ibid., 349.
[709] Ibid.
[710] Dawson, *A Mission Funding System for the 21st Century*, 7.

In the figure below, Presbyterian giving to Presbyterian local mission is presented as a constant, with the amount of giving to Presbyterian non-denominational giving presented relative to the constant. Presbyterian giving to non-Presbyterian local missions increased from 20% to 250% of giving to Presbyterian local missions. (Figure 20)

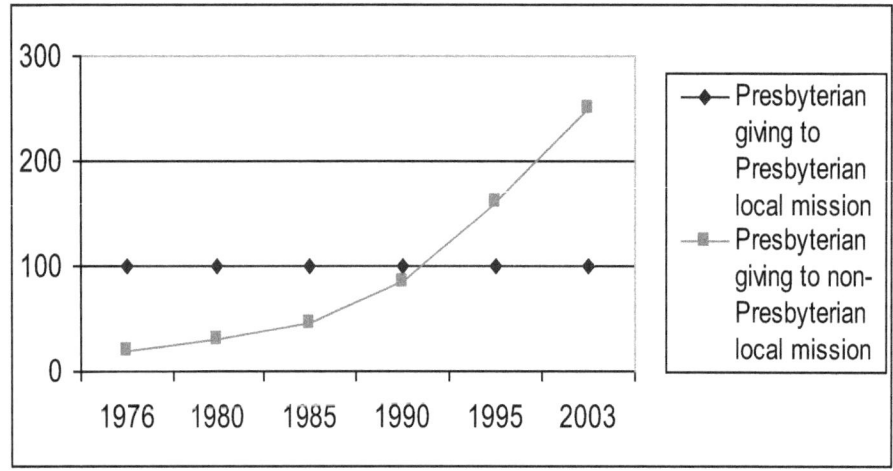

Figure 20. Presbyterian Giving to 1) Presbyterian and 2) Non-Presbyterian Local Missions--A Comparison

In the figure below, Dawson's data concerning Presbyterian giving to Presbyterian mission beyond local is presented as a constant. Over a period of 27 years, Presbyterian giving to non-Presbyterian beyond local increased from 20% to 110% of giving to Presbyterian beyond local (Figure 21):

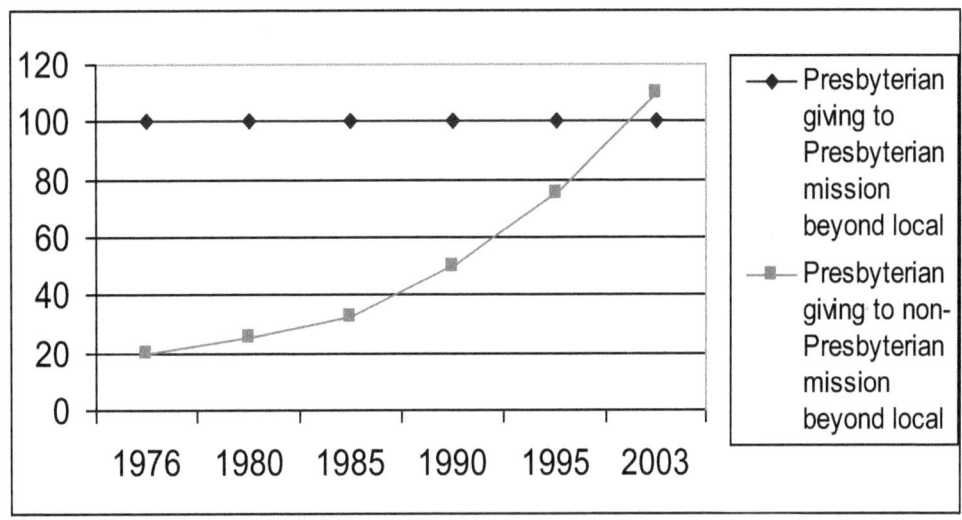

Figure 21. Presbyterian Giving to 1) Presbyterian and 2) Non-Presbyterian Mission beyond Local--A Comparison

In 1944, at the beginning of the period that Dawson studied, mission giving totaled 7.35 percent of congregational giving; it dropped 80% to 1.5 percent by 2003.[711] Dawson warns that "if we continue to live as if it is the 1950s and exert energy to cling to what has come and gone, we will simply construct more roadblocks to giving by faithful Presbyterians."[712] The denomination can continue to command and control an ever

---

[711] Dawson, "Counting the Cost," 47. G. Thompson Brown adds that the Presbyterian Church in the United States (Southern Church) spent 3.5 percent of all contributions for ministries in the other five continents in 1970, but by 1980 this percentage had slipped to 2.6 percent. G. Thompson Brown, "Rethinking Some Modern-Day Shibboleths," *Missiology* 12, (1984): 90-91.

[712] Dawson, "Counting the Cost," 47.

shrinking stream of revenue or it can negotiate a new social contract with its members who are designating their giving already. Future money will not flow upstream again to Presbyterian headquarters in Louisville, but Louisville can recognize and take pride in the widespread mission giving of its members.[713]

---

[713] The Church Mission Society made this needed transition: although organized in 1799, it was not until 1841 that CMS director Henry Venn formalized an agreement between the society and the Anglican Church hierarchy. This was made possible "when, on the suggestion of the bishop of London, the society agreed to add a clause to its rules and regulations to the effect "that all questions relating to matters of Ecclesiastical Order and Discipline respecting which a difference shall arise between any Colonial Bishop and any Committee of the S.M. Society shall be referred to the Archbishops and Bishops of the United church of England and Ireland, whose decision therein shall be final." Quoted in Ajayi: 51. Following this change the highest ranking officials in the Church of England—the archbishops of Canterbury and York, the bishop of London, and other bishops—joined the CMS as members. Ibid. 52. Granting this concession, Henry Venn felt confident that he could preserve what he called "the Voluntary Principle" of autonomy in the CMS.

Ratio of Presbyterian Overseas Missionaries to Home Staff, 1944-2007. The centralizing of budget decisions and management seems to proceed in step with *decreasing* efficiency as measured by cost per product. David Dawson, in his article "Counting the Cost" produces the following statistics[714] (Figure 22):

Year	Number of overseas missionaries	Number of home staff serving the missionaries	Ratio of missionaries to home staff
1944	1160	30	39
1955	1150	34	31
1957	1150	65	16
1967	1087	71	15
1987	505	30	17
2000	250	100	3
2006	250	89	3
2007	250	64	4

Figure 22. Ratio of Presbyterian Missionaries to Home Staff: Data

---

[714] Dawson, "Counting the Cost," 40.

The ideal of efficiency which centralization was supposed to achieve seems more realizable in a decentralized model. Here is the data presented in a time line (Figure 23):

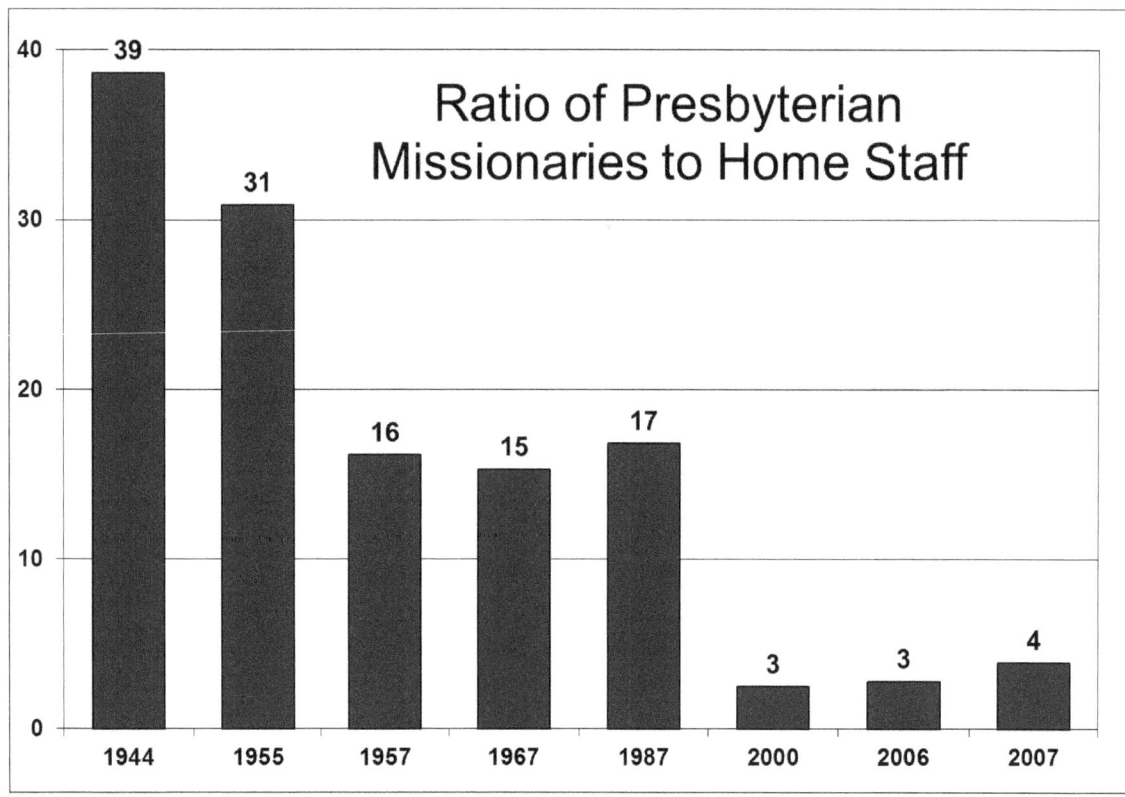

Figure 23. Ratio of Presbyterian Missionaries to Home Staff

The trend is also reflected in the declining number of Presbyterian missionaries in the Middle East; totals fell from 329 (in 1959) to 47 (1979) to 11 in 2007 (Figure 24):

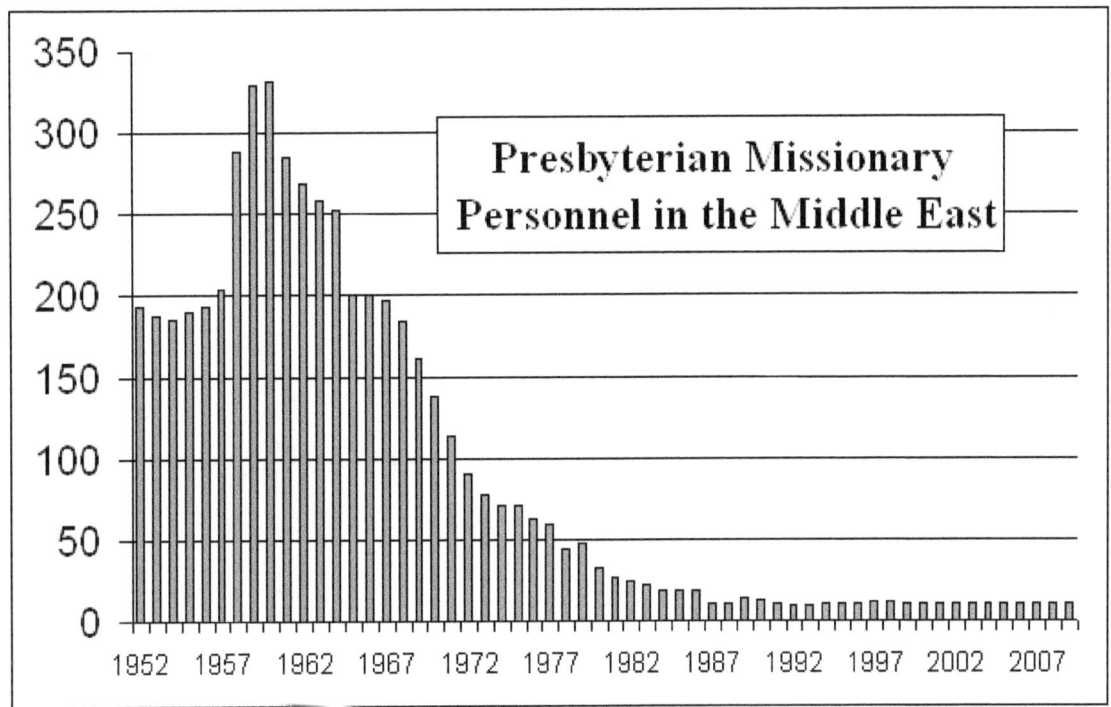

Figure 24. Presbyterian Missionaries in the Middle East

By contrast, Presbyterians and Christians from all kinds of Protestant churches are "finding more freedom, more effectiveness and more productive engagement" by forming themselves into voluntary mission societies such as Frontiers (Figure 25):

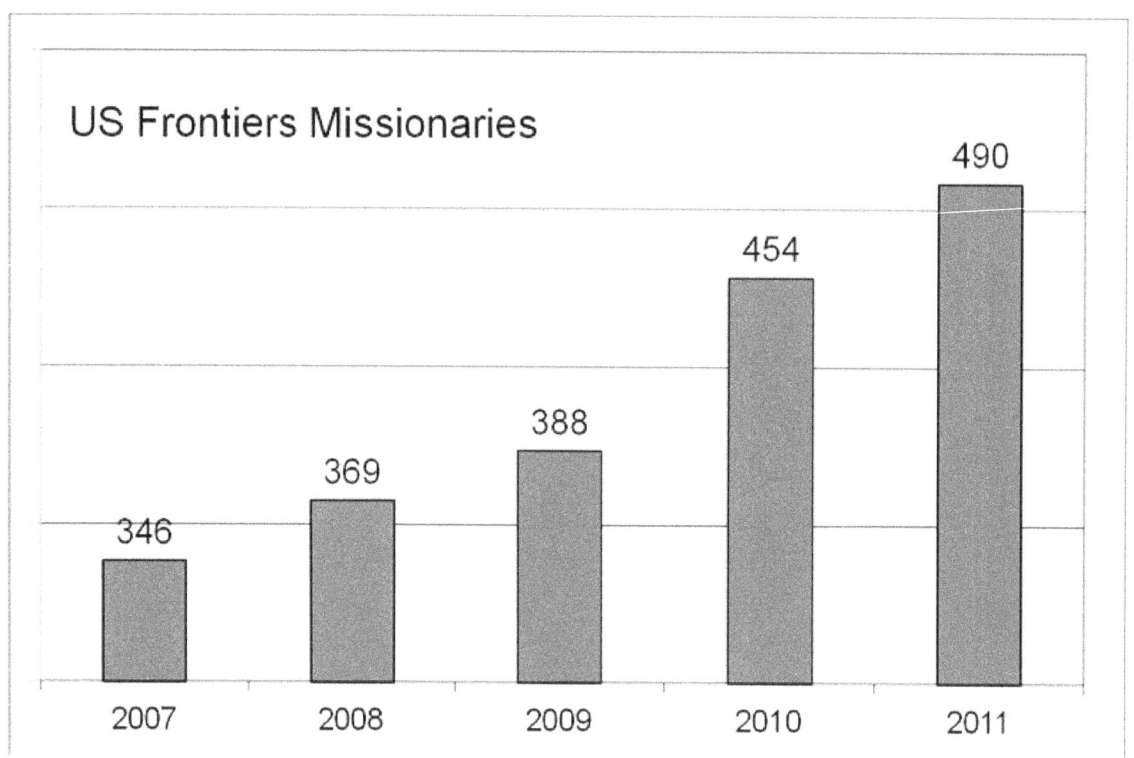

Figure 25. US Frontiers Field Workers

20th Century *Observations in Praise of Autonomous Mission Societies: Observations of Richard G. Hutcheson and William Weston.* In a 1977 *Christian Century* article, "Pluralism and Consensus: Why Mainline Church Mission Budgets Are in Trouble," Richard G. Hutcheson, Jr. explained why "once-powerful central denominational headquarters" had "fallen on hard times . . . The real income of national church agencies is less than half of what it was ten years ago."⁷¹⁵ But by means of voluntary associations, Hutcheson wrote, the classic pattern of missional activity and giving has re-appeared:

> Christian faith has always led to some kind of action: nourishing the Christian community, spreading the faith, teaching the young, feeding the hungry, healing the sick, challenging evil, changing society. For most of Christian history, this kind of missional activity has been *voluntary* and has taken place *outside* the formal church governmental structures. Voluntary missional activity has always depended on activists who do the work, and money-givers who support it. The historic pattern has been one in which the activists, with the approval of church authorities, have gone directly to the members to arouse enthusiasm, enlist support and collect funds [emphasis is in original].⁷¹⁶

Hutcheson suggests that we look to the Catholics for a self-governing missional model:

> The Roman Catholic Church developed admirable structures for carrying out these missional activities in the various lay and priestly religious orders. These have been permitted to be self-governing internally. Teaching orders, missionary orders, charitable and serving orders could focus on their own particular missional interests, and they have had free access to church members to develop support and collect funds.⁷¹⁷

"The Protestant equivalent of the Roman Catholic order," writes Hutcheson, "has been the voluntary association." These are "largely autonomous groups within the denominations, cultivating their own constituencies, raising their own funds with denominational cooperation, and carrying out their various kinds of mission."⁷¹⁸ But since World War II, Hutcheson continues, corporatized denominational structures

---

⁷¹⁵ Richard G. Hutcheson, "Pluralism and Consensus: Why Mainline Church Mission Budgets Are in Trouble," *Christian Century*, no. July 6-17 (1977): 618. This article is online: http://www.religion-online.org/showarticle.asp?title=1173. Accessed November 2006.
⁷¹⁶ Ibid., 619.
⁷¹⁷ Ibid.
⁷¹⁸ Ibid.

with their promise of efficiency have reached new levels of control over mission budgets. "Corporatized mission of mainline Protestant churches," he wrote,

> is probably best symbolized by its skyscraper monument in New York City, the Interchurch Center at 475 Riverside Drive. But corporatized mission began to collapse even before it was fully developed. Funds began to dry up before corporate headquarters buildings were paid for, and bureaucracies began to shrink even as "priority strategies" proliferated. The collapse was probably due chiefly to one basic flaw: the failure to take full account of the fact that *churches are voluntary organizations* [emphasis is in original].[719]

In a section called "The Flaw in the Unified Budget," Hutcheson attempts to persuade denominational leaders that a centrally administered mission structure prevents citizens with special interests from allocating any of the funds they contribute. "It is a curious anomaly," writes Hutcheson, "that it is precisely those inclusive, pluralistic denominations without a clear consensus which have gone furthest in corporatizing their denominational structures!"[720] The centralization of decision-making has left many members disaffected. But this perilous condition can be changed; a better future for

---

[719] Ibid., 620. Specifically, churches are voluntary associations at the local (congregational) level. More so than in Europe, U.S. churches hold their members by the will of the members; for this reason "the distinction between church and voluntary society, always fundamental in Europe, sometimes all but disappeared in America." Walls, "The American Dimension of the Missionary Movement," 299. Douglas W. Johnson writes, correctly, that "a denomination is a voluntary association which operates *locally* through programs that are useful to its members." Douglas W. Johnson, *Program Dissensus between Denominational Grass Roots and Leadership and Its Consequences.*, ed. Ross P. Scherer, American Denominational Organization (Pasadena: William Carey Library, 1980), 330.

Scholarly papers on the subject of churches as voluntary organizations have been published: Sheils and Wood, eds. From the introduction: "Church membership is subject to involuntary constraints, social, familial cultural. Nevertheless, . . . the conduct of a Christian life and the ongoing life of the Church, even in situations where the theological propositions of extreme predestinarian determinacy prevail, depends upon individual and group responses which in some measure and sense are deemed to be voluntary responses to a variety of invitations and exhortations . . . This is to conceive of the Church itself in voluntaristic and associative terms, an approach reflected in this volume." xi.

[720] Hutcheson, "Pluralism and Consensus: Why Mainline Church Mission Budgets Are in Trouble," 621.

denominations and churches is the social contract proposed in this dissertation.

In his informative 1987 book *Presbyterian Pluralism: Competition in a Protestant House,* William Weston contributes to this discussion. He advocates for "competitive pluralism," that is, a pluralism guided by the Presbyterian Church's ethos of catholicity and diversity, as embodied in its constitution.[721] "The triumph of constitutional tolerance," he writes, "made competitive pluralism the policy of the Presbyterian Church" early in the 20th century.[722]

For Weston, the loyal middle constituency pulls together when it senses that one extreme or another is attempting to normalize its position as policy for the entire church. The loyal middle reacts, marginalizing the extreme position and forcing it to decide whether it can remain within the church, but preserving the church from serious division. Weston applies his thesis to the C. A. Briggs judicial case that took place in the 1890s, and to the J. Gresham Machen challenge to the Princeton faculty in the 1930s, as well as to the Special Commission Report of 1925 and other provocations which threatened the unity of the denomination. In each crisis a loyal centrist majority pulled itself together to withstand a threat from single-interest members who wish to compel all the others to believe or behave as they do. Under the shepherding care of a loyal majority, like-minded members in a diverse constituency respectfully "compete" in the marketplace of ideas. "Competitive pluralism," Weston concludes, "under a Constitution is the best solution to

---

[721] Weston, xiii.

[722] Ibid., xii-xiii. Unfortunately, four years after Weston penned these words this policy fell out of favor when the 1991 General Assembly dissolved the reporting relationship of nineteen Presbyterian voluntary societies.

the problem of diversity."⁷²³ Hutcheson adds,

> A genuine pluralism, with a variety of activities freely supported by a variety of constituencies, held together not by political victories but by mutual acceptance, must be the direction of the future. There are plenty of data to demonstrate that voluntary funding is effective (1) where there is a freely gathered consensus on doing a particular task, and (2) where what is done reflects the intentions of the donors.⁷²⁴

The approach Weston advocates would significantly modify the unified approach to organizing mission. Weston's approach, Dawson says approvingly, "takes seriously the nature of the church as a voluntary organization, and it offers some hope of defining a useful missional role for central denominational headquarters."⁷²⁵

In his book *Change in the Church,* Robert C. Worley described two organizational paradigms, the "structuralist" and the "pluralist."⁷²⁶ In the "structuralist" or feudal paradigm it was Europe's princes, both Catholic or Protestant, who gave validity to the church in his domain. The "pluralist" paradigm began, Worley writes, in North America when the federal government disestablished the church, but offered to license its citizens to organize special-purpose associations. The "structuralist" paradigm of Europe yielded to the "pluralist" paradigm of the United States." Today "it is imperative," Worley writes, "that there be a political style that encourages the development of openness and visibility of these differences and enables minority groups to form coalitions and be active

---

[723] Ibid., 130ff.
[724] Hutcheson, "Pluralism and Consensus: Why Mainline Church Mission Budgets Are in Trouble," 624.
[725] Ibid., 625.
[726] Robert C. Worley, *Change in the Church: A Source of Hope* (Philadelphia: Westminster, 1976), 45ff.

politically without being labeled 'enemies.'"[727] In this way Worley supports the thesis of this dissertation. In a social contract, denominational leaders would recognize the right of mission agency boards to set budgets and raise funds and direct funding, thus validating the independent nature of voluntary societies. This would repair the breach after the manner of the Roman Catholic pattern. As Ralph Winter wrote,

> a single, highly centralized denominational board cannot by itself fully express the vision and energy of the whole constituency of the denomination, especially as the tradition becomes older and more diverse internally. It is likely that the most creative structural changes for U.S. denominations in the near future will be in this area.[728]

Shenango Presbytery—a Way Forward. Dawson describes how one presbytery in Pennsylvania, the Shenango Presbytery, funds its mission efforts. "First, the underlying principles are different," writes Dawson. "We have assumed that congregations do mission, not governing bodies (presbytery, synod, General Assembly). Therefore we welcome money for mission on the *donors' terms* [emphasis is in original]."[729] Dawson then recounts some success stories based on this model. "There is a high level of confidence in the churches," Dawson adds, "that money given for a particular purpose will quickly get to that place. Special funding opportunities are common practice and positively received."[730]

---

[727] Ibid., 46.
[728] Winter, "Churches Need Missions Because Modalities Need Sodalities," 199.
[729] Dawson, *A Mission Funding System for the 21st Century*, 14.
[730] Ibid.

The "fraternal workers" controversy. In his book, *Merging Mission and Unity*, Donald Black recounted how mission in the 1960s came to mean church-to-church relationships, or "mutuality in mission." The "sending" dimension has been "written off as an anachronism," wrote Beaver, and was "being phased out in a diminishing system of interchurch aid."[731] In fact, for twenty years the Presbyterian Church did not use the term "missionaries": they were re-designated "fraternal workers." Fred Wilson said the term "fraternal worker" was "an attempt to describe the assignment of a person to the management of a local national church."[732] Donald Black writes that "the term 'missionary' was changed to 'fraternal worker' as a way to express equality between those serving overseas and those being served."[733]

The term "fraternal worker" was accurate; by 1964 the work of all Presbyterian overseas personnel as administrated by national churches. By design, the Presbyterian Church suddenly had no more missionaries. D. T. Niles of Sri Lanka wrote, "To speak of a missionary is to speak in terms of the world; to speak of a fraternal worker is to speak in terms of the Church."[734] Later, the Presbyterian Church used the term "fraternal workers" and "missionaries" interchangeably because some overseas personnel,

---

[731] Beaver, "A Plea for a New Voluntarism," 2.

[732] "Conference Papers," in *Consultation on Voluntary Societies*, ed. Robert A. Blincoe (Evansville, IL: 1975, May 22-24), 22.

[733] Brown, "Structures for a Changing Church," 72. Mennonite Brethren also redesignated its missionaries as "fraternal workers." See: http://www.mennonitemission.net/Stories/BeyondOurselves/CanITrustYou/Pages/Willwethrowtheribbonaway.aspx.

[734] Daniel Thambyrajah Niles, *Upon the Earth; the Mission of God and the Missionary Enterprise of the Churches* (New York: McGraw-Hill, 1962), 264.

especially those in South Korea, wished to be known as missionaries[735] even though "fraternal workers" more accurately described their relationship to the national church.[736] By 1964 the General Assembly Minutes no longer listed the number "missionaries" *or* "fraternal workers" in its index. In fact, the Committee on Ecumenical Missions and Relations (COEMAR) report for 1964, writes Scott Sunquist, is

> an extensive analysis of the global situation and social shifts, with nothing on the work of our missionaries . . . The report discusses meetings, consultations and ecumenical gatherings in which the church is engaged, but nothing is said of missionary work.[737]

R. Pierce Beaver said that the Presbyterian Church (USA) shift to "fraternal worker" indicated that their enterprise was

> no longer, in most of its operations, still truly missionary to any great extent. It has relative little to do with direct confrontation with unbelief and non-belief. A "sending" enterprise has given way to a "lending" operation. What now exists is largely a system of interchurch aid.[738]

The policy of "mutuality in mission" brought the Presbyterian mission to Muslims to a close, because no national church in Lebanon, Iraq, Pakistan or Egypt with which the Presbyterian Church (USA) had a relationship would invite American missionaries to minister the gospel to Muslims.

---

[735] Eileen Moffett, "Mission Society! There Remains Very Much Land to Be Possessed!," *Global Church Growth Bulletin* 18, no. 1. Jan-Feb. (1981): 81ff.
[736] The Presbyterians serving the Church of Christ in Thailand are still called "fraternal workers." http://ero.cct.or.th/360.pdf
[737] Scott Sunquist and Caroline Becker Long, *A History of Presbyterian Missions, 1944-2007*, 1st ed. (Louisville: Geneva Press, 2008), 9.
[738] R. Pierce Beaver, *The Missionary between the Times*, 1st ed. (Garden City, NY: Doubleday, 1968), 80.

The "mutuality in mission" policy was intended to respect the leadership of the overseas churches, but seems to have deterred mission initiative in the Muslim world and elsewhere.[739] In 1975 the Presbyterian Church Program Agency stated:

> In response to a referral on "unevangelized people" the staff has been exploring the need and opportunity in order to recommend new strategies for evangelization that do not violate the principle of "mutuality in mission." . . . In countries where we work, evangelization and church development is done by established churches and our contributions undergird their efforts."[740]

Dawson goes on to say, "The cautious statement seems to preclude even a dialogue on such an issue being initiated by the UPCUSA. Mutuality in mission was not mutual in initiatives. The issue and mission of reaching the "unreached" was restarted outside the Program Agency."[741]

Partnering exclusively with ethnic minority national churches: an observation by Kenneth E. Bailey. One who foresaw the negative result of deterring missionaries from taking initiative was Kenneth E. Bailey. In his 1984 Don McClure Lectureship at Pittsburgh Seminary, *A Tale of Three Cities*.[742] Bailey told this story:

> Let us imagine that America was not Christian and Japan was. The Japanese then come to the United States and establish a church among the Navajo people. After one hundred years the Navajo church is well established, and the Japanese pledge

---

[739] One career missionary began his service in the Middle East in 1955 alongside 140 career Arabic-speaking Presbyterian missionaries; however, when he retired in 1995, only two who spoke Arabic remained. See Caroline N. Becker, "Missionaries Speak," in *A History of Presbyterian Missions 1944-2007* (Louisville: Geneva Press, 2008), 149.

[740] Dawson, "Counting the Cost," 45.

[741] Ibid.

[742] Kenneth E. Bailey, *A Tale of Three Cities: An Analysis of Presbyterian Mission Policies* (Pasadena: Presbyterian Center for Mission Studies, 1989).

to work exclusively in partnership with the Navajo in America. "We will do nothing within the fifty states except at your specific request and under your direct authority," the church leaders back in Japan promise. After a period of time the following dialogue occurs:

"What about witness and service to the Hopi people?" ask the Japanese. "The Hopi are our traditional enemies," comes the answer.

"Well, then, can we start work with white America?" say the Japanese. "White America?" the Navajo reply. "White Americans took our land, killed our grandfathers and shamelessly broke the treaties they made with us. White America is not on our agenda."

"Very well," continue the Japanese. "Perhaps we can do something for the Eskimos." "Eskimos," counter the Navajo, "are also native Americans. But our people look on them as inferiors. Our people will not be able to understand why resources available for the Navajo are being spent on Eskimos."

"The deeper question then must be put to the Japanese. Is it fair," Bailey asks, "to place on the Navajo churches the burden of providing the vision for witness and ministry for all of America? Would we want a similar burden placed upon us?"[743] Regarding this policy—that is, relying on ethnic minority church partners in countries such as Pakistan and Lebanon to evangelize great populations of Muslims —David Dawson comments, "This was going to be hard to do in countries where our partner church or institutions were small, highly ethnic or very young."[744] R. Pierce Beaver made this point when he said that the church in each land considers itself "to be sovereign there"; but "there is no church large or small, ancient or very young, in any country today which appears thoroughly adequate to its responsibilities in evangelism and ministry."[745]

---

[743] Ibid., 10. The entire lecture can be read online at www.pcms-usa.org.
[744] Dawson, "Counting the Cost," 45.
[745] Beaver, "A Plea for a New Voluntarism," 5.

Partnering exclusively with national churches: an observation by Ralph D. Winter. Ralph Winter wrote that the overseas church—"that small beachhead on the shores of the vast, exploding non-Western population"[746]—is a positive new fact of our time. But, Winter cautions,

> Some agencies of mission are so enthralled by this new fact that they are busily modifying their "initiative" structures so as to focus non-paternalistically and "responsively" upon the one sheep that has been found, rather than on the ninety-nine that are still lost. Church-to-church "relations" are appropriate for those peoples within whose midst an active, evangelizing national church exists. But "missions" are no less appropriate for the vast ethnic groups in whose midst there is not yet any adequate national church, much less internal mission sodalities reaching out to undertake the specialized tasks of mission. This fact has the gravest consequences for our fullest response in mission in this hour.[747]

Missiologically, Winter argues, "it would be far better to denote church movements by their culture base then their country."[748] The logic of granting to the national church leaders—all of whom may be part of a minority culture in that nation—the authority to accept or proscribe mission initiatives arising from an overseas partner would create unrealistic expectations that the nation's majority culture and other minority cultures can be reached only through partnership with the national church.

Partnership with national churches; an observation by Richard Shaull. Richard Shaull spoke at Princeton Seminary, on the occasion of his installation as professor of ecumenics and mission in 1963:

---

[746] Winter, "Churches Need Missions Because Modalities Need Sodalities," 200.
[747] Ibid.
[748] Ralph D. Winter, "Mission in the 1990s: Two Views," *International Bulletin of Missionary Research* 14, no. 3 (1990): 101.

Theologically speaking, the church may be a missionary community. In actual fact, however, it has become a major hindrance to the work of mission. . . Our ecclesiastical organizations are not the most striking examples of dynamic and flexible armies which direct their energies primarily toward witness and service to those outside. Missionary boards and organizations, in their justified desire to turn over increasing responsibility to their daughter churches, have become so bound in relatively static ecclesiastical organizations that, with rare exceptions, they have shown little possibility of thinking imaginatively about the vast new frontiers of mission or becoming engaged in new ventures on them."[749]

Former Presbyterian missionary Glenn Reed put it plainly, "We lost our initiative and the independents took up what we discarded."[750] But the errors of the past can be corrected in the future. The Presbyterian Church (USA) has at times turned to mission societies to provide the required national mission partner.[751] In this way the Presbyterian Church maintains its commitment to partnering, but now looks on occasion for those partners in mission societies.

The Presbyterian Order for World Evangelization.[752] In 1974 the General Assembly Mission Council recognized the Presbyterian Order for World Evangelization (POWE)

---

[749] M. Richard Shaull, "The Form of the Church in the Modern Diaspora," *Princeton Seminary Bulletin* (March 1964, reprinted in *New Theology No 2*, ed. Martin E. Marty and Dean G. Peerman (New York: Macmillan, 1965), 266-67 quoted in Anderson, "American Protestants in Pursuit of Missions: 1886-1986." 110

[750] Bailey, 13.

[751] Some mission agencies with which the Presbyterian Church (USA) partners today are: the Arabic Communication Center, Middle East Media, Pakistan Bible Correspondence School, Iranian Students International, Berlin Missionswerk, Evangelical Theological Seminary (Cairo), and Central Asia Development Agency, Summer Institute of Linguistics (Wycliffe) and the Wolof Church Partnership.

[752] The POWE's website is www.reconsecration.org, where visitors can read Ralph D. Winter's paper, "Reconsecration to a Wartime Lifestyle." In addition to beginning the POWE, Dr. Winter began, in the early 1970s, the Presbyterian Center for Mission Studies, Presbyterians United for Missions Advance, the Presbyterian Frontier Fellowship and the Association of Presbyterian Missionaries. All of them reported to the Presbyterian Church General Assembly through the Chapter 28 provision of the Book of Order.

under the "Right to Organize" provision for special interest groups.[753] Since 1991 the POWE has been recognized by the Internal Revenue Service as a religious order (ironically the very year that the Presbyterian Church General assembly voted to delete the "Right to Organize" provision). The POWE has two purposes: 1) "The evangelization of all the world's people groups, especially those which remain outside any active evangelistic effort." 2) "The cultivation of a lifestyle which prioritizes world evangelization." The POWE is not a sending agency but an association, like the CMS, of members who have voluntarily give their discretionary money away and live on a missionary budget. Dr. Ralph Winter's founding idea is that the POWE is the Presbyterian chapter of the Order for World Evangelization (OWE); members of other denominations are encouraged to begin their own chapters. The POWE's members pass over a high barrier in order to join: they "reconsecrate their lives to a wartime lifestyle."[754] Members of the POWE believe they can most effectively achieve this good when they are accountable to one another to give away their discretionary money to a warrantable cause.

4.7.6 The Conciliar Church Disadvantage

Since 1961, when the WCC absorbed the International Missionary Council (IMC), the WCC "modality" has decided which initiatives its mission arm may begin. If Herbert Workman is correct—that not once has the Catholic Church central hierarchy send out a

---

[753] The provision was reassigned to Chapter 9 at the time of the UPCUSA and PCUS merger in 1983.
[754] www.reconsecration.org

mission effort,[755]—then for the Protestant WCC to take control of the IMC was, as Mottinger said, "disastrous."[756] Arthur Glasser adds,

> Mission societies were seen as no longer needed. Enthusiasts coined a new slogan: "The Church is mission!" . . . This dismissal of parachurch agencies as irrelevant reflected abysmal indifference to two thousand years of church history with its long record of the fruitful organized labors of specific missionary vocations.[757]

The missionary involvement of the conciliar churches movement, as churches affiliated with the World Council of Churches have come to be called, went "almost immediately into sharp decline."[758]

---

[755] Workman, 12.
[756] Mottinger, 2.
[757] Arthur F. Glasser and Donald Anderson McGavran, *Contemporary Theologies of Mission* (Grand Rapids: Baker Book House, 1983), 95.
[758] Ibid.

(Figure 26)

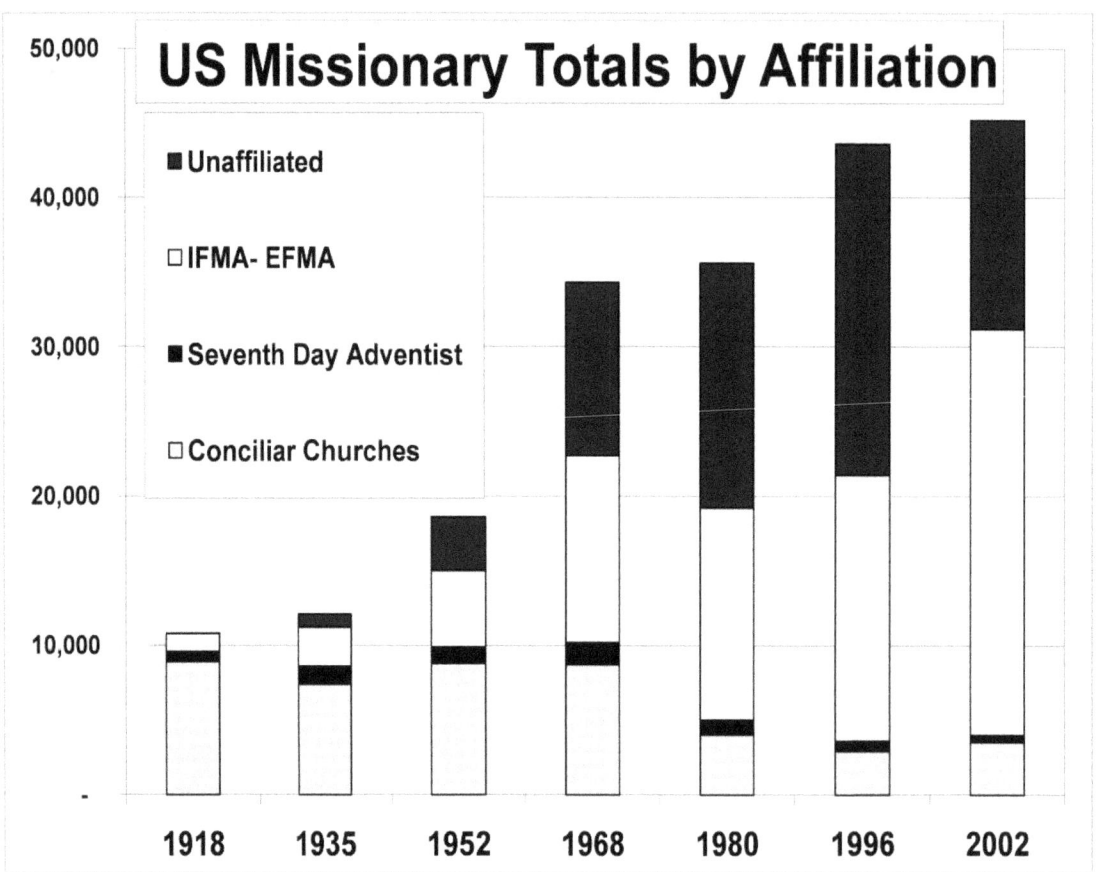

Figure 26. US Missionary Totals by Affiliation 1918-2002[759]

The conciliar church mission force is represented by the part of the graph nearest the base line. In 1918 the conciliar churches had 8900 missionaries, or 82% of the total. The conciliar churches had 8700 missionaries in 1968, but now this number fell to 25% of the total. The percentage fell to 7.5% in 2002 while the total US missionary force swelled to 45,600. Several thousand missionaries serving in non-conciliar mission agencies are from

---

[759] Chart created from data in Robert T. Coote, "Shifts in the North American Protestant Full-Time Missionary Community," *International Bulletin of Missionary Research* 29, no. 1 (2005): 12-13.

conciliar churches, though the presentation of exact data is beyond the scope of this dissertation.

How Mission Credenda Becomes Mission Agenda. Church leaders want to inspire their members to change the world. For example, at a Synod of the Pacific missions rally in February 1997, I listened to General Assembly Moderator John Buchanan wish aloud to the gathering for mission orders in the Presbyterian Church that would bring Presbyterians to work and live in decaying urban neighborhoods. Buchanan asked, "What if certain Presbyterians made a three year commitment to a mission order, and lived out their faith in poverty-wracked neighborhoods?"[760] He was saying, "We've got to do something!" through voluntary associations. By finding like-minded people, Buchanan or anyone can start such an initiative (though no headquarters ever has, according to Herbert Workman[761]). Keith Phillips started one—World Impact[762]—in 1972. It would be simple for the Presbyterian Church or any congregation or presbytery to negotiate a partnership agreement with World Impact or other special-interest associations.[763] Buchanan's wish can come true. So can a dream that Donald Black, Presbyterian Church (USA) mission executive during the 1960s and early 1970s, described at a staff meeting in December,

---

[760] John Buchanan, "Moderator's Address," (Synod Missions Rally, Bel Air Presbyterian Church, Los Angeles, CA February: 1997).
[761] Workman, 12.
[762] See www.worldimpact.org. Accessed November 2006.
[763] See Viv Grigg's article, "Apostolic Orders Among the Poor," http://www.urbana.org/articles/apostolic-orders-among-the-poor.

1972, when Black presented a remarkable paper, "Missionary Orders in the UPCUSA."[764] Here is what Black envisioned (I quote in full for the historical record):

> Appointment to missionary service under the Board of Foreign Missions and then the Commission on Ecumenical Mission and Relations had some characteristics of joining a missionary order.
>
> Over the past two decades these characteristics have been disappearing. The characteristics of the former pattern are still available, but not within the denominational structures. Independent missions and efforts to establish Protestant orders are signs of this concern. We find that a small but growing number of United Presbyterians of varied ages and backgrounds are expressing their eagerness to experience: 1) The discipline of belonging to a community of people covenanted together in such fashion that loyalty to one another within the fellowship is matched only by loyalty to the cause or task being undertaken at some point in the world; 2) The discipline of economic stringency where the goal is simple subsistence, ideally at the level of one's national colleagues; 3) The freedom, born of these disciplines, to be both personally and corporately highly mobile and thoroughly flexible. Can the United Presbyterian Church provide within its fellowship an alternative to present support patterns—available to those who feel a loyalty to the church and to a different approach to service? Should such an approach emerge, how would it be formed? What part could the present church structures play in encouraging it?
>
> The Program Agency can explore the possibilities and invite people to participate in a process by which a truly ecumenical, international missionary order can be devised. It can revise its own personnel policies and procedures so that those of its members who choose to may serve within this covenant community while retaining full relationship to the United Presbyterian Church. For the Program Agency to be an alert, sensitive observer of what may be emerging spontaneously is the essential first step. The second is the challenge: to be creative and supportive in appropriate ways and times in a movement which will run high risk but holds great promise for Christ's mission on earth (The CMS model warrants study).[765]

This "alternative to present support patterns" that are "not now available in denominational structures" would, if recognized by church administrations, achieve this

---

[764] Donald Black, "Missionary Orders in the UPCUSA." Reprinted in Watson, *Mission Orders and the Presbyterian Church*, 24-25.
[765] Ibid.

dissertation's desired symbiosis. Black's proposal may be acted on tomorrow; always we can begin again. "The restoration of the church," Bonhoeffer wrote to his brother,

> will surely come from a new kind of monasticism which will have nothing in common with the old but a life of uncompromising adherence to the Sermon on the Mount in imitation of Christ. I believe it is now time to rally people together for this.[766]

In Bishop Richard B. Wilke's pastoral critique of the Methodist Church, *And Are We Yet Alive?*, the author outlines the problem of declining membership facing his denomination. It was 1986 and the decline had continued for 22 years. But in his church in Wichita, Kansas, there was numerical growth. One of the places growth occurred was in the choir; it had tripled. Wilkes related how the choir director and the singers came to understand themselves as a committed community, studying the Bible and caring for one another in specific ways. The choir director asked people who were not in the church to join the choir; they started in the choir and subsequently joined the church. A church choir, of course, is a sodality. Thus, renewal in Wilke's church started with a special-interest group, the church choir.[767]

---

[766] From a letter to Karl-Friedrich Bonhoeffer, January 14, 1935 reprinted in Eberhard Bethge and Victoria Barnett, *Dietrich Bonhoeffer: Theologian, Christian, Man for His Times; a Biography*, Rev. ed. (Minneapolis: Fortress Press, 2000), 462. Bonhoeffer believed that the perilous times in which he and his colleagues lived necessitated "the creation of something for Protestants which, for centuries, they could only find under Roman Catholic auspices." 461. His biographer says that, while Bonhoeffer had contemplated the communal life for many years, his interest was academic until the value of organizing such a "community" in "a settlement" became what the church needed most during the Third Reich.

[767] Richard B. Wilke, *And Are We yet Alive? The Future of the United Methodist Church* (Nashville: Abingdon Press, 1986), 77-78. Church renewal often begins with the renewal of sodalities. For example, arriving at the monastery at Citeaux in 1112, where a Benedictine named Stephen Harding was abbot at the monastery, but where sickness had struck down most of the residents, a youth of twenty-two knocked on the door. With him were 30 companions, five of them his own brothers. Renewal was afoot; Workman writes, "That youth was the great medieval prophet and preacher, St. Bernard, for many years the

The outpouring of renewal has to be cupped with two hands, the one being liberality in licensing of special-interest associations by church administrations and the other the forming of associations themselves. This is the advantage enjoyed by the Catholic Church; by licensing the monastic associations to organize themselves and to hive off new mission efforts, the Catholic Church has achieved the desired symbiosis. But "by cutting off the orders," Winter suggested, "the Protestant body virtually put . . . renewal . . . out of reach."[768] Thus, Mark Noll could begin his essay "The Monastic Rescue of the Church" with a sweeping statement, "The rise of monasticism was, after Christ's commission, to his disciples, the most important—and in many ways, the most beneficial—institutional event in the history of Christianity."[769] It is no trouble for me to remind the church of its once and future advantage.

4.8. Mission Policies and Related Structural Issues—Findings in Seven Denominations

In this section I describe the policy of seven church administrations to special-interest mission associations: Anglican, Dutch Reformed, Episcopal, Quaker, Methodist, American Baptist and Lutheran Church Missouri Synod (LCMS). (The case of the Presbyterian Church USA has been taken up separately in 4.7 and 5.1 of this

---

uncrowned pope of the Church, almost the dictator of Europe—by whose influence and enthusiasm the order so grew that within forty years it had founded one hundred and sixty daughter-houses, sixty-eight of which were filiations of the most illustrious offshoot of Bernard's own foundation at Clairvaux." Workman, 239-40.

[768] Winter, "Protestant Mission Societies and the 'Other Protestant Schism'," 198.

[769] Mark A. Noll, "The Monastic Rescue of the Church: Benedict's Rule," in *Turning Points: Decisive Moments in the History of Christianity* (Grand Rapids: Baker, 1997), 84.

dissertation.) The LCMS has adopted what I am advocating in this dissertation, a new social contract relating the dozens of mission societies to ecclesiastical structures.

4.8.1 Anglican Mission Policy—The Church Mission Society

In 1975tThe director of the Church Mission Society (CMS), John V. Taylor (d. 2001) gave two historic addresses at "The Consultation on Voluntary Societies" held at First Presbyterian Church of Evanston, Illinois. He spoke to mission executives representing four mainline denominations[770]—Presbyterian, Episcopal, Methodist, and Baptist— on the relationship of the CMS to the Anglican Church. Taylor's talks were taped, then transcribed, but never published until now.[771] Taylor lectured on two subjects that relate to this thesis: 1) A relatively few members in pluralistic churches organize themselves into special-purpose associations and 2) ecclesiastical leaders should recognize and protect the autonomy of these associations.

Lay members of the Church of England, including William Wilberforce, founded the CMS in 1799, just seven years after Carey published his *Enquiry*. It was their stated ambition "to found a church society within the church" ("There is the principle of incorporation," commented Taylor), "without a charter from the crown" ("There is the

---

[770] For the historical record, present were Gary Demarest, Ralph Winter, Fred Wilson, Charles Mellis (Presbyterian); David Seamands (Methodist); Samuel van Culin, Frederick Phinney, Boone Porter, Walter Hannum (Episcopal); Ralph Covell (Baptist); and Jim Richardson, Paul Suzuki, and Ernie Lewis.

[771] John V. Taylor, "An Historical Comparison of American and British Voluntary Societies," in *Consultation on Voluntary Societies*, ed. Robert A. Blincoe (First Presbyterian Church, Evanston, IL: May 22-24, 1975). Unpublished manuscript. Taylor's paper will be published for the first time in the book referred to at the beginning of this dissertation, "Design of Project Given by Ralph D. Winter" (section 1.3).

interest in a certain withdrawal, a certain declaring of separate options").[772] The independent nature of the CMS gave it an advantage, Taylor said, over the older Society for the Propagation of the Gospel. "By creating a plurality of bodies, not subject to the same determinants," Taylor said, "it gives you your freedom—you increase in options."[773] Max Warren, who preceded Taylor as director of the CMS, had said the same thing:

> That is where, as I see it, the *Voluntary Principle* becomes important. The Church, *qua* Institution, has manifold tasks to discharge, not least the conservation of all that has been achieved in history, the guarding of the Faith; and the continuing ministry to the Christian community . . . [But] mission, understood as evangelism, calls for almost infinite *flexibility*, because no two situations are alike. And flexibility demands, in practice, special organs for action and a vital factor, a readiness to take initiatives which may be mistaken! Official bodies have an inbuilt hesitation about every taking risks [emphasis is in the original.]![774]

Taylor admired the advantage that voluntary societies afforded the Catholic Church during the era of the Crusades:

> You might say that during the Middle Ages, Christendom had its official line with regard to Islam. The official line was the Crusades. There were no other options, and all the determinants were such as to pressurize Christian people of Western Europe into a crusading attitude—a crusading solution to the problem. Then Francis of Assisi appeared, representing an alternative structure—the Catholic Order. Although a tiny minority in the whole situation, the coming into being of the Friars was highly significant. They were expressive of new attitudes about almost everything in that society, and specifically they were able to offer an alternative solution to the problem of Islam, one which we embrace as the essential missionary solution. It was Francis who made that fantastic Franciscan

---

[772] Ibid., 4.
[773] Ibid., 1.
[774] Max Warren's February 22, 1977 letter to Harvey Hoekstra. Quoted in Hoekstra, 45.

gesture, which only he could have made, of going right to the courts of Saladin;[775] and it was Francis later on who had the incredibly hopeless, but optimistic idea of one-man or two-man missions into Islam itself. It is a fabulous story, a story of high idealism and hopeless logistics. But one thanks God that there emerged a second option. It did not separate itself from Christendom, but within the body it offered an alternative option.[776]

Governance and Tension with Anglican Church Leadership. At the Consultation on Voluntary Societies, John V. Taylor spoke about ecclesiastical opposition to the CMS:

> The Church of England, on its side, was rather cool to this new organization, the CMS. There was considerable—very considerable—opposition at the beginning. This was true because the founders of the Society were already incurring that displeasure through being evangelicals of the Church of England. At that stage, evangelicals were a powerful body because they had many very powerful laymen who owed their conversion to the Evangelical Awakening. So right from the start the Society had its members of Parliament. I don't mean to say that they represented the CMS in Parliament, but people deeply concerned with the CMS were also members in Parliament, like Lord Wilberforce. But the CMS was definitely under a cloud from the point of view of the establishment. It was years before any bishop would admit a support of the CMS, and three or four did so, and then, after 40 years the CMS was at last recognized.[777]

Taylor contrasted the advantage of the independent CMS with the hindrances encountered by his colleagues in the older Anglican mission society, the Society for the Propagation of the Gospel (SPG):

> That first society, the SPG, had a royal charter and from the very start felt itself to be inherently part of the established church. Every one of its missionaries was given a sort of valedictory license by the Archbishop of Canterbury. That pattern has continued right up the present time. Had it remained the *only* Church of England missionary society, it would have been almost indistinguishable from the

---

[775] Actually, Saladin had died in 1193 when Francis was 11 years old. Francis addressed Sultan Malik al-Kamil at Damietta, Egypt. The year was 1219.
[776] Taylor, 1.
[777] Ibid., 6.

kind of structure we have in the Methodist Missionary Society in England, which is to all intents and purposes a department of the Church.[778]

Further contrasting the experience of the SPG to the independent CMS, Taylor said,

> A second missionary society, the CMS, came into being without a charter from the crown, subordinate to church authority (you see again the incorporation element) but upon the basis of voluntary action. There you see the voluntary principle in action, with a sort of tension, equipoised, if you like, which is absolutely central to our understanding of the voluntary society, and the CMS in particular. Henry Venn envisioned that the CMS, to be successful, must maintain a governing body that existed on a voluntary principle; and it could hold together its staff of missionaries by no stronger bond. That was a very interesting insight. That was part of Venn's argument.[779]

The Value of the Independent Critic. Taylor reminded his listeners of the contribution made by independent critics. In the following story Taylor himself confronted the British government over an issue of human rights in Africa. Taylor said:

> In my own time I can remember very well towards the end of the Mau Mau independence wars in Kenya, the British were rounding up vast numbers of Kikuyu into what were called "rehabilitation camps." The CMS became aware of the quite deplorable conditions and the treatment of prisoners in those camps under the heading of what was called "rehabilitation." After many attempts to get the Colonial Office to recognize this situation, we finally published a "white paper" describing what we knew to be true, and got a very wide circulation in

---

[778] Ibid.

[779] Ibid. Henry Venn (1796-1873) directed the work of the Church Missionary Society from 1841. (Venn's father, John Venn, was rector of the Clapham church and a member of the reform group, the Clapham Sect. Henry Venn was a contemporary of Rufus Anderson, director of the American Board of Commissioners for Foreign Mission.) As CMS director, Venn gave his reasons for rigorously protecting the autonomy—he called it "the Voluntary Principle"—of the CMS, "by which," Max Warren commented, "men and women agreed not only on the goal but on the means to reach it and were united to pursue it." See Henry Venn, *To Apply the Gospel; Selections from the Writings of Henry Venn* (Grand Rapids: Eerdmans, 1971), 105. This meant liberty to hold meetings anywhere, prudence and forbearance being necessary to not give offense. Thus, in 1871 when the Diocese of Salisbury resolved to "place the management of the Church Missionary Association and all other voluntary associations of Churchmen under the charge of a Synod elected for a variety of Church purposes," Venn opposed it, arguing that this new arrangement would place men over the CMS who would not be "specially interested in the Church Missionary Society or acquainted with its principles or its work." Ibid. 133. Venn persuaded the Diocese to drop its proposal.

Britain. Our action angered the Colonial Office enormously. It angered the Archbishop of Nairobi enormously. All of that you would expect. But here was a Society that was not obliged to the same determinants. In other words, it was free at an early stage to make that kind of protest. And we should always want to cling to that freedom, I think.[780]

"That is a nice balance between the voluntary and the official," Taylor commented, "The official must be angry; the official cannot encourage that kind of action. And the official Church could not have done that kind of thing."[781]

CMS Summary: "The essence of the voluntary society is to maintain its freedom." "It is of the essence of the voluntary society," Taylor said, "to maintain its freedom against the embrace of the central authority."[782] He said in conclusion,

> The voluntary missionary societies are derived from their conviction that, in practice, the institutional church does not consistently demonstrate the same degree of enthusiasm for its own outreach in mission. This is true not only of the historical moment in which some of the voluntary societies were born, but it's true of the whole history of the church. Even today, when a diocese or central executive body of a church finds its income diminishing, the first cuts are normally made in the area of outreach. Moreover the protracted processes of synodical forms of church government do not permit the immediate, quick action and response which is open to the voluntary society.[783]

4.8.2 The Reformed Church of America Mission Policy

I asked church leaders in five U.S. denominations how they start new mission initiatives. The question I e-mailed each of them was:

---

[780] Taylor, 9.
[781] Ibid., 10.
[782] Ibid.
[783] Ibid., 7-8.

Suppose your office wanted to begin sending missionaries to Muslims in a country where you presently do not have work—say, in Morocco or Iraq—how would your office go about doing this? In other words, how would you proceed to begin mission work in a new location?[784]

I heard back from all five church leaders, and followed these up with further emails or a phone conversation. An intriguing pattern emerged: Each of these denomination—Reformed, Presbyterian, Methodist, Quaker and Episcopal—defined its mission as "partnering with existing national churches;" but each has made allowance for members to form outside-the-headquarters structures that initiate missions "where there is no partner."[785] Each denomination understands its mission in terms of its relationship to an overseas national church, there was a reaction by some of its members to make up for what is lacking by starting an additional mission sending structures. These new structures sometimes begin against the will of the centralized denomination, though, as we will see, the Lutheran Church Missouri Synod has cordially resolved its differences with voluntary structures.[786]

---

[784] Robert A Blincoe, "Desired Symbiosis: Church and Mission Structures," *International Journal of Frontier Missions* 19, no. 3 (2002): 43.

[785] I asked a staff member of the Presbyterian Church (USA) Worldwide Ministries Division to describe the means of initiating new overseas missions "where there is no partner." He replied, "Our approach is generally to find a local church partner to work within the new area. We don't go in alone to initiate work." The spokesperson added, "However, if there is no local church to initiate a mission, or if it is too dangerous for the existing local church, or if governmental restrictions prohibit our working with a local church, then we would find a local Christian NGO." In other words, where there is no partner church, or where the minority church in a Muslim country cannot risk a mission outreach, other creative partnerships are being developed. This is a welcome corrective. Telephone interview, April 2002

[786] TeSelle writes, "In the nineteenth century it was the 'liberals' who defended the voluntary principle and the 'conservatives' who championed the ecclesiastical principle. In the 1930s it was the conservatives who objected to the church's attempting to bind the conscience and asserted the right to give free will gifts rather than taxes... Disputes over 'voluntary organizations' are not linked, then, to points on the theological spectrum." TeSelle, 6-7.

We begin with the mission of the Reformed Church of America. "The Reformed Church in America," wrote Wesley Granberg-Michaelson, "began as a missionary outpost."[787] He references the arrival in the new world of Dominie Jonas Michaelius in 1628, chaplain to the Dutch West Indies Company. But to characterize his ministry as "simply a chaplaincy," Granberg-Michaelson writes, "is dismissive of the missional DNA that is embedded in the core of that work—and of our historic denomination."[788] A frank assessment of the sagging witness of the in the late 20th century today follows, and then: "Something profound has happened to the place of the Christian faith in North America. The church needs to enter a new missional age. There is no other clear way to put this."[789] Unfortunately, in the fine appeal that follows this introduction, no reference is made to the "enabling technology" that Carey proposed and that Reformed missionary pioneers like Samuel Zwemer adopted

Samuel Zwemer Proposes to Start a Mission Society. The most well-known voluntary structure in the Reformed Church of America (RCA) was the American Arabian Mission. Samuel Zwemer and James Cantine started this mission after leadership in the RCA determined that the church did not have the funds to help them. Ira Scudder relates the story:

> The inspiring genius of the Arabian mission was Professor John G. Lansing, the Gardner Sage Professor of Old Testament Language and Exegesis at the Seminary

---

[787] Van Gelder, *The Missional Church and Denominations : Helping Congregations Develop a Missional Identity*, 265.
[788] Ibid.
[789] Ibid., 266.

of the Reformed Church in New Brunswick, New Jersey. It was his dream, his spiritual child. He it was who planted the seed; he it was who defended its organization as an autonomous mission project against those who would have let it languish for lack of official adoption; and he it was who marshaled its support.[790]

The RCA Board turns down Zwemer's Mission Proposal. On May 23, 1889, Lansing, Cantine, Phelps and Zwemer presented their plan to the Reformed Church Board of Foreign Missions. The board was already severely in debt with heavy commitments in India, China, and Japan. Scudder writes,

> The board "declined to assume responsibility in the matter." There the dream might well have died. But Lansing put the dream in writing, announcing the organization of a mission effort independent of the Reformed Church. "A responsibility Divinely imposed is not discharged by any admission of existing human difficulty . . . When God calls we must obey, not object." On this principle the fraternity proceeded to devise an "undenominational" plan for the Arabian Mission.[791]

John Beardslee recounted how the mission began:

> The swirl of student zeal blew into the narthexes of the mainline churches. Not that the fresh wind was uniformly welcomed; Lansing et al. comprised an autonomous group that the organized church was not ready to touch. "Lack of funds" was said to be the reason. So Zwemer and Cantine brought into being the American Arabian Mission, members of which pledged to give financial support.[792]

---

[790] Lewis R. Scudder, *The Arabian Mission's Story: In Search of Abraham's Other Son*, The Historical Series of the Reformed Church in America (Grand Rapids: Eerdmans, 1998), 135-136.

[791] Ibid., 141-142.

[792] John Beardslee, "American Arabian Mission Centennial Address," (New Brunswick Seminary, New Brunswick, NJ: April 1989). Unpublished. I was present at the Centennial as a reporter for the Zwemer Institute.

The two enthusiastic students raised money for each other: James Cantine raised money for Zwemer and Zwemer for Cantine.[793] On October 16, 1890 James Cantine departed for Arabia. "Zwemer and Lansing, meanwhile, continued to develop the financial base of the mission, with Zwemer concentrating his efforts in the Midwest and Lansing (as his now deteriorating health allowed) continued to work on his contacts in the East."[794]

The RCA Board Changes its Mind. Zwemer followed Cantine to Arabia in 1891. In 1894 the Reformed Church Board changed its mind and adopted the Arabian Mission as its own.[795] There was no cost to the Board, as the revenue needed for the mission was assured by private donors. This sequence is a familiar one in the RCA: John Piet, professor of missions in a Reformed Church college, told Ralph D. Winter that *every* RCA overseas mission initiative began as a voluntary effort outside the government of the church.[796] Gathering all of the RCA mission efforts together, Winter wrote in his "Protestant Mission Societies":

> The Reformed Church in America as a "church in mission" directly sponsors mission work in 24 countries. *In not a single case* were these locations *pioneered by denominational board initiatives*. In every case, *informal* initiative spearheaded the initial activity and the denominational board later shouldered

---
[793] Ibid.
[794] Scudder, 146.
[795] Ibid., xvii.
[796] Author's interview with Ralph D. Winter, autumn 2002. Piet was probably referring to pioneers like John and Harriet Scudder, who sailed for Ceylon in 1819 under the ABCFM, and Guido Verbeck and two medical companions, Samuel Robbins Brown and Danne B. Simmons, who organized themselves for the purpose of sailing to Nagasaki in 1859, thus opening the Reformed Church mission work in Japan. Ibid. 131, 134

ongoing responsibility. This is not to be considered ominous but does underscore the crucial importance of allowing breathing space for initiatives too small to gain a 51% approval in a democratic church body.[797]

Thus, every RCA mission apparently began when "restless people seeking to deal with problems that were not being successfully coped with by existing institutions escaped the old formats and were driven to invent new forms of organizations."[798]

In 1989 I attended the Zwemer Centennial Lectures at New Brunswick Theological Seminary. John Buteyn, director of the RCA mission 1962-1980 said in his prepared address, and later restated to me in private, that the RCA should have inclined itself more favorably to the initiatives proposed by its churches and members. "A smaller group of workers, with specialized focus, might have been able to initiate new ministries in some of those sensitive places, without burdening the national partner constituencies of the Reformed Church of America."[799] This dissertation is an effort to speed the day when church leaders recognize and regulate the initiatives that their members are forming or joining.

4.8.3 The Methodist Church Mission Policy

Early American Methodist mission societies were the Methodist Missionary Society (1819) and the New York Female Missionary Society (1825). Others formed, and in 1844

---

[797] Winter, "Protestant Mission Societies and the 'Other Protestant Schism'," 205-206.
[798] Bornstein, 4. Speaking of "inventing new forms of organizations", James Cantine operated the "Freed Slave School of the American Arabian Mission" between1899 and 1901, and Zwemer began a hospital in Bahrain that celebrated its centennial in 2005.
[799] Robert A Blincoe, "Quote by John Buteyn," in *Samuel Zwemer Centennial Report* (Samuel Zwemer Institute, Pasadena, California: May, 1989).

a new central structure, the General Missionary Committee, supervised their oversight,. Then, in 1872, the General Conference "transformed all voluntary societies in the church into denominational agencies," a change which started the church, Russell Richey argued, "down the road of centralized bureaucratization."[800] Dana L. Robert writes that the pioneering, restless types "began going outside the denomination to fulfill their missionary callings."[801] Methodist missionaries Helen and John Springer, for example, traveled from Zambia to Angola in the early part of the 20th century to found a string of mission stations "despite the explicit disapproval of the mission board."[802] But the Springers "raised such popular support for a mission in the Congo that the mission board capitulated to public sentiment."[803] Later, in 1936, John Springer was elected to serve as bishop of Africa.[804] Dana Robert comments:

> In John and Helen Springer's struggle to establish the Congo Mission, we see how spiritual conviction and entrepreneurial success—undergirded by grassroots support—permitted individuals to force changes in denominational priorities. The noteworthy successes of Methodists missions have often relied on a healthy if uncomfortable tension between expansion and consolidation, individual entrepreneurship and organization.[805]

---

[800] Richey, Russell E. "Methodism: Essentially a Missionary Movement, Domestic and Foreign?" unpublished paper presented at ISAE Missionary Impulse in north American History Conference, June 4, 1998, 23. Cited by Dana Lee Robert, "Innovation and Consolidation in American Methodist Mission History," in *World Mission in the Wesleyan Spirit*, ed. Darrell L.Whiteman and Gerald H. Anderson, American Society of Missilogy Series (Franklin, TN: Providence House Publishers, 2009), 130.
[801] Ibid.
[802] Ibid., 131.
[803] Ibid.
[804] Ibid.
[805] Ibid. Dana L. Robert credits persistent Methodist pioneers with opening the new fields of the Methodist Church, despite efforts by the mission board to deter them. See section 4.8.3.

During the 1960s the number of Methodist missionaries was falling. David Seamands said, "In 1960 there were 1575 missionaries, in 1971 there were 1070. We began 1974 with 841, and have suffered constant decline in income."[806] Seamands and other Methodists organized The Evangelical Missions Consortium on February 6-8, 1974 in Dallas for the purpose of raising new missionary funds and reversing the downward trend.[807] Seamands could not know in 1974 that the decline would continue. In 1980 this Consortium considered "becoming a separate sending agency in the United Methodist Church."[808] "It is time once again," the Methodist R. Pierce Beaver had said, "to look to voluntary association and action for rescue."[809] Finally, in October 1983, Gerald Anderson, a Methodist missionary and then for many years editor of the *International Bulletin of Missionary Research*, proposed starting a "second mission agency" for United Methodists. Anderson wrote,

> It seems clear that, over the last decade, the World Division of the General Board of Global Ministries has been unable—some would say unwilling—to serve the whole denomination as an agency for expressing our global witness and service. Unfortunately, there is increasingly widespread sentiment in the church that the World Division is theologically imprecise, not truly holistic in mission, and unresponsive to the pluralism in the denomination.[810]

---

[806] David Seamands, "Methodist Report," in *Consultation on Voluntary Societies*, ed. Robert A. Blincoe (Evansville, IL: 1974), 1.

[807] David A. Seamands correspondence to the United Presbyterian Church Center for Mission Studies, January 31, 1974.

[808] V. E. Maybray, "Letter to Frank Satterberg, United Presbyterian Center for Missions Studies," (Pasadena: Evangelical Missions Council, September 3, 1980).

[809] Beaver, "A Plea for a New Voluntarism," 5.

[810] Gerald H. Anderson, "Why We Need a Second Mission Agency," in *The Factors That Confront Us and the Faith That Compels Us* (Dallas: 1984, February), 1.

Consequently, Anderson said, "a good deal of money and personnel from our church is going to other mission agencies outside the United Methodist Church."[811] If the denomination was unresponsive to the wishes of a minority of its members, he went on to say, the Methodist church needed an independent mission agency. "I propose," Anderson said,

> that this new agency be created by and accountable to the General Conference as a voluntary, international, missionary society. It would be voluntary in that it would be dependent on voluntary support from churches and individuals. The model I have in mind is that of the Church Mission Society of the Anglican Church, and perhaps some of the Roman Catholic missionary societies, such as the Society of the Divine Word.[812]

The Mission Society Founded. Some members of the Board of Global Ministries opposed Anderson; but others, as well as some bishops and Methodist missionaries, including David Seamands, joined him. Thus, a second Methodist mission agency, The Mission Society of the United Methodist Church formed in 1984. In 2005 it shortened its name to The Mission Society. Today, it has more than 200 missionaries serving in 35 countries,[813] initiating mission "where there is no partner," such as in the Muslim countries of the former Soviet Union. Dana L. Robert says that The Mission Society recalls "the spirit of entrepreneurial voluntarism" that has "consistently shaped the history of Methodist missions."[814] In her article, "Innovation and Consolidation in Methodist Mission History," Dana Robert writes that when The Mission Society was founded "critics

---

[811] Ibid., 2.
[812] Ibid., 3.
[813] www.themissionsociety.org.
[814] Robert, "Innovation and Consolidation in American Methodist Mission History," 128.

condemned it as a violation of the *Book of Discipline* and a retro-evangelistic movement that would perpetuate missionary paternalism." But, in 2008 "delegates at the United Methodist General Conference passed a resolution praising The Mission Society for its perseverance, and urging cooperation between the Society and official agencies of the denomination."[815] This is a move in the right direction.

4.8.4 Quakers: The Friends Mission Policy

The Friends denomination in America is divided into six regions. Four of these regions send their own missionaries. "Regional offices do not have to ask permission of the national board," says Chuck Mylander of the Colorado-based national Friends office.[816] For example, the Northwest Friends have been sending missionaries to South America for six decades; that work has matured to the point where Quakers in Latin America are sending their own missionaries. Accordingly, the Northwest Friends turned their pioneering interests to the Muslim world, in a partnership with Frontiers. Here is the point: "We operate on the assumption that the Great Commission is our marching order," says Mylander. "We do not have to partner with a host church in a country; we are free to begin new works among the unreached."[817] Because the Friends denomination has no self-imposed requirement to partner with a national church, it follows that there is no apparent need for a second mission agency to emerge.

---

[815] Ibid., 127.
[816] Telephone interview, April 2002.
[817] Ibid.

4.8.5 The Episcopal Church Mission Policy

Four autonomous Episcopalian mission agencies are active today. They are the South American Mission Society, the Episcopal Church Missionary Community, Anglican Frontier Missions, and Global Teams. More than these four follows below.

South American Missionary Society (SAMS). Allan Gardiner organized the Patagonia Mission Society and sailed to Tierra del Fuego with six colleagues. Their deaths, by starvation in 1851, created a sensation in England when Gardiner's journal was published. The next missionaries were martyred in 1859 at the hands of the Yaghan indigenous people. The story of this tribe's conversion is part of SAMS' founding history. In 1976 SAMS-USA was founded.[818]

The Episcopal Church Missionary Community. There were 456 Episcopalian missionaries serving overseas in 1963; the number dropped 71% to 128 by 1974.[819] This precipitous decline prompted Walter and Jean Hannum to found the Episcopal Church Missionary Community (ECMC) in 1974. The Hannums had spent 20 years as missionaries in Alaska. The bishop of Alaska, David R. Cochran, endorsed Hannum's proposal.[820] So Hannum founded the ECMC on the model of the (Anglican) Church Mission Society (CMS), whose voluntary membership of 37,000 supported 488

---

[818] www.samsusa.org
[819] Sam Van Culin, "Episcopal Report," in *Consultation on Voluntary Societies*, ed. Robert A. Blincoe (First Presbyterian Church, Evanston, IL: 1975, May 22-24). Unpublished.
[820] Personal interview with Bishop David R. Cochran in Tacoma, Washington in 1987.

missionaries at that time.[821] Hence Hannum's interest in starting a mission agency that more closely imitated the "voluntary" membership of the CMS structure in his Episcopal context.

Anglican Frontier Missions. Anglican Frontier Missions (AFM) was founded in 1993 by Tad de Bordenave as a voluntary missionary agency of the Episcopal Church.[822] The AFM has identified the 25 largest unreached populations as its mission mandate. The AFM is cooperating with the Southern Baptists and with "all who are committed to the Task Remaining in World Evangelization."[823] Anglican Frontier Missions reports to the Episcopal Church headquarters on its activities, but is not governed by the headquarters. The AFM pioneers new mission work and educates the denomination about the least evangelized world. Its income for 2005 was $395,593 (2004 income totaled $364,947 and 2003 income totaled $320,258).

Global Teams. A fourth Episcopalian mission agency is Global Teams.[824] How does mission initiative begin with Global Teams? Kevin Higgins replied, "It happens when someone approaches us or we meet someone at a church, and we or they say, 'Let's do

---

[821] Walter and Louise Hannum, "The Development of a Voluntary Mission Society in the Episcopal Church" (Fuller Theological Seminary School of World Mission, 1975). Contact the Episcopal Church Missionary Community at P.O. Box 278, Ambridge, PA 15003, ecmc@usaor.net or on the web at www.episcopalian.org/ecmc/.

[822] Anglican Frontiers Mission P.O. Box 18038, Richmond, VA 23226, www.afm-us.org.

[823] Ibid.

[824] Visit Global Teams at www.ewmglobalteams.org.

it.' The process begins there."[825] Episcopalians (and non-Episcopalians) can partner with Global Teams "to see the heart of Christ in the skin of every culture." There is no restriction on Global Teams missionaries from initiating mission "where there is no local partner."

4.8.6 American Baptist Mission Policy

In 1906 150 Baptist leaders signed a petition asking the boards of the largest three (of eight) national (but independent) Baptist church conventions to meet and form a single convention. Paul Mansfield Harrison wrote that members opposing the formation of a single convention lost to the greater numbers of delegates who favored it. The majority held high hopes that a unified denomination would guarantee the independence of the local churches; "they believed there was no reason the essential autonomy of the churches should not be maintained."[826] Though the intent was for a central office to provide modest administrative support to the congregations, "the officers of the denomination have obtained a significant degree of influence over the affairs of local churches."[827] Today a central administration retains the exclusive authority to initiate American Baptist mission and program.[828] The founders of the National Convention "did not anticipate the *impossibility* of policy formulation by autonomous churches" [emphasis

---

[825] Email interview with Kevin Higgins, April 2002

[826] Paul Mansfield Harrison, *Authority and Power in the Free Church Tradition; a Social Case Study of the American Baptist Convention* (Princeton, NJ: Princeton University Press, 1959), 43.

[827] Ibid., viii.

[828] Ibid., ix. Regarding the power of the Convention to make policy, see pages 90-95

is in original],[829] nor "that the executive leadership would feel a constant need to strive for that informal power which they were not officially given."[830] Harrison determined that the Baptist ideal of local church autonomy was usurped by organization of the denominational structure formed in 1907. The church hierarchy was organized "on an *ad hoc* basis as an efficient money-raising technique and to serve certain sectional and partisan concerns."[831] The accepted myth that "the existing denominational organization is derived from Biblical precepts or from historic Baptist principles simply is not true."[832]

The author sympathizes with local churches and their regional mission societies for the loss of freedom and local initiative they have experienced. The centralizing of initiative in the American Baptist church headquarters has opened a breach between it and the local churches it serves. I believe a new social contract between them would heal that breach.

4.8.7 The Lutheran Church Missouri Synod—A Model Mission Policy

Until 1996 leaders in the Lutheran Church Missouri Synod (LCMS) were proponents of centralized mission planning and budgeting. No pastor or church member could initiate a mission effort. But this has changed; since 1996 LCMS pastors and church members have formed a galaxy of mission agencies; ecclesiastical leaders, for their part, recognize and promote these mission agencies. The LCMS has even assigned a staff

---

[829] Ibid., 94.
[830] Ibid., 95.
[831] Ibid., 18. 18. Quoting Winthrop S. Hudson, "Stumbling into Disorder," *Foundations* 2, no. 1 (April 1958): 45.
[832] Harrison, 18.

administrator to coach LCMS members through the legal process of forming corporations and opening bank accounts.

How Lutherans Today Recognize and Regulate Voluntary Societies. In 1996 the Lutheran Church Missouri Synod sponsored a meeting of twelve mission agencies. These twelve subsequently organized the Association of Lutheran Mission Agencies (ALMA). The number of new mission initiatives began to increase. (Figure 27)

Figure 27. New Mission Initiatives, Lutheran Church World Mission

The number of mission agencies grew to 52 agencies in 1999, to 65 in 2003 and 75 by 2008. These voluntary societies are doing specialized work with the official consent and promotion of the Missouri Synod headquarters, but without its control. Some of the seventy-five ALMA-related mission agencies are[833]:

- *Alaska Mission for Christ*: sharing Christ in the last frontier through the use of well trained laity, especially in areas too remote or sparsely populated to allow service by ordained clergy.
- *Apple of His Eye Ministries*: Planting messianic congregations among Jewish people
- *Friends of Indonesia*: Helping Indonesian believers grow in body, mind and spirit, as well as partnering with them to share Jesus' love with those around them.
- *Hmong Mission Society*: Proclaiming of the Gospel to the Hmong people of North America and throughout the world.
- *Missio Dei Network*: providing theological materials to foster learning communities that encourage, form and equip mission leaders for missiological bridge-building in the 21st century.
- *Sudanese Lutheran Mission Society*: telling the Good News to the Sudanese who do not know about Jesus
- *Tien Shan Mission Society*: Spreading the Gospel of Jesus Christ among the Dungan people of the Tien Shan Mountain region of Central Asia (Kyrgyzstan).

Each Lutheran mission agency has its own board and its own by-laws. Each agency obtains from the IRS its own Tax Identity Number in order to open up its own bank account. Once a new mission initiative obtains its 501(c)(3) status, the society can apply to the LCMS headquarters in St. Louis to become a Recognized Service Organization (RSO). RSO status allows an agency to solicit funding and provides a number of privileges, such as the opportunity to include its staff in the denomination's pension and health-care plan. Organizations with RSO status agree to submit an annual audit and

---

[833] http://www.alma-online.org ALMA lists only those agencies that pay the annual $85 membership fee and agree to work in cooperation with the member agencies and with the LCMS. There are 35 additional LCMS mission agencies that have not joined ALMA.

promise to work in ways that support the aims of the denomination. Mission groups that seek a partnership status with the denomination's mission arm enter into a five to seven year agreement to work together in mutually beneficial ways. Some ALMA agencies choose not to participate in RSO.

An LCMS staff member advises pastors and lay members on the process of incorporation, and provides a starter kit for setting up a mission agency. ALMA also helps new mission agencies to effectively raise funds and communicate to Lutheran churches.

ALMA hosts an annual gathering of its member agencies to help them network with one another and to interface with the mission staff of LCMS World Mission. It's a win-win for denomination and the mission agencies. "In a time of financial limitations and in response to the initiative of many different mission groups in the LCMS it makes sense to work closely with the independent Lutheran mission agencies,"[834] said Steve Hughey, Director for Mission Partnership and Involvement at the Lutheran church headquarters.

The LCMS mission structure: An Example for Other Denominations. Lutheran Church Missouri Synod has validated the right of its members to form "little republics." "Our concern," Hughey said, "is to get the task of missions done" by partnering with small voluntary associations.[835] In a pluralistic church such as the LCMS, members with ideas that interest only a minority of the entire church membership can work in harmony with

---

[834] Telephone interview with Steve Hughey in March 2002
[835] Ibid.

church officials. This pattern *should encourage other denominations to do likewise.* Paul Pierson concurs: "Ecclesiastical structures (Presbyterian and Anglican) are suited for stability and stationary organization—not conducive to the frontier situation which required more freedom."[836] The historical data supports these statements, as we have seen. The data does not corroborate the statement by Paul A. Beals that "normally the local church initiates the sending of missionaries."[837] I think Beals pulled this thought out of the air; all empirical evidence is to the contrary. An individual or a group may approach a church board and persuade it to act; but in that case the board is responding to an initiative begun elsewhere. As long as there are new missions to undertake, men and women must organize themselves into voluntary societies.

---

[836] Paul E. Pierson, "Historical Development of the Christian Movement," (Pasadena: Fuller Theological Seminary, 1985), 204.
[837] Beals, 115.

4.8.8 Four Types of Denomination-Mission Agency Relationships

At the May 22-24 1975 "Consultation on Voluntary Societies" Ralph Winter presented a graph depicting presented four kinds of relationships between denominations and mission agencies[838] (Figure 28):

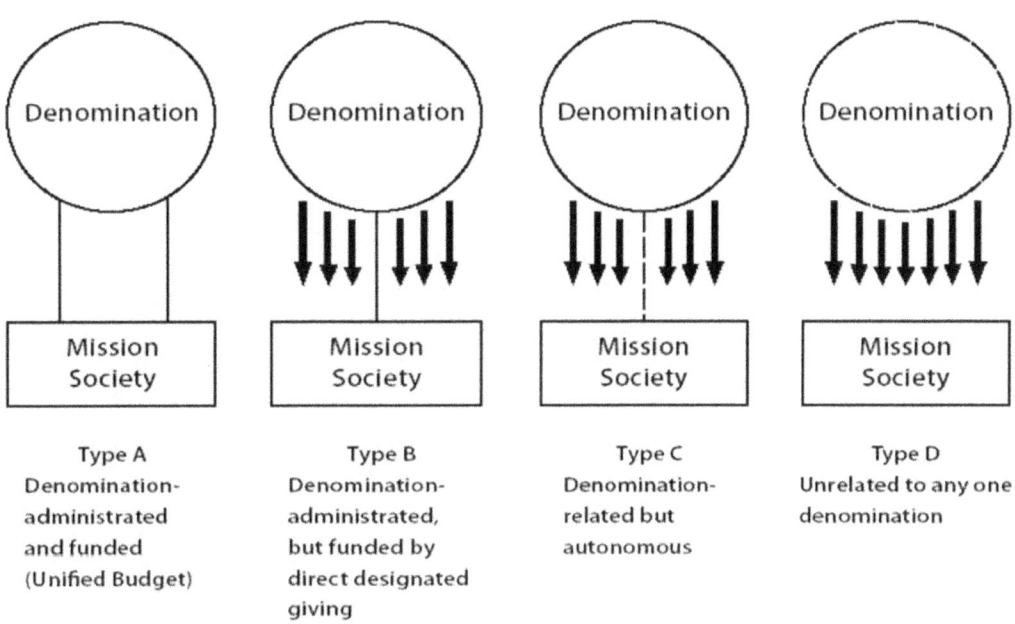

Figure 28. Four Kinds of Mission-Church Relationships

Winter explains the four kinds of relationships:

> *Type A Missions* are (1) related to a specific church body; this is signified by the large circle; (2) administrated by that church through a board appointed by ecclesiastical processes; this is signified by the vertical bar on the left; and (3) funded by that church through a unified budget which discourages (or prevents) local churches from affecting the percentage going to the mission structure; this is

---

[838] Ralph D. Winter, "Seeing the Task Graphically," *Evangelical Missions Quarterly* 10, no. 1 (1974): 11ff.; and Ralph D. Winter, "Four Kinds of Church-Agency Relationships," (*Missiology* 7 no. 2, 1979). See also Winter, "Protestant Mission Societies and the 'Other Protestant Schism'," 203.

signified by the vertical bar on the right and the *absence* of small arrows of relationship between the church and the mission.[839]

Type B Missions differ from Type A missions only in the elimination of the third characteristic mentioned. This type of mission raises its own support. It does not depend on a certain percentage of a church budget. Most Type A missions used to be of this kind.[840]

A *Type C Missions,* such as the Conservative Baptist Foreign Mission Society [today World Venture], sustain a close relation to a church body (the Conservative Baptist Association) but neither its administration nor its budget are determined by the official processes of that church.[841]

Type D Missions acknowledge no special relation to any specific church (although churches may choose to regard a certain Type D mission as their official expression in overseas work). Members of Missio Nexus (the IFMA-EFMA merger) includes all four types, while the National Council of Churches includes mainly Type A structures.

The first three types, A, B, and C, are similar in that they are all denominationally-related mission agencies. William Carey's "Baptist Missionary Society" was of Type C, barely escaping from Type D when Carey "secured the limp backing of a local Baptist conference of churches."[842] Winter favors Types B and C, but especially Type C. In "A Plea for Mission Orders," Winter's first paper on the subject, he writes,

---

[839] These denominations have a "Type A" mission society: Presbyterian Church (USA), Episcopalian, Methodist, and Reformed Church. At the May 1975 "Consultation on Voluntary Societies" the Episcopalian representative, Sam van Culin said, "We have a Type A organization in our church. It is funded directly through an organized method in the church, and it is directly related administratively to the Church through a thing called the Executive Council. Within our charter, every baptized member of the Episcopal Church is described as a member of this Domestic and Foreign Missionary Society (DFMS)." Van Culin.

[840] The Presbyterian Church (USA) has three Type B mission societies: Presbyterian Frontier Fellowship, The Outreach Foundation, and the Medical Benevolence Foundation.

[841] Type C mission societies include the Episcopal Church Missionary Community, the Presbyterian Order for World Evangelization, the ALMA mission societies of the LCMS, and the Anglican Church Mission Society.

[842] Winter, "Protestant Mission Societies and the 'Other Protestant Schism'," 204. In his *Enquiry* Carey

> We do not suggest additional [Presbyterian] General Assembly agencies of mission of the present type but rather semi-autonomous mission structures similar to the Church Mission Society of the Anglican Church that would report to and be subject to the General Assembly of our church and such other appropriate General Assemblies of sister churches.
>
> In so saying we do not envision this decentralization as dividing the church but knitting it together, since by allowing the fuller expression of mission within the various sub-communities of our church we would surely tend to reduce tensions rather than create them.[843]

All Catholic orders are Type C. American Protestant mission agencies mostly fall into Type A or Type D, extremes that Winter refers to as "the Bear Hug or Abandonment Syndrome."[844] In Type A, the church hierarchy understands itself to be a missionary society, and the only missionary organization to which its members should join or fund, a paradigm that in this dissertation I have referred to as *sola synodica*. In Type B, the church administration has negotiated an agreement with certain mission associations to accept designated giving in exchange for certain administrative controls. In Type C, a church administration recognizes and names the mission associations that church members are initiating or joining, in exchange for an annual report. When Robert Weingartner describes the 19th century Presbyterian women's societies as "a loose

---

suggested that members of each denomination organize a mission agency particular to their own church. William Carey suggested that each denomination begin its own mission society (the Baptist Missionary Society sent Carey to India) He writes that "each denomination should engage separately in the work. There is room enough for us all without interfering with each other." Carey, *An Enquiry into the Obligations of Christians to Use Means for the Conversion of the Heathens*, 83. Carey had no desire to promote one denomination's theology or organization over another. Carey, Walls comments, "has no theological objection to a united mission; indeed, he invites all Christians to the work. But to form a society you must begin where you are, with people who already form a nucleus, with people who already have some cohesion, mutual trust and fellowship. Let suspicion and lack of trust enter, and the society is doomed." Walls, "The Fortunate Subversion of the Church," 248.

[843] Ralph D. Winter, "A Plea for Mission Orders," (Chicago: COEMAR Conference, August, 1970).
[844] Winter, "Protestant Mission Societies and the 'Other Protestant Schism'," 204.

confederation of quasi-independent groups and agencies"[845] he is referring to a Type C denomination-mission relationship. I am advocating for Type C denomination-missions' relations in this dissertation.

---

[845] Weingartner, 111.

CHAPTER 5: CONCLUSION TO THE DISSERTATION

The people of God have always formed themselves into voluntary associations in order to create durable and effective solutions for many of humanity's great problems. Church leaders will more readily validate their members' voluntary societies when careful students of the Bible and history replace the *sola synodica* mission paradigm with the William Carey / Ralph D. Winter "Two Structures" paradigm. Sociological data indicate that it is the nature of societies everywhere for its members to join other likeminded members to achieve particular outcomes. In addition, the historical data indicates that Carey's 1792 publication of *An Enquiry into the Use of Means* did bring to a sudden end the 275 year period of Protestant mission doldrums and inaugurate the Protestant mission era. Therefore, the Carey / Winter "Two Structures" paradigm is closer to what is in the Bible, and to what is in nature, and what history teaches. As Bruce L. Bauer wrote, "The Christian movement has the best potential for expansion and growth when the congregational structure and the mission structure symbiotically relate to each other in order that both may accomplish their functions."[846]

Thomas Kuhn's theory of "paradigm shift and resistance" helps us to understand why ecclesiastical structures reacted against Carey's paradigm. But Kuhn also wrote, encouragingly, that "people are persuaded to change paradigms if they believe that the new model is closer to nature, closer to what is 'really there.'"[847] I hope I have persuaded

---

[846] Bauer, 15, 20.
[847] Kuhn, 206.

my readers that the "Two Structures" model is closer to what is "really there" in order to make straight a highway for church administrators and the people of God to more effectively carry out the *missio Dei*. Thankfully, one denomination has repaired the breach; other ecclesiastical structures can follow the lead of the Lutheran Church Missouri Synod (LCMS). At LCMS headquarters the church validates the special-interest associations that its citizens initiate.

5.1 A New Social Contract for Presbyterians

The history of Presbyterian mission is a repeating cycle of private mission initiative, administrative reaction, creation of central organizations to displace private mission organizations, and more private mission initiatives. We can do better; the Presbyterian Church can learn a lesson from the Catholic Church "Two Structures" social contract which Winter describes as "the ultimate synthesis, delicately achieved, whereby Catholic orders were able to function along with Catholic parishes and dioceses without the two structures conflicting with each other to the point of a setback to the movement."[848] The presbyteries and congregations should take responsibility to register and regulate voluntary mission societies, in the manner that free-world governments register and regulate the non-profit corporations that their citizens are forming or joining. To illustrate, a presbytery would adopt a registration procedure:

> The Presbytery of the Grand Canyon, in order to maintain the standards of faith and practice and to promote the mission of the church, has determined that the

---

[848]Winter, "The Two Structures of God's Redemptive Mission," 128.

following non-profit corporations meet the requirements described in "The Missional Guidelines" and summarized by the Great Ends of the Church[849] and are in good standing with this Presbytery.

The guidelines would be written by the office of each presbytery. Hutcheson suggests that such guidelines would contain most of the following elements:[850]

> 1. Acceptance of the existence, within the denomination, of special-interest mission associations.
>
> 2. Integrated planning of a full range of mission activities, substantively as well as nominally responsive to the intentions of various groups of donors.
>
> 3. Integrated promotion by the denomination of a full range of mission activities, together with acceptance of promotion by consensus groups of their own mission goals.
>
> 4. Full utilization of the widespread Christian commitment to the church itself, which leads to generalized giving to the whole mission of the church by many, but with full acceptance also of designated giving to particular causes.
>
> 5. A guarantee that all designated contributions go to the cause designated.
>
> 6. A willingness for the constituency to affect the missional priorities through its designated giving, without the kind of ecclesiastical shell game which compensates for increased giving in one area by shifting an equivalent amount of no designated money away from that area.
>
> 7. An intention to serve the needs and reflect the concerns of *all* groups within the constituency [Emphasis is in original].

The presbytery would normalize its relationship with the mission societies to which members of the presbytery belonged. Without this advantage the Presbytery is busy taking full-time care of its churches and ministers, a worthy but partial fulfillment of the

---

[849] The Presbyterian *Book of Order* has defined the Great Ends of the Presbyterian Church, which is to say its mission. Mission societies that aim to promote one or more of these great ends would normally be recognized by a Presbytery.

[850] Hutcheson, "Pluralism and Consensus: Why Mainline Church Mission Budgets Are in Trouble," 624.

missio Dei. For example, the mission of the Presbytery of the Grand Canyon, of which I am a member, is "to celebrate and proclaim the Gospel of Jesus Christ"[851] by:

- nurturing each congregation and minister member
- assisting and challenging each congregation to engage in ministry and mission with other congregations and denominations
- developing and redeveloping worship communities
- being a connectional, communicative link in the Presbyterian Church (U.S.A.)[852]

Thus, the Grand Canyon Presbytery, in this example, understands its mission to be nurturing, developing and connecting congregations. But, as George Hunter has cautioned, "no major denomination in the United States regards apostolic ministry to pre-Christian outsiders as its 'priority' or even as 'normal' ministry."[853] By validating the mission initiatives that its members are joining, the presbytery signals that special-interest associations are acceptable means for achieving the great ends of the church. Jerry White is one who has thought about what this validating could look like.[854] Pellowe has summarized White's key elements for successful relations:

- Affirm the theological legitimacy of self-governing agencies;
- Count the work of agency staff as part of the legitimate ministry of their local churches;
- Agencies should clearly define their purposes and goals so they can determine their effectiveness and be held accountable to them;
- Agency staff should relate to a local congregation and volunteer there as well;
- Agency leaders should give sound teaching on responsibility to local congregations;
- Emphasize the ministry of the laity; and

---

[851] www.pbygrandcanyon.org. Accessed September 2010
[852] Ibid.
[853] Hunter, 24.
[854] Jerry White, *The Church and Parachurch: An Uneasy Marriage* (Portland: Multnomah, 1983).

- Use the skills and specialties of agencies to build the local church.[855]

The presbytery or similar judicatory body in other denominations could enhance its mission by encouraging the formation of societies for doing good, as happened in the Philadelphia Presbytery in 1707. Likewise, a local church session would normally recognize all the mission societies of which any member of the congregation belonged.

The Presbyterian Church can regain those members whose interests are not represented by the majority, members who are leaving for lack of a voice; but this means that the Presbyterian Church must stop seeing itself as "one large mission society."[856] The assumed effectiveness of centrally-administered mission monopolies is at odds with how things really are. The Presbyterian Church must accept its governance role *vis á vis* special-purpose associations. The one condition for a new social contract is mutual respect based on the good will of presbytery and church sessions to recognize the right of Presbyterians to initiate or join mission agencies, so long as those agencies are in good standing as described in a registration document or memo of understanding. Each presbytery or church session will maintain a list of validated mission agencies and make the list available to its members on the church's website. It is agencies such as these to which David Dawson refers when he writes,

> We believe that there is a much larger number to be included, and those are the Presbyterian missionaries who serve overseas through other sending agencies. We get a glimpse of how large that number might be when we note that the largest

---

[855] Found in Pellowe, *A Practical Theology for Relations between Churches and Self-Governing Agencies*, 114-15.

[856] This is a recurring phrase. See http://missional.info/wp-content/uploads/2010/02/Mission-Invitation-FINAL-2008.pdf. Accessed September 2010.

single group of attendees at the triennial Urbana mission conference is PC (USA) members. Most of those "Urbana Presbyterians" who go into full-time missionary service do so through parachurch groups like World Vision, Habitat for Humanity, Frontiers, Heifer Project, SIM International, World Harvest and countless others. Furthermore, our estimates of Presbyterian giving to mission need to expand greatly for a large portion of these who are supported by Presbyterian congregations.[857]

For its part, the mission agency agrees to report annually on its activities, and to concede to a church administration the right to remove a mission agency from its registry if the mission agency fails to report or acts in a manner that is inconsistent with the purposes of the church.

Voluntary associations, like corporations, become centers of power, "little republics" that responsible governments are bound to regulate but not manage. But "it is imperative, Robert Worley wrote, "that there be a political style that encourages the development of openness and visibility of these differences and enables minority groups to form coalitions and be active politically without being labeled 'enemies.'"[858] Bonaventure, St. Francis' immediate successor, offers an apt illustration; he compared the friars of his day to the unnamed fishermen in "the second boat," the one that aided Peter in hauling in the extraordinary catch of fish.[859] "Without the help of the second boat," Bonaventure said, "the catch of fishes would surely be lost."[860] For the sake bringing in the extraordinary

---

[857] Dawson, "Counting the Cost," 45. *Voluntary Societies in my local church.* One Sunday in November 2007 at First Presbyterian Church of Mesa I wrote down the names of the several organizations that our pastor mentioned in his report on the mission of First Presbyterian Church of Mesa: The Ronald McDonald House; Lutheran Resettlement Services; Christhaven; Bibles for the World; and the Mark Center.[857]
[858] Worley, 46.
[859] Luke 5:4-11
[860] Moorman, 141.

catch William Carey launched a second boat. Those passionate, in the imitation of Christ, to overcome evil with good, pray that we might be wise to initiate special-purpose associations in order to address and eradicate the great problems of our day.

The tension between ecclesiastical structures and voluntary societies can be resolved by mutual respect and recognition. The day of centralized command and control is nearly over. A day of denominational mission "may still be possible," Hutcheson offers, "if its basis is *affirmation of rather than resistance to the pluralism of the constituency* [emphasis is in original]."[861] Such an approach, Hutcheson goes on to say,

> involves some loss in the area of a unified approach to mission, and some surrender to the constituency-at-large of decision-making now exercised . . . by church bureaucrats. [But] it offers some hope of defining a useful missional role for central denominational headquarters.[862]

This dissertation is a humble effort to persuade the reader that now is the time for ecclesiastical adminsitrations to validate mission structures, the structures by which men and women can perform what John Cotton called a "warrantable calling" that "tends to the public good."[863] Cotton drew the idea of a warrantable calling from the Bible: "Seek not every man his own things, but every man the good of his brother" (I Cor. 10. 24); and "Seek one another's welfare" (Phil. 2. 4). Voluntary associations seem to be the most predictably effective means for persons to achieve a warrantable calling, as evidenced by a study of history and sociology. William Carey had a "warrantable calling" in mind

---

[861] Hutcheson, "Pluralism and Consensus: Why Mainline Church Mission Budgets Are in Trouble," 623.
[862] Ibid., 624.
[863] Carl N. Degler, *Out of Our Past; the Forces That Shaped Modern America*, Rev. ed. (New York: Harper & Row, 1970), 7. 7

when he proposed that Christians organize special-purpose associations in order to eradicate certain root evils in the world, evils that are subjugating "our fellow creatures, whose souls are as immortal as ours" to "ignorance and barbarism"[864] De Tocqueville said that "the art of association" is "the mother science" because it enables restless people to invent special-purpose agencies that will change the world.[865] "The voluntary societies," Andrew Walls writes, "have been as revolutionary in their effect as ever the monasteries were in their sphere. The sodalities we now need may prove equally disturbing."[866]

Voluntary societies are merely cloth sails, but it is these sails that catch the wind. Hoist a thousand more, and they will take the Protestant Church where our theology informs us that we should go. A great new fleet of ships is sailing out of the harbor to "attempt great things for God."

---

[864] Carey, *An Enquiry into the Obligations of Christians to Use Means for the Conversion of the Heathens*, 68. The particular works to which Carey put his hand on behalf of the people of India are well-known and beyond the subject of this dissertation. For an essay on Carey's good works see Vishal Mangalwadi and Ruth Mangalwadi, *The Legacy of William Carey: A Model for the Transformation of a Culture*, 1st U.S. ed. (Wheaton, IL: Crossway Books, 1999), 71ff.
[865] Tocqueville, 496.
[866] Walls, "The Fortunate Subversion of the Church," 253-54.

APPENDIX 1 **Protestant missionary biographies before and after Carey in *EDWM***

A comparison of two time periods: 1522-1792 and 1792-2000

Missionaries who went out before William Carey

Name-	date of death
1 Heyling, Peter	1652
2 Eliot, John	1690
3 Ziegenbald, B.	1719
4 Brainerd, David	1747
5 Egedes, Hans	1758
6 Dober, Leonhard	1766
7 Whitefield, George	1770
8 Thompson, Thomas	1773
9 Schmidt, Georg	1785
10 Wesley, John	1791
11 Schwartz, Christian	1798
12 Asbury, Francis	1816
13 Johnson, Richard	1827

Missionaries who went out after William Carey

Name-	date of death
1 Van der Kemp, J.	1811
2 Henry Martyn	1816
3 Ward, William	1823
4 Fisk, Pliny	1825
5 Carey, Lott	1828
6 Carey, William	1834
7 Morrison, Robert	1834
8 Wilson, Margaret	1835
9 Marshman, Joshua	1837
10 Marsden, Samuel	1838
11 Williams, John	1839
12 Macomber, Eleanor	1840
13 Cargill, Margaret	1840
14 Jones, David	1841
15 Evans, James	1846
16 Hunt, John	1848
17 Judson, Adoniram	1850
18 Gardiner, Allen F.	1851
19 Gützlaff, Karl F.	1851
20 Groves, Anthony	1853
21 Riis, Andreas	1854
22 Thomson, J. Diego	1854
23 Anderson, John	1855
24 Gossner, Johannes	1858
25 Farrar, Cynthia	1862
26 Boone, William J.	1864
27 Graul, Karl	1864
28 Fisk, Fidelia	1864
29 Stockton, Betsy	1865
30 Pfander, Karl G.	1866
31 Cary, Maude	1867
32 Aldersey, Mary Ann	1868
33 Burns, William	1868
34 Wilson, Mary Ann	1868
35 Bingham, Hiram	1869
36 Perkins, Justin	1869
37 Thompson, Elizabeth	1869
38 Hinderer, Anna	1870
39 Bridgman, Eliza Jane	1871
40 Patteson, John	1871
41 Geddie, John	1872
42 Livingstone, David	1873
43 Wilson, John, L.	1875
44 Bulu, Joeli	1877
45 Selwyn, George A.	1878
46 Duff, Alexander	1878
47 Baldwin, Mary B.	1879
48 Gobat, Maria	1879
49 Fjellstedt, Peter	1881
50 Krapf, Johann L.	1881
51 Schreuder, Hans P.	1882
52 Jaeschke, Heinrich	1883
53 Moffat, Robert	1883
54 Posselt, Wilhelm	1885
55 Stern, Henry	1885
56 McDougall, Francis	1886
57 Baker, Amelia D.	1888
58 Kalley, Robert R.	1888
59 Parker, Peter	1888
60 Trumbull, David	1889
61 Whately, Mary Louisa	1889

62	Butler, Fanny Jane	1889	107	Jessup, Henry H.	1910
63	Freeman, Thomas	1890	108	Kropf, Albert	1910
64	Mackay, Alexander	1890	109	Williams, Channing	1910
65	Niijima, Jom	1890	110	Abrams, Anna	1910
66	Casalis, Eugene	1891	111	Farrow, Lucy F.	1910
67	Crowther, Samuel	1891	112	Swain, Clara A.	1910
68	Gilmour, James	1891	113	Hepburn, James	1911
69	Lavigerie, Charles	1892	114	Hyde, John	1912
70	McGeorge, Mary	1892	115	John, Griffith	1912
71	Agnew, Eliza	1893	116	Kasatkin, Nicholas	1912
72	Tucker, Charlotte	1893	117	Moon, Lottie	1912
73	Nevius, John	1893	118	Minnie Abrams	1912
74	Mabile, Adolphe	1894	119	Morton, John	1912
75	Gorham, Sarah	1894	120	McLaren, Agnes	1913
76	Gordon, A. Judson	1895	121	Coppin, Fanny J.	1913
77	Waddell, Hope M.	1895	122	Tucker Alfred Robert	1914
78	Stewart, Louisa	1895	123	Arnot, Frederick	1914
79	Hill, David	1896	124	Marks, John E.	1915
80	Hinz, Hansina	1896	125	Pollard, Samuel	1915
81	Scott, Peter C.	1896	126	Slessor, Mary	1915
82	Legge, James	1897	127	Smith, Amanda	1915
83	Pilkington, George	1897	128	Bliss, Daniel	1916
84	Verbeck, Guido F.	1898	129	Martin, William	1916
85	Haygood, Laura	1900	130	Nuttall, Enos	1916
86	Chalmers, James	1901	131	Fearing, Adele M.	1916
87	Mackay, George	1901	132	Underwood, Horace	1916
88	Thoburn, Isabella	1901	133	Chambers, Oswald	1917
89	Taylor, William	1902	134	Forsyth, Christina	1918
90	Coillard, Francois	1904	135	Merensky, Alexander	1918
91	Francois Coillard	1904	136	Richard, Timothy	1919
92	Chestnut, Eleanor	1905	137	Simpson, Albert B.	1919
93	Taylor, J. Hudson	1905	138	Coppock, Grace	1921
94	Bompas, William	1906	139	Codrington, Robert	1922
95	Grenfell, George	1906	140	Weston, Frank	1924
96	Schereschewsky, S.	1906	141	Penzotti, Francisco	1925
97	Baedeker, Friedrick	1906	142	Crawford, Daniel	1926
98	Fison, Lorimer	1907	143	Gairdner, William	1928
99	Lawes, William G.	1907	14	Torrey, Reuben A.	1928
100	Paton, John	1907	145	Trotter, Isabelle L.	1928
101	Chamberlain, Jacob	1908	146	Kinsolving, Lucien	1929
102	Franson, Fredrik	1908	147	Harris, William W.	1929
103	Jackson, Sheldon	1909	148	Grubb, Wilfred B.	1930
104	Clough, John E.	1910	149	Kumm, Karl W.	1930
105	Greene, Mary Jane	1910	150	Stevenson, Marion	1930
106	Guinness, Henry	1910	151	Paul, Kanakarayan	1931

#	Name	Year
152	Studd, Charles T.	1931
153	Booth, Joseph	1932
154	Morris, William	1932
155	Waterston, Jane E.	1932
156	Beach, Harlan P.	1933
157	Fraser, Donald	1933
158	Veenstra, Johanna	1933
159	White, John	1933
160	Laws, Robert	1934
161	Sisson, Elizabeth	1934
162	Kunst, Irene	1934
163	Barclay, Thomas	1935
164	Bender, Carl J.	1935
165	Hoover, James M.	1935
166	Goforth, Jonathan	1936
167	Hoover, Willis C.	1936
168	Fearing, Maria	1937
169	Armstrong, Annie	1938
170	Moffett, Samuel A.	1939
171	Chitambar J. R.	1940
172	Grenfell, Wilfrid	1940
173	Ricther, Julius	1940
174	Young, Florence	1940
175	Allan, George	1941
176	Bill, Samuel A.	1942
177	Bingham, Rowland	1942
178	Gregg, Jessie	1942
179	Gofroth, Rosalind	1942
180	Patton, William	1943
181	Reed, Mary	1943
182	Sung, John	1944
183	Haining, Jane M.	1944
184	Rodgers, James B.	1944
185	Azariah Vedanayakam	1945
186	Jaffray, Robert	1945
187	Liddell, Eric	1945
188	Hoste, Dixon E.	1946
189	Shellabear, William	1947
190	Abraham Mar Thoma	1947
191	Allan, Roland	1947
192	Small, Mary	1947
193	Peabody, Lucy	1949
194	Andrews, Charles	1950
195	Moninger, Mary	1950
196	Carmichael, Amy	1951
197	Flynn, John	1951
198	Cable, (Alice) Mildred	1952
199	Parrish, Sarah	1952
200	Zwemer, Samuel	1952
201	Keller, Mirian W.	1953
202	Luce, Alice E.	1955
203	Mott, John R.	1955
20	Trotman, Dawson	1956
205	Brown, Edith	1956
206	Rouse, Ruth	1956
207	Kuhn, Isobel	1957
208	Smith, Edwin	1957
209	Higgenbotham, Sam	1958
210	Hamer, Lillian	1959
211	Huey, Mary Alice	1960
212	Scudder, Ida S.	1960
213	Clark, Charles A.	1961
214	Crawford, Isabel	1961
215	Keysser, Christian	1961
216	Trasher, Lillian	1961
217	Buchman, Frank	1961
218	Steidel, Florence	1962
219	Bavinck, Johan H,	1964
220	Schweitzer, Albert	1965
221	Starched, Kenneth	1965
222	Kraemer, Hendrik	1965
224	Strachan, R. Kenneth	1965
225	Gutmann, Bruno	1966
226	Padwick, Constance	1968
227	Hewat, Elizabeth	1968
228	Oldham, Joseph H.	1969
229	Braden, Charles S.	1970
230	Calverley, Edwin E.	1971
231	Bell, Lemuel Nelson	1973
232	Wilson, J. Christy	1973
233	Jones, Eli Stanley	1973
234	Wang, Leland	1975
235	Mabel, Francis	1975
236	Das, R. Chandra	1976
237	George, Eliza Davis	1979
238	Jones, Lina Maude	1979
239	Doke, Clement M.	1980
240	Grubb, Sir Kenneth	1980
241	Townsend, Cameron	1982
242	Mackay, John A.	1983

243 Neill, Stephen Charles 1984
244 Ridderhof, Joy 1984
245 Gih, Andrew 1985
246 Harvey, Esther B. 1986
247 Beaver, R. Pierce 1987
248 Hodges, Melvin Lyle 1988
249 Kivengere, Festo 1988
250 Tippett, Alan R. 1988
251 Penman, David 1989
252 McGavran, Donald 1991
253 Bernsten, Annie S. 1992
254 Kane, J. Herbert 1992
255 Whitman, Leroy F. 1992
256 Whiteman, Leroy F. 1992
257 Greene, Betty 1997
258 Mother Teresa 1997
259 Smalley, William A 1997
260 Foreman, Charles 1997
261 Pike, Kenneth Lee 2000
262 Taylor, John Vernon 2001
263 Verkuyl, Johannes 2002
264 Baba, Panya **
265 Brother Andrew **
266 Evans, Helen E. **
267 Loewen, Jacob A. **
268 Nida, Eugene A. **
269 Padilla, Carlos Rene **
270 Pudaite, Rochunga **
271 Roberts, W. Dayton **
272 Roseveare, Helen **
273 Elisabeth Eliot **
274 Anderson, Gerald H. **
275 Finkbinder, Paul Edwin **
276 Glasser, Arthur F. **
277 Howard, David Morris **
278 Shedd, Russell **
279 Walls, Andrew F. **

APPENDIX 2 Protestant missionary biographies before and after Carey in *BDCM*

A comparison of two time periods: 1522-1792 and 1792-2000

Missionaries who went out before William Carey (Date is date of death)

1 Hut, Hans   1527
2 Riedemann, Peter   1556
3 Schmid, Hans   1558
4 Candidius, Georgius 1647
5 Heurnius, Justus   1652
6 Heyling, Peter   1652
7 Junius, Robertus   1655
8 Mayhew, Thomas   1657
9 Hambroeck, Antonius 1661
10 Baldaeus, Philippus 1671
11 Williams, Roger   1683
12 Eliot, John   1690
13 Makemie, Francis   1708
14 Ziegenbalg, Barthol. 1719
15 Grundler, Johann   1720
16 Westen, Thomas von   1727
17 Walther, Christoph   1741
18 Brainerd, David   1747
19 Martin, Frederick   1750
20 Plutschau, Heinrich 1752
21 Edwards, Jonathan   1758
22 Egede, Hans   1758
23 Mayhew, Experience   1758
24 Schultze, Benjamin   1760
25 Bohnisch, Frederick 1763
26 Rauch, Christian   1763
27 Dober, Johann   1766
28 Callenberg, Johann   1769
29 Protten, Christian   1769
30 Thompson, Thomas   1773
31 Schultz, Stephan   1776
32 Horton, Azariah   1777
33 Lieberkuhn, Samuel   1777
34 Brainerd, John   1781
35 Grassman, Andrew   1783
36 Moulton, Ebenezer   1783
37 Mack, Johann   1784
38 Coughlan, Laurence   1785
39 Schmidt, Georg   1785
40 Stach, Matthew   1787
41 Fabricius, Johann   1791
42 Occom, Samson   1792
43 Haven, Jens   1796
44 Schwartz, Christian 1798
45 Braun, Peter   1800
46 Gericke, Christian   1803
47 Govan, William   1804
48 Hawley, Gideon   1807
49 Jefferson, John   1807
50 Zeisberger, David   1808
51 Asbury, Francis   1818

Missionaries who went out after William Carey (Date is date of death)

1 Martyn, Henry   1812
2 Newell, Harriet   1812
3 John, Christoph   1813
4 Coke, Thomas   1814
5 Ringeltaube, Wilhelm 1816
6 Obookiah, Henry   1818
7 Milne, Rachel   1819
8 Bicknell, Henry   1820
9 Schnarre, Johannes   1820
10 Chamberlain, John   1821
11 Morrison, Mary   1821
12 Newell, Samuel   1821
13 Renner, Melchior   1821
14 Carey, Felix   1822
15 Milne, William   1822
16 Parsons, Levi   1822
17 Heckewelder, John   1823
18 Johnson, William   1823
19 Srewart, John   1823
20 Crosby, Aaron   1824
21 Nylander, Gustavus   1824
22 Smith, John   1824
23 Fisk, Pliny   1825

#	Name	Year	#	Name	Year
24	Hall, Gordon	1826	69	Crowe, Frederick	1846
25	Judson, Ann	1826	70	McCoy, Isaac	1846
26	Carey, Lott	1828	71	Hill, Mary	1847
27	Liele, George	1828	72	Jameson, William	1847
28	Price, Jonathan	1828	73	Richards, William	1847
29	Boardman, George	1831	74	Whitman, Marcus	1847
30	Newell, Maria	1831	75	Whitman, Narcissa	1847
31	Holmes, Elkanah	1832	76	Bingham, Sybil	1848
32	Ronne, Bone	1832	77	Fox, Henry	1848
33	Cox, Melville	1833	78	Hunt, John	1848
34	Winslow, Harriet	1833	79	Schmelen, Johann	1848
35	Black, William	1834	80	Glen, William	1849
36	Carey, William	1834	81	Bickersteth, Edward	1850
37	Morrison, Robert	1834	82	Frey, Joseph	1850
38	Ellis, Mary	1835	83	Hodgson, Thomas	1850
39	Mackenzie, John	1835	84	Judson, Adoniram	1850
40	Wilson, Margaret	1835	85	Reeve, William	1850
41	Rottler, John	1836	86	Gardiner, Allen	1851
42	Marshmn, Joshua	1837	87	Gützlaff, Karl	1851
43	Stevens, Edwin	1837	88	Jones, John	1851
44	Rhenius, Carl	1838	89	Anderson, William	1852
45	Blumhardt, Christian	1839	90	Case, Isaac	1852
46	Boudinot, Elias	1839	92	Collins, Judson	1852
47	Grant, Judith	1839	92	Duchesne, Rose	1852
48	Loveless, Sarah	1839	93	Read, James	1852
49	Teague, Colin	1839	94	Schurmann, J.	1852
50	Williams, John	1839	95	Hartmann, Maria	1853
51	Campbell, John	1840	96	Robinson, William	1853
52	Hallbeck, Hans	1840	97	Goddard, Josiah	1854
53	Jones, David	1841	98	Hume, Robert	1854
54	McDowell, Robert	1841	99	Riis, Andreas	1854
55	Raban, John	1841	100	Sutton, Amos	1854
56	Cross, William	1842	101	Anderson, John	1855
57	Cargill, David	1843	102	Case, William	1855
58	Dyer, Samuel	1843	103	Davies, John	1855
59	Johns, David	1843	104	Jowett, William	1855
60	Bacon, Sumner	1844	105	Nesbit, Robert	1855
61	Condit, Azubah	1844	106	Walker, William	1855
62	Nott, Henry	1844	107	Chapdelaine, Auguste	1856
63	Shuck, Henrietta	1844	108	Nicolayson, John	1856
64	Judson, Sarah	1845	109	Butler, Elizur	1857
65	Lee, Jason	1845	110	Medhurst, Walter	1857
66	Abeel, David	1846	111	Peck, John	1857
67	Coker, Daniel	1846	112	Smith, Eli	1857
68	Crook, William	1846	113	Wilkins, Ann	1857

114	Ragland, Thomas	1858
115	Vinton, Justus	1858
116	Hough, George	1859
117	Schwarz, Johann	1859
118	Threlkeld, Lancelot	1859
119	Worcester, Samuel	1859
120	Huc, Evariste Regis	1860
121	Macgowan, Edward	1860
122	Riedel, Johann	1860
123	Adam, William	1861
124	Boaz, Thomas	1861
125	Bridgman, Elijah	1861
126	Mullens, Hannah	1861
127	Dwight, Harrison	1862
128	Gogerly, Daniel	1862
129	Mackenzie, Charles	1862
130	Tellstrom, Carl	1862
131	Wolff, Joseph	1862
132	Allen, David	1863
133	Giffiths, David	1863
134	Hislop, Stephen	1863
135	Jones, Charles	1863
136	McCaul, Alexander	1863
137	Shuck, Jehu	1863
138	Boone, William	1864
139	Buzcott, Aaron	1864
140	Devasahayam, John	1864
141	Evans, James	1864
142	Fiske, Fidelia	1864
143	Herschell, Ridley	1864
144	Isenberg, Karl	1864
145	Mazzuchelli, Samuel	1864
146	Vinton, Calista	1864
147	Winslow, Miron	1864
148	Ballantine, Henry	1865
149	Hamlin, James	1865
150	Jones, Edward	1865
151	Noble, Robert	1865
152	Peet, Joseph	1865
153	Pfander, Karl	1865
154	Stockton, Betsey	1865
155	Archbell, James	1866
156	Ball, Dyer	1866
157	Merrick, James	1866
158	Rundle, Robert	1866
159	Stockfleth, Nils	1866
160	Swan, William	1866
161	Thomas, Robert	1866
162	Tucker, John	1866
163	Watson, William	1866
164	Darling, David	1867
165	Goodell, William	1867
166	Papeiha	1867
167	Sharkey, John	1867
168	Williams, Henry	1867
169	Aldersey, Mary Ann	1868
170	Andrews, Lorring	1868
171	Burns, William	1868
172	Byington, Cyrus	1868
173	Feller, Henriette	1868
174	Hardy, Robert	1868
175	Thurston, Asa	1868
176	Wade, Deborah	1868
177	Wilson, Mary	1868
178	Bingham, Hiram	1869
179	Gilmour, John	1869
180	Nott, Samuel	1869
181	Perkins, Justin	1869
182	Bettelheim, Bernard	1870
183	Hinderer, Anna	1870
184	Lemue, Prosper	1870
185	Schwartz, Carl	1870
186	Taylor, Maria	1870
187	Thomas, John	1870
188	Aea, Hezekiah	1871
189	Bridgman, Eliza	1871
190	Cochran, Joseph	1871
191	Day, Samuel	1871
192	Patteson, John	1871
193	Roberts, Issachar	1871
194	Smith, George	1871
195	Turton, William	1871
196	Williams, William	1871
197	Bishop, Artemas	1872
198	Ellis, William	1872
199	Elmslie, William	1872
200	Geddie, John	1872
201	Wade, Jonathan	1872
202	Wardlaw, John	1872
203	Bradley, Dan Beach	1873

204	Heyer, John	1873
205	Hobson, Benjamin	1873
206	Jones, Evan	1873
207	Judd, Gerrit	1873
208	Livingstone, David	1873
209	Pettitt, George	1873
210	Rolland, Samuel	1873
211	Spaulding, Levi	1873
212	Taylor, Richard	1873
213	Dole, Charlotte	1874
214	Mason, Francis	1874
215	Officer, Morris	1874
216	Scott, George	1874
217	Spalding, Henry	1874
218	Zaremba, Felician	1874
219	Bowen, Thomas	1875
220	Marston, Sarah	1875
221	New, Charles	1875
222	Smith, William	1875
223	Wilson, John	1875
224	Bessieux, Jean	1876
225	Breck, James	1876
226	Calhoun, Simeon	1876
227	Jones, John	1876
228	Nisbet, Henry	1876
229	Rebmann, Johannes	1876
230	Teava	1876
231	Thurston, Lucy	1876
232	Welch, James	1876
233	Zimmermann, J.	1876
234	Arbousset, J. T.	1877
235	Bulu, Joeli	1877
236	Douglas, Carstairs	1877
237	Gulick, Peter	1877
238	Mather, Robert	1877
239	Yate, William	1877
240	Clark, Ephraim	1878
241	Duff, Alexander	1878
242	Ridley, William	1878
243	Sharkey, Ann	1878
244	Williams, William	1878
245	Brown, Samuel	1879
246	Clarke, John	1879
247	Gobat, Samuel	1879
248	Mullens, Joseph	1879
249	Phillippo, James	1879
250	Phillips, Jeremiah	1879
251	Russell, William	1879
252	Stronach, Alexander	1879
253	Williamson, Thomas	1879
254	Bird, Mark	1880
255	Farrington, Sophronia	1880
256	Lindley, Daniel	1880
257	Maretu	1880
258	Saker, Alfred	1880
259	Snow, Benjamin	1880
260	Tomlin, Jacob	1880
261	Fjellstedt, Peter	1881
262	Thomas, John	1881
263	Anderson, Louisa	1882
264	Coan, Titus	1882
265	Elmslie, Margaret	1882
266	Hill, John	1882
267	Percival, Peter	1882
268	Schreuder, Hans	1882
269	Steere, Edward	1882
270	Agnew, Eliza	1883
271	Bronson, Miles	1883
272	Gulick, Fanny	1883
273	Jaechke, Heinrich	1883
274	Moffat, Robert	1883
275	Priest, James	1883
276	Riggs, Stephen	1883
277	Schauffler, William	1883
278	Alexander, William	1884
279	Brown, Alfred	1884
280	Green, Samuel	1884
281	Leupolt, Charles	1884
282	Lyman, David	1884
283	Pitman, Charles	1884
284	Stallybrass, Edward	1884
285	Williams, Samuel	1884
286	Bennett, Cephas	1885
287	Stern, Henry	1885
288	Timpany, Americus	1885
289	Brett, William	1886
290	Brown, Nathan	1886
291	Clark, William	1886
292	Gollmer, Charles	1886
293	Hogg, John	1886

#	Name	Year
294	Lyons, Lorenzo	1886
295	McDougall, Francis	1886
296	Townsend, Henry	1886
297	Wilson, John	1886
298	Woolston, Beulah	1886
299	Carpenter, Chapin	1887
300	Comber, Thomas	1887
301	Donders, Peter	1887
302	Gordon, Andrew	1887
303	Long, James	1887
304	Rice, Benjamin	1887
305	Sturges, Albert	1887
306	Wilder, Royal	1887
307	Wylie, Alexander	1887
308	Baker, Amelia	1888
309	Bowen, George	1888
310	Mackenzie, John	1888
311	Parker, Peter	1888
312	Rankin, Melinda	1888
313	Stronach, John	1888
314	Bliss, Isaac	1889
315	Boyce, William	1889
316	Butler, Fanny	1889
317	Sargent, Edward	1889
318	Schon, Jakob	1889
319	Trumbull, David	1889
320	Callaway, Henry	1890
321	Doane, Edward	1890
322	Freeman, Thomas	1890
323	Hastings, Eurotas	1890
324	Hinderer, David	1890
325	Lewis, Marianne	1890
326	Mackay, Alexander	1890
327	Safford, Anna	1890
328	Shreve, Elizabeth	1890
329	Williamson, A.	1890
330	Caldwell, Robert	1891
331	Casalis, Eugene	1891
332	Crowther, Samuel	1891
333	Droese, Ernest	1891
334	French, Thomas	1891
335	Gilmour, James	1891
336	Guilick, Luther	1891
337	Inglis, John	1891
338	Maclaren, Albert	1891
339	Newton, John	1891
340	Thomson, William	1891
341	Turner, George	1891
342	Brooke, Graham	1892
343	Calvert, James	1892
344	Gomer, Joseph	1892
345	Lapsley, Samuel	1892
346	Lowe, John	1892
347	Murray, Archibald	1892
348	Talmage, John	1892
349	Dauble, Carl	1893
350	Gribble, John	1893
351	Hepburn, James	1893
352	McBeth, Sue	1893
353	Nevius, John	1893
354	Tucker, Charlotte	1893
355	Alli, Janni	1894
356	Fleming, John	1894
357	Forman, Charles	1894
358	Good, Adolphus	1894
359	Gorham, Sarah	1894
360	Gowans, Walter	1894
361	Gulick, Lousia	1894
362	Happer, Andrew	1894
363	Mabille, Adolphe	1894
364	Maunsell, Robert	1894
365	Pratt, George	1894
366	Anderson, William	1895
367	Christaller, Johannes	1895
368	Dean, William	1895
369	Goldie, Hugh	1895
370	Hahn, Carl	1895
371	Hale, Mathew	1895
372	Tyler, Josiah	1895
373	Van Dyck, Cornelius	1895
374	Waddell, Hope	1895
375	Bisseux, Isaac	1896
376	Gill, William	1896
377	Goble, Jonathan	1896
378	Gomer, Mary	1896
379	Hill, David	1896
380	Lee, Daniel	1896
381	Lockhart, William	1896
382	Meyer, Theodore	1896
383	Schnelle, Johann	1896

384 Bickersteth, Edward 1897
385 Day, David 1897
386 Laurie, Thomas 1897
387 Legge, James 1897
388 McFarland, Samuel 1897
389 Petrie, Irene 1897
390 Pilkington, George 1897
391 Simonton, Ashbel 1897
392 Crummell, Alexander 1898
393 Rowe, Phoebe 1898
394 Sale, Elizabeth 1898
395 Ta'unga 1898
396 Verbeck, Guido 1898
397 Butler, William 1899
398 Chalmers, John 1899
399 Colenso, William 1899
400 Fleming, Louise 1899
401 Thomas, Mary 1899
402 Clark, Robert 1900
403 Fuller, Jennie 1900
404 Lowrie, John 1900
405 McCartee, Divie 1900
406 Price, Roger 1900
407 White, Moses 1900
408 Cochran, George 1901
409 Fliedner, Federico 1901
410 Mackay, George 1901
411 Riggs, Elias 1901
412 Thoburn, Isabella 1901
413 Underhill, Edward 1901
414 Wakefield, Thomas 1901
415 Appenzeller, Henry 1902
416 Crawford, Tarleton 1902
417 Ingalls, Marilla 1902
418 Matthews, Daniel 1902
419 Taylor, William 1902
420 Gulick, Alice 1903
421 Buchan, Jane 1904
422 Coillard, Francois 1904
423 Colenso, Elizabeth 1904
424 Fernbaugh, Hettie 1904
425 Hadfield, Octavius 1904
426 Jansz, Pieter 1904
427 Johnson, Amelia 1904
428 Machray, Robert 1904

429 Mitchell, John 1904
430 Taylor, Jenny 1904
431 Bentley, William 1905
432 Bohner, Heinrich 1905
433 Chestnut, Eleanor 1905
434 Cochran, Joeseh 1905
435 Edkins, Joseph 1905
436 Favier, Pierre Marie 1905
437 Graybill, Anthony 1905
438 Hofmeyr, Stefanus 1905
439 Muir, William 1905
440 Stewart, James 1905
441 Taylor, James H. 1905
442 Bompas, William 1906
443 Grenfall, George 1906
444 Isherwood, Annie 1906
445 Ramseyer, Rosa 1906
446 Ruatoka 1906
447 Schereschewsky, S. 1906
448 Allen, Young 1907
449 Fison, Lorimer 1907
450 Lawes, William 1907
451 Lohr, Oscar 1907
452 Maclay, Robert 1907
453 Paton, John 1907
454 Scott, David 1907
455 Thornton, Douglas 1907
456 Barton, John 1908
457 Bingham, Hiram Jr. 1908
458 Chamberlain, Jacob 1908
459 Franson, Fredik 1908
460 Hemans, John 1908
461 Mateer, Calvin 1908
462 Pope, George 1908
463 Widemann, Rosina 1908
464 Ashmore, William 1909
465 Colley William 1909
466 Crawford, Martha 1909
467 Darling, Thomas 1909
468 Hagenauer, Friedrich 1909
469 Jackson, Sheldon 1909
470 Janes, Leroy 1909
471 Rouse, George 1909
472 Clough, John 1910
473 Dubose, Hampden 1910

474	Jessup, Henry	1910
475	Newell, James	1910
476	Shattuck, Corinna	1910
477	Skrefsrud, Lars	1910
478	Swain, Clara	1910
479	Williams, Channing	1910
480	Woolston, Sarah	1910
481	Holly, James	1911
482	Hughes, Thomas	1911
483	Lloyd, Arthur	1911
484	McDonald, Alexander	1911
485	McFarlande, Samuel	1911
486	McGilvary, Daniel	1911
487	Price, William	1911
488	Stuart, Edward	1911
489	Wilder, Grace	1911
490	Abrams, Minnie F.	1912
491	Hore, Edward	1912
492	Hyde, John	1912
493	John, Griffith	1912
494	Liggins, John	1912
495	McLaurin, John	1912
496	Moon, Charlotte	1912
497	Moule, George	1912
498	Pennell, Theodor	1912
499	Pratt, Henry	1912
500	Slater, Thomas	1912
501	Walker, Thomas	1912
502	Borden, William	1913
503	Bulmer, John	1913
504	Butler, Clementina	1913
505	Coppin, Fanny	1913
506	Doke, Joseph	1913
507	Ely, Mary Ann	1913
508	McDonald, Robert	1913
509	Schrenk, Elias	1913
510	Arnot, Fredrick	1914
511	Bird, Mary	1914
512	Crosby, Thomas	1914
513	Dennis, James	1914
514	Gerard, Joseph	1914
515	Ramseyer, Fritz	1914
516	Spieth, Andreas	1914
517	Cushing, Ellen	1915
518	Dirks, Heinrich	1915
519	Ely, Charlotte	1915
520	Flad, Johann	1915
521	Marks, John	1915
522	Pollard, Samuel	1915
523	Ross, John	1915
524	Slessor, Mary	1915
525	Smith, Amanda	1915
526	Vernier, Frederic	1915
527	Wilson, Edward	1915
528	Bliss, Daniel	1916
529	Clark, Henry	1916
530	Ferguson, Samuel	1916
531	Fielde, Adele	1916
532	Foucauld, Charles	1916
533	Guerrant, Edward	1916
534	Jones, John	1916
535	Martin, William	1916
536	Moore, Joanna	1916
537	Underwood, Horace	1916
538	Wilson, Samuel	1916
539	Bickel, Luke	1917
540	Brown, George	1917
541	Dennis, Thomas	1917
542	Loosdrecht, Antoine	1917
543	Armstrong, William	1918
544	Davidson, Andrew	1918
545	Duncan, William	1918
546	Gilman, Frank	1918
547	Merensky, Alexander	1918
548	Moffat, John	1918
549	Morrison, William	1918
550	Moule, Arthur	1918
551	Nommensen, Ingwer	1918
552	Shedd, William	1918
553	Spinner, Wilfried	1918
554	Armstrong, Hannah	1919
555	Bliss, Edwin	1919
556	Camphor, Alexander	1919
557	Coombs, Lucinda	1919
558	Forsyth, Christina	1919
559	Gibson, John	1919
560	Hitchcock, John	1919
561	Jones, George	1919
562	Lefroy, George	1919
563	Richard, Timothy	1919

#	Name	Year
564	Corbett, Hunter	1920
565	Fisher, George	1920
566	Friesen, Abraham	1920
567	Harris, Merriman	1921
568	Lucas, Bernard	1921
569	Baller, Frederick	1922
570	Codrington, Robert	1922
571	Delany, Emma	1922
572	Scranton, William	1922
573	Strehlow, Carl	1922
574	Thoburn, James	1922
575	Wood, Thomas	1922
576	Eddy, Mary	1923
577	Gulick, Orramel	1923
578	Miller, William	1923
579	Stirling, Waite	1923
580	Torrance, David	1923
581	Tule, Mary	1923
582	Cowman, Charles	1924
583	Evans, Robert	1924
584	Gurney, Samuel	1924
585	Noyes, Harriet	1924
586	Payne, William	1924
587	Peck, Edmund	1924
588	Smith, Henry	1924
589	Weston, Frank	1924
590	Cassels, William	1925
591	Dahle, Lars	1925
592	Ewing, James	1925
593	Howard, Leonora	1925
594	Adriani, Nicolaus	1926
595	Cook, J.A.B	1926
596	Crawford, Daniel	1926
597	Elliot, Benjamin	1926
598	Nelson, Daniel	1926
599	Sheppard, William	1926
600	Edwards, Mary	1927
601	Hoy, William	1927
602	Reid, Gilbert	1927
603	Wherry, Elwood	1927
604	Young, Samuel	1927
605	Gairdner, William	1928
606	Howe, Gertrude	1928
607	Johnson, William	1928
608	Matthews, Thomas	1928
609	Nau, Semisi	1928
610	Richards, Henry	1928
611	Stock, Eugene	1928
612	Tisdall, William	1928
613	Trotter, Isabelle	1928
614	Winans, Ester	1928
615	Brent, Charles	1929
616	Bromilow, William	1929
617	Creux, Ernest	1929
618	Farquhar, John	1929
619	Hume, Robert	1929
620	Lewis, Thomas	1929
621	MacDonald, Duff	1929
622	Matthopoulos, Eus.	1929
623	Schmelzenbach, H.	1929
624	Sibree, James	1929
625	Abel, Charles W.	1930
626	Barber, Margaret	1930
627	Berthoud, Paul	1930
628	Francke, August	1930
629	Grubb, Wilfrid	1930
630	Henderson, James	1930
631	Stevenson, Marion	1930
632	Stover, Wilbur	1930
633	Trollope, Mark	1930
634	Weinland, William	1930
635	Baird, William	1931
636	Goward, William	1931
637	Limbrock, Eberhard	1931
638	Macdonald, Annie	1931
639	MacGillivray, Donald	1931
640	McCandliss, Henry	1931
641	Voth, Henry	1931
642	Whittemore, Emma	1931
643	Allen, Horace	1932
644	Bakker, Dirk	1932
645	Besson, Pablo	1932
646	Boothe, Joseph	1932
647	Giffen, John	1932
648	Makichan, Dugald	1932
649	Sell, Edward	1932
650	Smith, Arthur	1932
651	Bearch, Harlan	1933
652	Fraser, Donald	1933
653	Hall, Elizabeth	1933

#	Name	Year
654	Hodgkin, Henry	1933
655	Mather, Percy	1933
656	Thomson, Jon	1933
657	Veenstra, Johanna	1933
658	Vingren, Adolf	1933
659	Wanless, William	1933
660	Weir, Andrew	1933
661	White, John	1933
662	Johanssen, Ernst	1934
663	Junod, Henri	1934
664	Main, David	1934
665	Montgomery, Helen	1934
666	Peery, Rufus	1934
667	Stam, John	1934
668	Stam, Elizabeth	1934
669	Wilkes, Paget	1934
670	Barclay, Thomas	1935
671	Bender, Carl	1935
672	Davidson, Hannah	1935
673	Elmslie, Walter	1935
674	Fraser, Kenneth	1935
675	Miner, Luella	1935
676	Barton, James	1936
677	Christie, Dugald	1936
678	Clifford, James	1936
679	Goforth, Jonathan	1936
680	Hurlburt, Charles	1936
681	Jones, David	1936
682	Mackenzie, Jean	1936
683	Bailey, Wellesley	1937
684	Broomhall, Marshall	1937
685	Edmiston, Althea	1937
686	Gale, James	1937
687	Gulliford, Henry	1937
688	Oldham, William	1937
689	Pott, Francis	1937
690	Voskamp, Carl	1937
691	Bodding, Paul	1938
692	Fraser, James	1938
693	Gulick, Ann	1938
694	Le Roy, Alexander	1938
695	Paton, Francis	1938
696	Polhill, Cecil	1938
697	Schneder, David	1938
698	Willoughby, William	1938
699	Bagby, William	1939
700	Baldwin, Elizabeth	1939
701	Cousins, William	1939
702	Hetherwick, A.	1939
703	Matthews, Janet	1939
704	McKechnie, Elizabeth	1939
705	Moffett, Samuel	1939
706	Prip, Einar	1939
707	Takle, John	1939
708	Andrews, Charles F.	1940
709	Buxton, Alfred	1940
710	Clough, Emma	1940
711	Grenfall, Wilfred	1940
712	Larsen, Lars	1940
713	Moody, Campbell	1940
714	Richter, Julius	1940
715	Sheppard, Lucy	1940
716	Allan, George	1941
717	Dalman, Gustav	1941
718	Frame, Alice	1941
719	Luce, Henry	1941
720	Vautrin, Wilhelmina	1941
721	Belksma, Johannes	1942
722	Bill, Samuel	1942
723	Bingham, Rowland	1942
724	Edwins, August	1942
725	Futon, Thomas	1942
726	Goforth, Rosalind	1942
727	Graham, John	1942
728	Meeuwsen, Johanna	1942
729	Yi, Ki Poong	1942
730	Lock, Annie	1943
731	Molnar, Maria	1943
732	Reed, Mary	1943
733	Waller, Edward	1943
734	Brockman, Fletcher	1944
735	Garr, Alfred	1944
736	Heine, Carl	1944
737	Lorrain, James	1944
738	Mebius, Frederick	1944
739	Monnier, Henri	1944
740	Rodgers, James	1944
741	Scherer, James	1944
742	Stauffacher, John	1944
743	Staunton, John	1944

#	Name	Year
744	Warneck, Johannes	1944
745	Blackmore, Sophia	1945
746	Frost, Henry	1945
747	Gaebelein, Arno	1945
748	Griswold, Hervey	1945
749	Grossman, Guido	1945
750	Jaffray, Robert	1945
751	Liddell, Eric	1945
752	Lohrenz, Henry	1945
753	Lucas, William	1945
754	Owen, Walter	1945
755	Schellenberg, K.	1945
756	Schiller, Karl	1945
757	Schomerus, Hilko	1945
758	Schuurman, Barend	1945
759	Small, Ann	1945
760	Tewksbury, Elwood	1945
761	Fisch, Rudolf	1946
762	Hoste, Dixon	1946
763	Hunter, George	1946
764	Springer, Helen	1946
765	Flierl, Johann	1947
766	Furman, Charles	1947
767	Glover, Robert	1947
768	Murray, William	1947
769	Petter, Rodolphe	1947
770	Scharer, Hans	1947
771	Shellabear, William	1947
772	Speer, Robert	1947
773	Whitehead, Henry	1947
774	Bachman, Traugott	1948
775	Haymaker, Edward	1948
776	Baldwin, Jane	1949
777	Hulbert, Homer	1949
778	Lyon, David	1949
779	MacVicar, Neil	1949
780	Neumann, Johan	1949
781	Thevenoud, Joanny	1949
782	Tyndale Biscoe, Cecil	1949
783	Watson, Minnie	1949
784	Westcott, Foss	1949
785	Allshorn, Florence	1950
786	Anderson, William H	1950
787	Fleming, Paul	1950
788	Gamewell, Frank	1950
789	Moninger, Mary	1950
790	Ronning, Halvor	1950
791	Stahl, Ferdinand	1950
792	Carmichael, Amy	1951
793	Cook, Albert	1951
794	Hastings, Harry	1951
795	Melrose, Margaret	1951
796	Petersen, Anne	1951
797	Arthur, John W	1952
798	Birkeli, Emil	1952
799	Cable, Alice	1952
800	MacNicol, Nicol	1952
801	McLaurin, John	1952
802	Miller, Walter	1952
803	O'Niell, Frederick	1952
804	Parrish, Sarah	1952
805	Reichelt, Karl	1952
806	Ritchie, John	1952
807	Streicher, Henri	1952
808	Zwemer, Samuel	1952
809	Cochrane, Thomas	1953
810	Eastman, Elaine	1953
811	Fleming, Archibald	1953
812	Magee, John	1953
813	McNarin, Stuart	1953
814	Moe, Malla	1953
815	Glover, Archibald	1954
816	Goldie, John	1954
817	Hogg, Alfred	1954
818	Leenhardt, Maurice	1954
819	Willis, John	1954
820	Cash, William	1955
821	Christoffel, Ernest	1955
822	Howells, George	1955
823	Luce, Alice	1955
824	Yoder, Charles	1955
825	Young, Thomas	1955
826	Avison Oliver, R.	1956
827	Brown, Edith	1956
828	Elliot, Phillip "Jim"	1956
829	Fleming, Peter	1956
830	Heath, George	1956
831	Louw, Andries	1956
832	Myers, Estellia	1956
833	Plymire, Victor	1956

#	Name	Year
834	Rouse, Clara	1956
835	Saint, Nathanael	1956
836	Shaw, Archibald	1956
837	Bouey, Elizabeth	1957
838	Deck, John	1957
839	Goldsack, William	1957
840	Gribble, Ernest	1957
841	Gwynne, Llewellyn	1957
842	Hiebert, Nikolas	1957
843	Smith, Edwin	1957
844	Burgess, Paul	1958
845	Higginbottom, Sam	1958
846	Porter, Lucious	1958
847	Thurston, Matilda	1958
848	Tucker, John	1958
849	Warnshuis, Abbe	1958
850	Cheese, John	1959
851	Mills, Wilson	1959
852	Stauffacher, Florence	1959
853	Torrance, Thomas	1959
854	Cowman, Lettie	1960
855	Davis, John	1960
856	Jones, Lewis	1960
857	Popley, Herbert	1960
858	Scudder, Ida	1960
859	Clark, Charles	1961
860	Crawford, Isabelle	1961
861	French, Evangeline	1961
862	French, Francesca	1961
863	Hueting, Andre	1961
864	Simpson, William	1961
865	Stockwell, Bowman	1961
866	Trasher, Lillian	1961
867	Wiser, William	1961
868	Fraser, Alexander	1962
869	Fraser, John	1962
870	Halliwell, Jessie	1962
871	Harris, George	1962
872	Harrison, Paul	1962
873	Hunnicutt, Benjamin	1962
874	Monsen, Marie	1962
875	Sandegren, Johannes	1962
876	Steidel, Florence	1962
877	Stuart, John	1962
878	Atkinson Maria	1963
879	Axling, William	1963
880	Bach, Thomas	1963
881	Benigneus, Pierre	1963
882	Brown, Arthur	1963
883	Eddy, George	1963
884	Lanneau, Sophie	1963
885	Mabie, Catherine	1963
886	Nielsen, Alfred	1963
887	Springer, John	1963
888	Bavinck, Johan	1964
889	Carlson, Paul	1964
890	Chawner, Charles	1964
891	Cheek, Landon	1964
892	Elwin, Harry	1964
893	Herron, Walter	1964
894	Titus, Murray	1964
895	Tucker, J.	1964
896	Vories, William	1964
897	Bartel, Henry	1965
898	Holland, Henry	1965
899	Sabatier, Ernst	1965
900	Seagrave, Gordon	1965
901	Bronnum, Niels	1966
902	Hooper, Handley	1966
903	Reed, George	1966
904	Sambeek, Jan van	1966
905	Tollefsen, Gunnerius	1966
906	Williamson, Henry	1966
907	Cary, Maude	1967
908	Dickson, James	1967
909	Halliwell, Leo	1967
910	Willson, Robert	1967
911	Dyer, Alfred	1968
912	Padwick, Constance	1968
913	Iglehart, Charles	1969
914	Oldham, Joseph	1969
915	Aylward, Gladys	1970
916	Braden, Charles	1970
917	Burton, John	1970
918	Laubach, Frank	1970
919	Macdonald, Andrew	1970
920	Burton, William	1971
921	Calverley, Edwin	1971
922	Huegel, Frederick	1971
923	Litwiller, John	1971

924 Wuhrmann, Anna 1971
925 Reischauer, August 1971
926 Schurhammer, Georg 1971
927 Sedat, William 1971
928 Shepherd, Robert 1971
929 Webster Smith, Irene 1971
930 Trenchard, Ernest 1972
931 Vedder, Hermann 1972
932 Bell, Lemuel 1973
933 Buck, Pearl 1973
934 Jones, Stanley 1973
935 Pihofer, Georg 1973
936 Wilson, J. Christy 1973
937 Brand, Evelyn 1974
938 Eastman, George 1974
939 Price, Francis 1974
940 Winslow, John 1974
941 Caffray, Daisy 1975
942 Francis, Mabel 1975
943 Winans, Roger 1975
944 Donaldson, Dwight 1976
945 Fox, Charles 1977
946 Gebauer, Paul 1977
947 McClure, William 1977
948 Bates, Miner 1978
949 Jones, Mabel 1978
950 Lombard, Eva 1978
951 Petersen, Paul 1978
952 Smith, Algernon 1978
953 Strauss, Hermann 1978
954 Wangerin, Theodora 1978
955 Dick, Amos 1979
956 Sargent, Douglas 1979
957 Trobisch, Walter 1979
958 Fisher, Welthy 1980
959 George, Eliza 1980
960 Grubb, Kenneth 1980
961 Rowlands, John 1980
962 Drebert, Ferdinand 1981
963 Larson, Reuben 1981
964 Pickett, Jarrell 1981
965 Wiser, Charlotte 1981
966 Graham, James 1982
967 Malinki, James 1982
968 Townsend, Cameron 1982

969 Williams, Ralph 1982
970 Birkeli, Fridtjov 1983
971 Chesterman, Clement 1983
972 Dickson, Lillian 1983
973 Jocz, Jakob 1983
974 Scott, Michael 1983
975 Lehmann, E. Arno 1984
976 Neill, Stephen 1984
977 Smith, John 1984
978 Goodall, Norman 1985
979 Lindell, Jonathan 1985
980 Jones, Clarence 1986
981 Proksch, Georg 1986
982 Beaver R. Pierce 1987
983 Bergmann, Wilhelm 1987
984 Boberg, Folke 1987
985 Hayward, Victor 1988
986 Hodges, Melvin 1988
987 Taylor, Clyde 1988
988 Taylor, Richard 1988
989 Tippett, Alan 1988
990 Buntain, Daniel 1989
991 McDowell, Henry 1989
992 Ramsey, Evelyn 1989
993 Stanway, Alfred 1989
994 Wood, Alfred 1989
995 Becker, Carl 1990
996 Haines, Byron 1990
997 Martin, Marie Louise 1990
998 Moomaw, Ira 1990
999 Hall, Martin 1991
1000 Hall, Sherwood 1991
1001 Hynd, David 1991
1002 Pean, Charles 1991
1003 Young, George 1991
1004 Buker, Raymond 1992
1005 Hunt, Bruce 1992
1006 Paton, David 1992
1007 Bosshardt, Rudolf 1993
1008 Miller, WIlliam 1993
1009 Raaflaub, Fritz 1993
1010 Rycroft, William 1993
1011 Adeney, David H. 1994
1012 Broomhall, Anthony 1994
1013 Judd, Walter 1994

1014 Saint, Rachel	1994	
1015 Dahl, Otto	1995	
1016 Ibiam, Francis	1995	
1017 Lozada, Jorgelina	1995	
1018 Sundkler, Bengt	1995	
1019 Lyall, Leslie	1996	
1020 Money, Herbert	1996	
1021 Motta, Waldomiro	1996	
1022 Stockwell, Eugene	1996	
1023 Brand, Paul	2003	
1024 Luzbetak, Louis	2005	
1025 Taylor, John	2001	
1026 Trobisch, Ingrid	2007	
1027 Verkuyl, Johannes	2005	
1028 Winter, Ralph D.	2009	
1029 Bang Ji Il	**	
1030 Baughman, Burr	**	
1031 Block Hoell, Niles	**	
1032 Broger, John	**	
1033 Choi Chan Young	**	
1034 Cook Gonzales, E.	**	
1035 Danbolt, Erling	**	
1036 Dodge, Ralph	**	
1037 Doig, Andrew	**	
1038 Dunger, George	**	
1039 Hernandez, V	**	
1040 Hogan, James	**	
1041 Jones, Nancy	**	
1042 Ledyard, Gleason	**	
1043 Liggett, Thomas	**	
1044 Mackenzie, Helen	**	
1045 Mamora, Lucius	**	
1046 Newbigin, James	**	
1047 Rossel, Jacques	**	
1048 Sedat, Elizabeth	**	
1049 Smith, Stanley	**	

BIBLIOGRAPHY

Adger, J. B. "The General Assembly of 1860." *The Southern Presbyterian Review*, no. 13 (1861).

Ajayi, J. F. A. "From Mission to Church: The Heritage of the Church Mission Society." *International Bulletin of Missionary Research* 23, no. 2 (1999): 50-55.

Allen, John L. *Opus Dei: An Objective Look Behind the Myths and Reality of the Most Controversial Force in the Catholic Church*. 1st ed. New York: Doubleday, 2005.

Allen, Roland. *The Spontaneous Expansion of the Church and the Causes Which Hinder It*. London: World Dominion Press, 1927.

The American Heritage Dictionary of the English Language. 3rd ed. Boston: Houghton Mifflin, 1996.

Anderson, Gerald H. "Why We Need a Second Mission Agency." In *The Factors That Confront Us and the Faith That Compels Us* Dallas, 1984, February.

————. "American Protestants in Pursuit of Missions: 1886-1986." *International Bulletin of Missionary Research* 2, no. 3 (1988): 98-118.

————. *Biographical Dictionary of Christian Missions*. New York: Macmillan, 1998.

Anderson, Robert and Barbara Gallatin. "Voluntary Associations and Urbanization." *American Journal of Sociology* 65, (1959): 265-273.

Baegert, Jacob, Brandenburg, M. M., Baumann, Carl L. *Observations in Lower California*. Berkeley: University of California Press, 1952.

Bailey, Kenneth E. *A Tale of Three Cities: An Analysis of Presbyterian Mission Policies*. Pasadena: Presbyterian Center for Mission Studies, 1989.

Bainton, Roland Herbert. *Christianity*. New York: American Heritage; Distributed by Houghton Mifflin, 1964.

Baker, Dwight P. "William Carey and the Business Model for Mission: Reflections on the Conduct of Mission at the Opening of the 21st Century." Pasadena, CA: William Carey International University, 2001.

Barth, Karl. *Church Dogmatics*. Vol. IV/3. Edinburgh: T. & T. Clark, 1957.

Bauer, Bruce L. "Congregational and Mission Structures." D. Miss. Dissertation, Fuller Theological Seminary, 1982.

Bavinck, Johan Herman. *An Introduction to the Science of Missions*. Philadelphia: Presbyterian and Reformed, 1960.

Beals, Paul A. *A People for His Name: A Church Based Missions Strategy*. Rev. ed. Pasadena, CA: William Carey Library, 1985.

Beardslee, John. "American Arabian Mission Centennial Address." New Brunswick Seminary, New Brunswick, NJ, April 1989.

Beaver, R. Pierce. "The Genevan Mission to Brazil." *The Reformed Journal* 17, no. 6 (1967): 14-20.

_____. *To Advance the Gospel; Selections from the Writings of Rufus Anderson*. Grand Rapids: Eerdmans, 1967.

_____. *All Loves Excelling; American Protestant Women in World Mission*. Grand Rapids: Eerdmans, 1968.

_____. *The Missionary between the Times*. 1st ed. Garden City, NY: Doubleday, 1968.

_____. "The Christian Mission, a Look into the Future." *Concordia Theological Monthly* 42, (1971): 345-352.

_____. *American Protestant Women in World Mission: A History of the First Feminist Movement in North America*. Rev. ed. Grand Rapids: Eerdmans, 1980.

_____. "A Plea for a New Voluntarism." *Concordia Theological Monthly*, (June 1971).

Becker, Caroline N. "Missionaries Speak." In *A History of Presbyterian Missions 1944-2007* Louisville: Geneva Press, 2008.

Bede. *A History of the English Church and People*. Harmondsworth, Middlesex: Penguin Books, 1968.

Behrhorst, Wallace. "New Mission Initiatives, Lutheran Church World Mission." Pasadena: US Center for World Mission, 1997.

Bellah, Robert Neelly. *Habits of the Heart: Individualism and Commitment in American Life*. Berkeley, CA: University of California Press, 1985.

Benthall, Jonathan, and Jérôme Bellion-Jourdan. *The Charitable Crescent: Politics of Aid in the Muslim World*. London ; New York: I.B. Tauris, 2003.

Benz, Ernst. "Pietist and Puritan Sources of Early Protestant World Missions (Cotton Mather and H. Francke)." *Church History*, (1951): 28-55.

Berkhof, Louis. *Systematic Theology*. 2d rev. and enl. ed. Grand Rapids, Mich.,: Wm. B. Eerdmans publishing co., 1982.

Bethge, Eberhard, and Victoria Barnett. *Dietrich Bonhoeffer: Theologian, Christian, Man for His Times; a Biography*. Rev. ed. Minneapolis: Fortress Press, 2000.

Beyreuther, Erich. *Zinzendorf Und Die Christenheit 1732-1760*. Marburg an der Lahn: Francke, 1961.

Bliese, Richard H., and Horst Rzepkowski, eds. *Missionary Societies*. Edited by Karl Muller SVD, Dictionary of Mission: Theology, History, Perspectives. Maryknoll, NY: Orbis Books, 1997.

Blincoe, Robert A. "Desired Symbiosis: Church and Mission Structures." *International Journal of Frontier Missions* 19, no. 3 (2002): 43-46.

_____. "U.S. Missionary Totals by Affiliation 1918-2002." *International Bulletin of Missionary Research*, January 2005, 2009.

_____. "Warp and Woof." In *http://www.sarkisian.com/images/warpweft.jpg*, 2010.

_____. "Quote by John Buteyn." In *Samuel Zwemer Centennial Report*. Samuel Zwemer Institute, Pasadena, California, May, 1989.

Blincoe, Robert A. "Timeline: Luther to Carey, Plus 30 Remarkable Years." 2009.

_____. *Interview with T.J.: My Experience Working for an Afghan N.G.O.* Mesa, Arizona, August 2007.

Board, Stephen. "The Great Evangelical Power Shift." *Eternity* 30:6, (1979): 17-21.

Boer, Harry R. *Pentecost and Missions.* Grand Rapids: Eerdmans, 1961.

Book of Order. Louisville, KY: Office of the General Assembly, Presbyterian Church USA, 1992.

Bornstein, David. *How to Change the World: Social Entrepreneurs and the Power of New Ideas*: Oxford University Press, 2004.

Bosch, David Jacobus. *Transforming Mission: Paradigm Shifts in Theology of Mission*. Maryknoll, NY: Orbis Books, 1991.

Boyd, Lois A., R. Douglas Brackenridge, and The Presbyterian Historical Society. *Presbyterian Women in America: Two Centuries of a Quest for Status*. 2nd ed. Contributions to the Study of Religion. Westport, CT: Greenwood Press, 1996.

Brauer, Jerald C., and B. A. Gerrish. *The Westminster Dictionary of Church History*. Philadelphia: Westminster Press, 1971.

Breckenridge, Robert J. "Facts and Considerations in Regard to Ecclesiastical Control in Benevolent Operations." *The Baltimore Literary and Religious Magazine*, no. 5 (1839): 378.

Brown, Arthur Judson. *One Hundred Years: A History of the Foreign Missionary Work of the Presbyterian Church in the USA*. New York: Revell, 1936.

Brown, G. Thompson. "Rethinking Some Modern-Day Shibboleths." *Missiology* 12, (1984): 87-95.

Brown, G. Thompson and Donald T. Black. "Structures for a Changing Church." In *A History of Presbyterian Missions 1944-2007*. Louisville: Geneva Press, 2008.

Bruce, F. F. *New Testament History*. London: Nelson, 1969.

Brumberg-Kraus, Jonathan, "Were the Pharisees a Conversionist Sect? Table Fellowship as a Strategy of Conversion" http://acunix.wheatonma.edu/jkraus/articles/Pharisees.htm.

Buchanan, John. "Moderator's Address." Synod Missions Rally, Bel Air Presbyterian Church, Los Angeles, CA February, 1997.

Burke, Edmund, and J. C. D. Clark. *Reflections on the Revolution in France*. Stanford, CA: Stanford University Press, 2001.

Burrows, William R. "Catholics, Carey's "Means," and Twenty-First Century Mission." *International Bulletin of Missionary Research* 34, no. 3 (2010): 131-138.

C., Joseph and Michele. "Field-Governed Structures: New Testament." *International Journal of Frontier Missions* 18, no. 2 (2001): 59-66.

Cahill, Thomas. *How the Irish Saved Civilization: The Untold Story of Ireland's Heroic Role from the Fall of Rome to the Rise of Medieval Europe*. 1st ed. New York: Nan A. Talese, Doubleday, 1995.

Calvin, Jean. *Institutes of the Christian Religion*. Vol. 2. Philadelphia: Westminster Press, 1960.

Camp, Bruce. "Scripturally Considered, the Local Church Has Primary Responsibility for World Evangelization." In *School of Intercultural Studies* Doctor of Missiology. La Mirada: Biola University, 1992.

⎯⎯⎯⎯. "Paradigm Shifts in World Evangelization." *Mobilizer* 5, no. 1 (1994).

⎯⎯⎯⎯. "A Theological Examination of the Two-Structure Theory." *Missiology* 21, no. 2 (1995): 197-209.

Carey, Eustace, and Jeremiah Chaplin. *Memoir of William Carey, D, D., Late Missionary to Bengal, Professor of Oriental Languages in the College of Fort William, Calcutta*. Hartford,: Canfield and Robins, 1837.

Carey, William. *An Enquiry into the Obligations of Christians to Use Means for the Conversion of the Heathens*. Pre-1801 Imprint Collection (Library of Congress), ed. Leicester: Baptist Missionary Society London; reprinted by Ann Ireland, 1792.

Carver, John, and Miriam Mayhew Carver. *Reinventing Your Board: A Step-by-Step Guide to Implementing Policy Governance*. Rev. ed. San Francisco: John Wiley, 2006.

Chadwick, Nora K. *The Celts*. Harmondsworth, England: Penguin Books, 1970.

Chadwick, Owen. *A History of Christianity*. 1st U.S. ed. New York: St. Martin's Press, 1996.

Clark, Francis E. *Christian Endeavor in All Lands*. Boston: The United Society of Christian Endeavor, 1886.

⎯⎯⎯⎯. *Memories of Many Men in Many Lands: An Autobiography*. Boston: United Society of Christian Endeavor, 1922.

Coalter, Milton J., John M. Mulder, and Louis B. Weeks. "Introduction." In *The Organizational Revolution: Presbyterians and American Denominationalism* Louisville, KY: Westminster/John Knox, 1992.

Collins, Michael, and Matthew Arlen Price. *The Story of Christianity*. 1st American ed. New York: DK Press, 1999.

Colson, Charles W., and Richard John Neuhaus. *Evangelicals and Catholics Together: Toward a Common Mission*. Dallas: Word, 1995.

"Conference Papers." In *Consultation on Voluntary Societies*, edited by Robert A. Blincoe. Evansville, IL, 1975, May 22-24.

Conn, Harvie M. *Theological Perspectives on Church Growth*. Nutley, NJ: Presbyterian and Reformed, 1976.

Cook, Harold R. "Who Really Sent the First Missionaries?" *Evangelical Missions Quarterly* 11, no. 4 (1975): 233-239.

Coote, Robert T. "Shifts in the North American Protestant Full-Time Missionary Community." *International Bulletin of Missionary Research* 29, no. 1 (2005): 12-13.

Cormode, D. Scott. "A Financial History of Presbyterian Congregations since World War Two." In *The Organizational Revolution: Presbyterians and American Denominationalism* Louisville, KY: Westminster/John Knox Press, 1992.

Costas, Orlando E. *The Church and Its Mission: A Shattering Critique from the Third World*. Wheaton, IL: Tyndale House Publishers, 1974.

Cummings, Joe. "Jacob Baegert's Region of Baja California--Guaycura." Avalon Travel, 2008.

Danker, William J. *Profit for the Lord; Economic Activities in Moravian Missions and the Basel Mission Trading Company*. Grand Rapids: Eerdmans, 1971.

Dawson, David G. "A Recurring Issue of Mission Administration." *Missiology* 25, no. 4 (1997): 457-465.

———. *A Mission Funding System for the 21st Century*. New College, University of Edinburgh, Scotland, 2004.

———. "The Evolving Role of Presbytery after Christendom." Unpublished, (2005, March 23).

———. "Counting the Cost." In *A History of Presbyterian Missions, 1944-2007* Louisville: Geneva Press, 2008.

De Ridder, Richard. *Discipling the Nations*. Grand Rapids: Baker Book House, 1975.

Degler, Carl N. *Out of Our Past; the Forces That Shaped Modern America*. Rev. ed. New York: Harper & Row, 1970.

Douglas, Stephen A., and Paul Pedersen. *Blood, Believer, and Brother: The Development of Voluntary Associations in Malaysia*. Athens: Ohio University, 1973.

Dowley, Tim. *The History of Christianity* A Lion Handbook. Berkhamsted, England: Lion Publishing, 1977.

Dries, Angelyn. *The Missionary Movement in American Catholic History* American Society of Missiology Series; No. 26. Maryknoll, NY: Orbis Books, 1998.

Drury, Clifford Merrill. *Presbyterian Panorama; One Hundred and Fifty Years of National Missions History*. Philadelphia,: Board of Christian Education, Presbyterian Church in the United States of America, 1952.

Eberly, Don E., and Ryan Streeter. *The Soul of Civil Society: Voluntary Associations and the Public Value of Moral Habits*. Lanham, Md.: Lexington Books, 2002.

Edersheim, Alfred. *Sketches of Jewish Social Life in the Days of Christ*. London: The Religious Tract Society, 1876.

Eisenman, Robert. *The Dead Sea Scrolls and the First Christians*. Rockport, MA: Element Books, 1996.

Elazar, Daniel J. "Patterns of Jewish Organization in the United States." In *American Denominational Organizations* Pasadena: William Carey Library, 1980.

Eller, Gary S. "Special Interest Groups and American Presbyterianism." In *The Organizational Revolution: Presbyterians and American Denominationalism* Louisville, KY: Westminster/John Knox, 1992.

Ellingsen, Mark. *The Evangelical Movement: Growth, Impact, Controversy, Dialog*. Minneapolis: Augsburg, 1988.

Encyclopaedia Britannica Inc. *The New Encyclopædia Britannica*. Vol. 10. 15th ed. Chicago, Ill., 1991.

Evans, Greg. "We Should Be Doing Something!", Luann: *Arizona Republic*, 2008, May 19.

Fialka, John J. *Sisters: Catholic Nuns and the Making of America*. 1st ed. New York: St. Martin's Press, 2003.

Fletcher, R. A. *The Barbarian Conversion: From Paganism to Christianity*. 1st American ed. New York: H. Holt and Co., 1998.

Flett, John G. *The Witness of God : The Trinity, Missio Dei, Karl Barth, and the Nature of Christian Community*. Grand Rapids, Mich.: W.B. Eerdmans Pub., 2010.

Fogel, Robert William. *The Fourth Great Awakening & the Future of Egalitarianism*: University of Chicago Press, 2000.

Frizen, E. L. *75 Years of I.F.M.A., 1917-1992: The Nondenominational Missions Movement*. Pasadena, CA: William Carey Library, 1992.

Fuller, Lon L. "Two Principles of Human Association " In *Voluntary Associations* New York: Atherton Press, 1969.

Gallagher, John. "Private Groups Push Detroit Ahead." *The Detroit Free Press*, April 6, 2008.

Gensichen, Hans-Werner. "Justinian Von Welz." In *Biographical Dictionary of Christian Missions*, edited by Gerald H. Anderson. New York: Simon and Schuster, 1998.

Gensichen, Hans Werner. *Missionsgeschichte Der Neueren Zeit*. Göttingen,: Vandenhoeck & Ruprecht, 1961.

George, Sherron. "Faithfulness through the Storm: Changing Theology of Mission." In *A History of Presbyterian Mission, 1944-2007* Louisville: Geneva Press, 2008.

Gilbert, Martin, and Josephine Bacon. *The Illustrated Atlas of Jewish Civilization*. London: A. Deutsch, 1990.

"Giving Back." *US News and World Report* November 2010.

Glasser, Arthur F., and Donald Anderson McGavran. *Contemporary Theologies of Mission*. Grand Rapids: Baker Book House, 1983.

Glover, Robert H. *The Progress of World-Wide Missions*. New York: Harper, Brown 1953.

Golden, Don R. "A Study of the Local Church in Evangelical Cross-Cultural Mission." University of Wales, 1998.

Guder, Darrell L. "Missional Structures: The Particular Community." In *Missional Church: A Vision for the Sending of the Church in North America*. Grand Rapids: Eerdmans, 1998.

────────. *The Continuing Conversion of the Church* The Gospel and Our Culture Series. Grand Rapids: Eerdmans, 2000.

────────. "Para-Parochial Movements: The Religious Order Revisited." Vanderbilt University, September, 1994.

Guder, Darrell L., and Lois Barrett. *Missional Church: A Vision for the Sending of the Church in North America*, Edited by Darrell L. Guder. Grand Rapids: Eerdmans, 1998.

Hannum, Walter and Louise. "The Development of a Voluntary Mission Society in the Episcopal Church." Fuller Theological Seminary School of World Mission, 1975.

Harrison, Paul Mansfield. *Authority and Power in the Free Church Tradition; a Social Case Study of the American Baptist Convention*. Princeton, NJ: Princeton University Press, 1959.

Hart, D. G., and Mark A. Noll, eds. *Dictionary of the Presbyterian & Reformed Tradition in America*. Downers Grove, IL: Intervarsity Press, 1999.

Hay, Alexander Rattray. *The New Testament Order for Church and Missionary*. Temperley, Argentina ; St. Louis: New Testament Missionary Union, 1947.

Hayek, Friedrich A. von. *The Road to Serfdom*. 50th anniversary ed.: University of Chicago Press, 1994.

Heisenberg, Werner. *Physics and Beyond: Encounters and Conversations* World Perspectives. London: G. Allen & Unwin, 1971.

Herbermann, Charles George, Edward A. Pace, Condé Benoist Pallen, Thomas Joseph Shahan, John J. Wynne, and Knights of Columbus. Catholic truth committee. *The Catholic Encyclopedia*. New York: The Encyclopedia Press, 1913.

Hill, Thomas E. *Hill's Manual of Business and Social Information*. Chicago: W. B. Conkey, 1915.

Hoekstra, Harvey Thomas. *The World Council of Churches and the Demise of Evangelism*. Wheaton, Ill.: Tyndale House Publishers, 1979.

Horace, and John Carew Rolfe. *Q. Horati Flacci Sermones Et Epistulae* Allyn and Bacon's College Latin Series. Boston: Allyn and Bacon, 1901.

Hudson, Winthrop S. "Stumbling into Disorder." *Foundations* 2, no. 1 (April 1958).

Hudson, Winthrop Still. *American Protestantism* The Chicago History of American Civilization: University of Chicago Press, 1961.

Hunter, George G. *The Celtic Way of Evangelism: How Christianity Can Reach the West Again*. Nashville, TN: Abingdon Press, 2000.

Hutcheson, Richard G. "Pluralism and Consensus: Why Mainline Church Mission Budgets Are in Trouble." *Christian Century*, no. July 6-17 (1977): 618 ff.

_____. *Wheel within the Wheel: Confronting the Management Crisis of the Pluralistic Church*. Atlanta: John Knox Press, 1979.

Hybels, Bill. *Holy Discontent: Fueling the Fire That Ignites Personal Vision*. Grand Rapids: Zondervan, 2007.

Inc., Merriam-Webster. *Merriam-Webster's Collegiate Dictionary*. 10th ed. Springfield, MA: Merriam-Webster, 1997.

Jeffrey, Cox. "What I Have Learned About Missions from Writing *the British Missionary Enterprise since 1700*." *International Bulletin of Missionary Research* 32 no. 2 (2008): 86-87.

Johnson, Douglas W. *Program Dissensus between Denominational Grass Roots and Leadership and Its Consequences*. American Denominational Organization, Edited by Ross P. Scherer. Pasadena: William Carey Library, 1980.

Johnson, R. Park. "The Legacy of Arthur Judson Brown." *International Bulletin of Missionary Research* 10, no. 2 (1986): 71-75.

Julien, Tom. *Antioch Revisited: Reuniting the Church with Her Mission*. Winona Lake, IN: BMH Books, 2006.

Kaiser, Walter C., Jr. "Israel's Missionary Call." In *Perspectives on the World Christian Movement*, edited by Ralph D. Winter and Steve Hawthorne. Pasadena: William Carey Library, 1999.

Kärkkäinen, Veli-Matti. *Introduction to Ecclesiology: Ecumenical, Historical & Global Perspectives*. Downers Grove, Ill.: InterVarsity Press, 2002.

Kasdorf, Hans. *Christian Conversion in Context*. Scottdale, Pa.: Herald Press, 1980.

_____. "The Reformation and Mission: A Bibliographical Survey of Secondary Literature." *Occasional Bulletin of Missionary Research* 4, no. 4 (1980): 169-175.

Kraft, Charles H. *A Hausa Reader; Cultural Materials with Helps for Use in Teaching Intermediate and Advanced Hausa*. Berkeley, CA: University of California Press, 1973.

Kuhn, Thomas S. *The Structure of Scientific Revolutions*: University of Chicago Press, 1962.

Kuiper, B. K. *The Church in History*. Grand Rapids: National Union of Christian Schools, 1951.

Küng, Hans. *The Church*. London: Burns & Oates, 1967.

LaFollette, Joan C. "Presbyterian Women's Organizations." In *The Organizational Revolution: Presbyterians and American Denominationalism* Louisville, KY: Westminster Press, John Knox, 1992.

Latourette, Kenneth Scott. *A History of the Expansion of Christianity*. New York; London: Harper & Brothers, 1937.

_____. *A History of Christianity*. 2 vols. Revised ed. New York: Harper & Row, 1975.

Lausanne. *Cooperating in World Evangelization: A Handbook on Church/Parachurch Relationships*. Pattaya: Lausanne Movement, 1980.

Lewis, Jonathan. "Modality and Sodality." In *World Mission: An Analysis of the World Christian Movement*. Pasadena, CA: William Carey Library, 1994.

Locke, John, and J. W. Gough. *The Second Treatise of Civil Government, and, a Letter Concerning Toleration*. Oxford: Basil Blackwell, 1948.

Loetscher, Lefferts Augustine. *A Brief History of the Presbyterians*. 4th ed. Philadelphia: Westminster Press, 1958.

Luther, Martin, and John Dillenberger. *Martin Luther, Selections from His Writings*. 1st ed. Garden City, NY: Doubleday, 1961.

MacCormac, Earl R. "Missions and the Presbyterian Schism of 1837." *Church History* 32, no. 1 (1963): 32-45.

Machen, J. Gresham. *The Origin of Paul's Religion*. New York: Macmillan, 1921.

Mangalwadi, Vishal and Ruth. *Who Was William Carey?* 3rd ed. Perspectives on the World Christian Movement, Edited by Ralph D. Winter and Steven C. Hawthorne. Pasadena: William Carey Library, 1999.

Mangalwadi, Vishal, and Ruth Mangalwadi. *The Legacy of William Carey: A Model for the Transformation of a Culture*. 1st U.S. ed. Wheaton, IL: Crossway Books, 1999.

Marnell, William H. *Light from the West: The Irish Mission and the Emergence of Modern Europe*. New York: Seabury Press, 1978.

Marsden, George M. *The Evangelical Mind and the New School Presbyterian Experience; a Case Study of Thought and Theology in Nineteenth-Century America* Yale Publications in American Studies, 20. New Haven,: Yale University Press, 1970.

_____. *Evangelicalism and Modern America*. Grand Rapids: Eerdmans, 1984.

Marshall, David. *The Celtic Connection*. Grantham, Lincolnshire, England: The Stanborough Press, 1994.

Martin, Ralph P. *New Testament Foundations: A Guide for Christian Students*. Grand Rapids: Eerdmans, 1975.

Maybray, V. E. "Letter to Frank Satterberg, United Presbyterian Center for Missions Studies." Pasadena: Evangelical Missions Council, September 3, 1980.

McKnight, Scot. *A Light among the Gentiles: Jewish Missionary Activity in the Second Temple Period*. Minneapolis: Fortress Press, 1991.

McManners, John. *The Oxford Illustrated History of Christianity*. New York: Oxford University Press, 1990.

McNeill, John Thomas. *The Celtic Churches; a History A.D. 200 to 1200*: University of Chicago Press, 1974.

Meek, Donald E. "Protestant Missions and the Evangelization of the Scottish Highlands, 1700-1850." *International Bulletin of Missionary Research* 21, no. 2 (1997): 67-72.

Mellis, Charles J. *Committed Communities: Fresh Streams for World Missions*. South Pasadena, CA: William Carey Library, 1976.

Merriam-Webster Inc. *Merriam-Webster's Dictionary of English Usage*. Springfield, MA: Merriam-Webster, Inc., 1994.

Micklethwait, John, and Adrian Wooldridge. *The Company: A Short History of a Revolutionary Idea*. New York: Modern Library, 2003.

Miley, George. *Loving the Church--Blessing the Nations: Pursuing the Role of Local Churches in Global Mission*. Waynesboro, GA: Gabriel, 2003.

Mill, John Stuart. *Utilitarianism, Liberty, and Representative Government*. London, New York: J.M. Dent & sons E.P. Dutton & Co., 1931.

Miller, Basil. *John Wesley: The World His Parish*. 3d ed. Grand Rapids: Zondervan, 1943.

Minutes of the General Assembly of the Presbyterian Church of the United States of America. Edited by Stated Clerk. Philadelphia, 1875.

Minutes of the General Assembly of the Presbyterian Church of the United States of America. Edited by Stated Clerk. Philadelphia, 1880.

Minutes of the General Assembly of the Presbyterian Church of the United States of America. Edited by Stated Clerk. Philadelphia, 1883.

Minutes of the General Assembly of the Presbyterian Church of the United States of America. Edited by Stated Clerk. Philadelphia, 1893.

Minutes of the General Assembly of the Presbyterian Church of the United States of America. Edited by Stated Clerk. Philadelphia, 1897.

Minutes of the General Assembly of the Presbyterian Church of the United States of America. Edited by Stated Clerk. Philadelphia, 1902.

Minutes of the General Assembly of the Presbyterian Church of the United States of America. Edited by Stated Clerk. Philadelphia, 1991.

Moffett, Eileen. "Mission Society! There Remains Very Much Land to Be Possessed!" *Global Church Growth Bulletin* 18, no. 1. Jan-Feb. (1981).

Moffett, Samuel H. *A History of Christianity in Asia Vol. 2*. Vol. 2. Maryknoll, NY: Orbis Books, 2005.

Moorhead, James E. "Presbyterians and the Mystique of Organizational Efficiency." In *Reimagining Denominationalism* 264-287. New York: Oxford University Press, 1994.

Moorman, John R. H. *A History of the Franciscan Order: From Its Origins to the Year 1517*. Chicago, Ill.: Franciscan Herald Press, 1988.

Mottinger, William Douglas. "Readings in Church/Mission Structures." MA Thesis, Fuller Theological Seminary, 1986.

Moynahan, Brian. *The Faith : A History of Christianity*. 1st ed. New York: Doubleday, 2002.

Mulholland, Kenneth B. "From Luther to Carey: Pietism and the Modern Missionary Movement." *Bibliotecha Sacra* 156, no. 1 (1999): 85-95.

Neill, Stephen. *A History of Christian Missions*. 2nd ed. New York: Penguin Books, 1986.

Niles, Daniel Thambyrajah. *Upon the Earth; the Mission of God and the Missionary Enterprise of the Churches*. New York: McGraw-Hill, 1962.

Nissen, Johannes. *New Testament and Mission: Historical and Hermeneutical Perspectives*. Frankfurt am Main; New York: P. Lang, 1999.

Noll, Mark A. "The Monastic Rescue of the Church: Benedict's Rule." In *Turning Points: Decisive Moments in the History of Christianity* Grand Rapids: Baker, 1997.

Nyquist, John. "Parachurch Agencies and Mission." In *Evangelical Dictionary of World Missions* Grand Rapids: Baker Books, 2000.

Okholm, Dennis L. *Monk Habits for Everyday People: Benedictine Spirituality for Protestants*. Grand Rapids: Brazos Press, 2007.

Oort, J. van, and Rijksuniversiteit te Utrecht. Faculteit der Godgeleerdheid. *De Onbekende Voetius: Voordrachten Wetenschappelijk Symposium, Utrecht, 3 Maart 1989*. Kampen: J.H. Kok, 1989.

The Oxford Encyclopedia of the Reformation. Edited by Hans J. Hillerbrand. New York, 1996.

Pellowe, John. *A Practical Theology for Relations between Churches and Self-Governing Agencies*. Gordon-Conwell Theological Seminary, 2007.

──────. *A Theological Understanding of the Place of Independent, Organized Ministry in Relation to the Institutional Church*. Canadian Councl of Christian Charities, 2007.

──────. "Leading Ministries into Christian Community: A Practical Theology for Church-Agency Relations." D. Min. Dissertation, Gordon-Conwell Theological Seminary, 2008.

Peters, George W. *A Biblical Theology of Missions*. Chicago,: Moody Press, 1972.

Pierard, Richard V. "William Wilberforce and the Abolition of the Slave Trade." *Christian History* 16, no. 1 (1997).

Piercy, LaRue W. *Hawaii's Missionary Saga: Sacrifice and Godliness in Paradise*. Honolulu: Mutual Publishing, 1992.

Pierson, Paul E. "Historical Development of the Christian Movement." Pasadena: Fuller Theological Seminary, 1985.

──────. "Why Did the 1800s Explode with Missions?" *Christian History* 11, no. 4 (1992).

──────. "American Board of Commissioners for Foreign Mission." In *Evangelical Dictionary of World Missions* Grand Rapids: Baker Books, 2000.

──────. "Presbyterian Missions." In *Evangelical Dictionary of World Missions* Grand Rapids: Baker Books, 2000.

──────. "The Reformation and Mission." In *Evangelical Dictionary of World Missions* Grand Rapids: Baker Books, 2000.

──────. *The Dynamics of Christian Mission: History through a Missiological Perspective*. Pasadena, CA: William Carey International University Press, 2009.

Polack, William Gustave. *The Handbook to the Lutheran Hymnal*. Saint Louis, Mo.,: Concordia Publishing House, 1942.

Quebedeaux, Richard. *The Young Evangelicals: Revolution in Orthodoxy*. 1st ed. New York: Harper & Row, 1974.

Rengstorf, Karl Heinrich. "Apostolos." In *Theological Dictionary of the New Testament* Vol. 1. Grand Rapids: Eerdmans, 1965.

Rice, Ronald B. "Congregational Giving to Denominational Mission within the United Presbyterian Church." Doctoral of Ministry thesis, San Francisco Theological Seminary, 1978.

Robert, Dana Lee. *American Women in Mission: A Social History of Their Thought and Practice*, Edited by Wilbert R. Shenk. Macon, Ga.: Mercer University Press, 1997.

_____. "Innovation and Consolidation in American Methodist Mission History." In *World Mission in the Wesleyan Spirit*, edited by Darrell L.Whiteman and Gerald H. Anderson. Franklin, TN: Providence House Publishers, 2009.

Roberts, M. J. D. *Making English Morals: Voluntary Association and Moral Reform in England, 1787-1886* Cambridge Social and Cultural Histories: Cambridge University Press, 2004.

Robertson, Archibald, and Alfred Plummer. *A Critical and Exegetical Commentary on the First Epistle of St. Paul to the Corinthians*. 2nd ed. The International Critical Commentary on the Holy Scriptures of the Old and New Testaments. Edinburgh: T. & T. Clark, 1914.

Robertson, D. B., and James Luther Adams. *Voluntary Associations, a Study of Groups in Free Societies; Essays in Honor of James Luther Adams*. Richmond, VA: John Knox Press, 1966.

Rousseau, Jean-Jacques. *The Social Contract, and Discourses*. New York: Dutton, 1950.

Rycroft, W. Stanley. *The Ecumenical Witness of the United Presbyterian Church in the U.S.A*. New York: Commission on Ecumenical Mission and Relations, United Presbyterian Church in the U.S.A., 1968.

Sanders, Van. "The Mission of God and the Local Church." In *Pursuing the Mission of God in Church Planting* Alpharetta, GA: North American Mission Board (Southern Baptist Convention), 2006.

Sanneh, Lamin O. "Christian Missions and the Western Guilt Complex." *The Christian Century* April 8, (1987): 331-334.

Scanlon, Leslie. "New Strategies for Raising Mission Dollars Considered by P.C.U.S.A. Officials." *The Presbyterian Outlook*, (February 25, 2002).

Schattschneider, David A. "William Carey, Modern Missions, and the Moravian Influence." *International Bulletin of Missionary Research* 22, no. 1 (1998): 8-12.

Scherer, James A. "Lutheran Missions." In *Evangelical Dictionary of World Missions* Grand Rapids: Baker Books, 2000.

Scherer, Ross P. *American Denominational Organization: A Sociological View*. Pasadena, CA: William Carey Library, 1980.

Schmidt, K. L. "Ekklesia." In *Theological Dictionary of the New Testament* 3. Grand Rapids: Eerdmans, 1965.

Schnabel, Eckhard J. *Early Christian Mission*. 2 vols. Downers Grove, Ill.: InterVarsity Press, 2004.

_____. *Paul, the Missionary: Realities, Strategies and Methods*. Downers Grove, IL: IVP Academic, 2008.

Schrage, Wolfgang. "Synagogue." In *Theological Dictionary of the New Testament* 7. Grand Rapids: Eerdmans, 1965.

Scott, Waldron. "Karl Barth's Theology of Mission." *Missiology* 3, no. 2 (1975): 209-224.

Scudder, Lewis R. *The Arabian Mission's Story: In Search of Abraham's Other Son* The Historical Series of the Reformed Church in America. Grand Rapids: Eerdmans, 1998.

Seamands, David. "Methodist Report." In *Consultation on Voluntary Societies*, edited by Robert A. Blincoe. Evansville, IL, 1974.

Segal, Alan F. *Paul the Convert: The Apostolate and Apostasy of Saul the Pharisee*. New Haven: Yale University Press, 1990.

Service, Elman Rogers. *Primitive Social Organization: An Evolutionary Perspective*. 2nd ed. New York: Random House, 1971.

_____. *Profiles in Ethnology*. 3d ed. New York: Harper & Row, 1978.

Severn, Frank M. "Mission Societies: Are They Biblical?" *Evangelical Missions Quarterly* 36, no. 3 (2000): 320-326.

Shedd, Clarence Prouty. *Two Centuries of Student Christian Movements, Their Origin and Intercollegiate Life*. New York: Association press, 1934.

Sheils, W. J., and Diana Wood, eds. *Voluntary Religion*. Vol. 23. Oxford: UK: Published for the Ecclesiastical History Society by B. Blackwell, 1986.

Shenk, Wilbert R. *Write the Vision: The Church Renewed*. 1st U.S. ed. Christian Mission and Modern Culture. Valley Forge, Pa.: Trinity Press International;, 1995.

Simmons, Scott J. "John Calvin and Missions: A Historical Study." *www.aplacefortruth.org/calvin.missions1.htm*.

Sklar, Eileen Mayer. "Westminster Fellowship." edited by Email to Robert Blincoe. Philadelphia: Presbyterian Historical Society, 24 November 2009.

Skreslet, Stanley H. "Impending Transformation: Mission Structures for a New Century." *International Bulletin of Missionary Research* 23, no. 1 (1999): 2-6.

Smith, A. Christopher. "The Legacy of William Carey." *International Bulletin of Missionary Research* 16, no. 1 (1992): 2-9.

Smith, Constance E., and Anne E. Freedman. *Voluntary Associations: Perspectives on the Literature*. Cambridge, MA: Harvard University Press, 1972.

Smylie, James H., Dean K. Thompson, Cary Patrick, and Presbyterian Church (U.S.A.). *Go Therefore: 150 Years of Presbyterians in Global Mission*. Atlanta: Produced for the General Assembly Mission Board, Presbyterian Church (U.S.A.), by the Presbyterian Publishing House, 1987.

Stamoolis, James J. "History of Missions." In *Evangelical Dictionary of World Missions* Grand Rapids: Baker Books, 2000.

Stanley, Brian. "Winning the World: Carey and the Modern Missionary Movement." *Christian History* 5, no. 1 (1986 January).

Stark, Rodney. *Cities of God: Christianizing the Urban Empire*. 1st ed. San Francisco: Harper, 2006.

Sullivan, Amy. "Jesuit Message Drives Detroit's Last Catholic School." *Time Magazine*, November 10 2009.

Sunquist, Scott, and Caroline Becker Long. *A History of Presbyterian Missions, 1944-2007*. 1st ed. Louisville: Geneva Press, 2008.

Taylor, John V. "An Historical Comparison of American and British Voluntary Societies." In *Consultation on Voluntary Societies*, edited by Robert A. Blincoe. First Presbyterian Church, Evanston, IL, May 22-24, 1975.

TeSelle, Eugene. "Church and Parachurch: Christian Freedom, Ecclesiastical Order, and the Problem of Voluntary Organizations (Unpublished)." Nashville: Vanderbilt University, 1994.

Theriault, Judy. "Presbyterian Women." Pasadena: Presbyterian Center for Mission Studies, 1995.

Thornwell, James Henley. "A Memorial to the Synod of South Carolina and Georgia on the Subject of Ecclesiastical Boards." *The Baltimore Literary and Religious Magazine*, no. 4 (1840).

Tinsley, Ambrose. *Pax: The Benedictine Way*. Collegeville, MN: The Liturgical Press, 1994.

Tocqueville, Alexis de. *Democracy in America / Translated, Edited, and with an Introduction by Harvey C. Mansfield and Delba Winthrop*: University of Chicago Press, 1833.

Tönnies, Ferdinand, and Charles Price Loomis. *Community & Society (Gemeinschaft Und Gesellschaft)*. East Lansing,: Michigan State University Press, 1957.

"Tönnies, Ferdinand." In *The New Encyclopedia Britannica* vol. 11: University of Chicago Press, 1991.

Towns, Elmer L. *Towns' Sunday School Encyclopedia*. Wheaton, Ill.: Tyndale House, 1993.

Treadgold, Donald W. *A History of Christianity*. Belmont, MA: Nordland, 1979.

Van Culin, Sam. "Episcopal Report." In *Consultation on Voluntary Societies*, edited by Robert A. Blincoe. First Presbyterian Church, Evanston, IL, 1975, May 22-24.

Van Engen, Charles Edward. *Mission on the Way: Issues in Mission Theology*. Grand Rapids: Baker Books, 1996.

Van Gelder, Craig. "Local and Mobile--a Study of Two Functions (Unpublished Dissertation)." Jackson, MS: Reformed Theological Seminary, 1975.

_____. "Understanding the Church in North America." In *Missional Church* Grand Rapids: Eerdmans, 1998.

_____. *The Missional Church and Denominations : Helping Congregations Develop a Missional Identity* Missional Church Series. Grand Rapids, Mich.: William B. Eerdmans Pub., 2008.

Vander Werff, Lyle L. *Christian Mission to Muslims: The Record: Anglican and Reformed Approaches in India and the near East, 1800-1938*. South Pasadena, CA: William Carey Library, 1977.

Venn, Henry. *To Apply the Gospel; Selections from the Writings of Henry Venn*. Grand Rapids: Eerdmans, 1971.

Walls, Andrew F. "Societies for Mission." In *The History of Christianity* Berkhamsted, England: Lion Publishing, 1977.

_____. "The American Dimension of the Missionary Movement." In *The Missionary Movement in Christian History* Maryknoll: Orbis, 1996.

_____. "The Fortunate Subversion of the Church." In *The Missionary Movement in Christian History: Studies in the Transmission of Faith* Maryknoll, NY: Orbis Books, 1996.

_____. "Structural Problems in Mission Studies." In *The Missionary Movement in Christian History* Maryknoll: Orbis, 1996.

_____. *The Cross-Cultural Process in Christian History: Studies in the Transmission and Appropriation of Faith*. Maryknoll, NY: Orbis Books, 2002.

_____. "The Missionary Movement: A Lay Fiefdom?" In *The Cross-Cultural Process in Christian History* Maryknoll: Orbis, 2002.

Wallstrom, Timothy Clarke. *The Creation of a Student Movement to Evangelize the World*. Pasadena, CA: William Carey International University Press, 1980.

Warneck, Gustav. *Outline of a History of Protestant Missions from the Reformation to the Present Time*. New York: Revell, 1901.

Warren, Max. *Crowded Canvas: Some Experiences of a Life-Time*. London: Hodder & Stoughton, 1974.

Watson, Cody U. *Mission Orders and the Presbyterian Church*. Pasadena: Presbyterian Center for Mission Studies, 1989.

Watson, Francis Crick and James. "Letter." *Nature*, April 25 1953.

Weingartner, Robert. "Missions within the Mission." In *A History of Presbyterian Missions, 1944-2007* Louisville: Geneva Press, 2008.

Welz, Justinian Ernst von, Scherer, James A. *Justinian Welz: Essays by an Early Prophet of Mission*. Grand Rapids: Eerdmans, 1969.

Weston, William J. *Presbyterian Pluralism: Competition in a Protestant House*. 1st ed. Knoxville, TN: University of Tennessee Press, 1997.

Westphal, Merold. *Suspicion and Faith: The Religious Uses of Modern Atheism*. Grand Rapids: Eerdmans, 1993.

White, Jerry. *The Church and Parachurch: An Uneasy Marriage*. Portland: Multnomah, 1983.

White, Lyman Cromwell. *International Non-Governmental Organizations; Their Purposes, Methods, and Accomplishments*. New Brunswick, NJ: Rutgers University Press, 1951.

Wilke, Richard B. *And Are We yet Alive? The Future of the United Methodist Church*. Nashville: Abingdon Press, 1986.

Willmer, Wesley Kenneth, J. David Schmidt, and Martyn Smith. *The Prospering Parachurch: Enlarging the Boundaries of God's Work*. 1st ed. San Francisco, CA: Jossey-Bass, 1998.

Winter, Ralph D. "The Anatomy of the Christian Mission." *Evangelical Missions Quarterly* 5:74-89, (1969).

———. "A Plea for Mission Orders." Chicago: COEMAR Conference, August, 1970.

———. "The New Missions and the Mission of the Church." *International Review of Mission* 60, no. 1 (1971, January): 89-100.

———. "Churches Need Missions Because Modalities Need Sodalities." *Evangelical Missions Quarterly* Vol. 7, (1971, July).

———. "The Planting of Younger Missions." In *Christian/Mission Tensions Today* Grand Rapids: Moody Press, 1972.

———. "Seeing the Task Graphically." *Evangelical Missions Quarterly* 10, no. 1 (1974).

———. "The Two Structures of God's Redemptive Mission." *Missiology* 2, no. 1 (1974): 121-139.

———. "Ghana: Preparation for Marriage." *International Review of Mission* 17, (1978): 338-353.

———. "Four Kinds of Church-Agency Relationships." *Missiology* 7 no. 2, 1979.

———. "Protestant Mission Societies: The American Experience." *Missiology* 7, no. 2 (1979): 139-178.

———. "Paul and the Regions Beyond." *Asia Missions Advance*, (1979 July 11-15).

———. "Protestant Mission Societies and the 'Other Protestant Schism'." In *American Denominational Organization* Pasadena: William Carey Library, 1980.

———. "Mission in the 1990s: Two Views." *International Bulletin of Missionary Research* 14, no. 3 (1990): 98-105.

———. "Four Men, Three Eras." (1996). http://williamcareylibrary.com/ebooks/Four_Men_Three_Eras%20.pdf

_____. "Four Men, Three Eras, Two Transitions: Modern Missions." In *Perspectives on the World Christian Movement*, edited by Ralph D. Winter and Steve Hawthorne. Pasadena: William Carey Library, 1999.

_____. "Sodality and Modality." In *Evangelical Dictionary of World Missions* Grand Rapids: Baker Books, 2000.

_____. "Theodore of Tarsus." In *Evangelical Dictionary of World Missions* Grand Rapids: Baker House, 2000.

_____. "Doctoral Learning Contract." Pasadena: William Carey International University, 2002.

_____. *Frontiers in Mission: Discovering and Surmounting Barriers to the Missio Dei*. Pasadena: William Carey International University Press, 2005.

_____. "Global Cross-Cultural Mission Collaboration: 1910 to 2010." Pasadena: William Carey International University, 2008.

_____. "Opening Remarks." In *Consultation on Voluntary Societies*. First Presbyterian Church, Evanston, IL: Unpublished, May 22, 1975.

_____. *The Story of the P.C.M.S., P.U.M.A., P.O.W.E., and the P.F.F.*: Worldwide Ministries Division of the P.C.U.S.A., Louisville, KY, October 26, 1995.

Winter, Ralph D., and R. Pierce Beaver. *The Warp and the Woof; Organizing for Mission*. South Pasadena, CA: William Carey Library, 1970.

Workman, Herbert B. *The Evolution of the Monastic Ideal from the Earliest Times Down to the Coming of the Friars*. London: C. H. Kelly., 1913.

Worley, Robert C. *Change in the Church: A Source of Hope*. Philadelphia: Westminster, 1976.

Wuthnow, Robert. "The Growth of Special Purpose Groups." In *The Restructuring of American Religion: Society and Faith since World War 2*. Princeton, NJ: Princeton University Press, 1988.

_____. *The Restructuring of American Religion: Society and Faith since World War 2*. Princeton, NJ: Princeton University Press, 1988.